Do You Like Jesus - Not the Church?

Do You Like Jesus - Not the Church?

JESUS: HIS TRUE MESSAGE - NOT THE LIE OF CHRISTIANITY

**Exposing the Lie Crumbles
the Foundation of Christianity**

Rev. Dr. JC Husfelt

ISBN: 0692357408
ISBN 13: 9780692357408
Library of Congress Control Number: 2015903218
Snowy Owl, Ludlow WA

For my family—
Sherry, Jamie, Jessie, and LilyRose
The Bee Clan

Acknowledgments

would like to express my love, gratitude, and appreciation to my family for their love, spirited companionship, support, help, and belief in my quest. Without doubt, my wife and soulmate, whom I met at thirteen, has been my partner once again with her love and support through a journey I would not have wanted to take without her by my side.

Additionally, without the support of Sir Alfred Darby, III, this book would have not been published in a timely manner. Thank you.

Contents

Life Eternal

Once again our earthly journey,
Separating from the loving womb of mother.
We take our first breath of life, of God's breath,
And we remember
The love and purity of the heavens,
The perfection and oneness of all.
With our cry our journey of life,
Of life's joys and struggles, begins,
And remembrance slowly fades
But is never totally gone.
Throughout the joys and struggles,
The joys of family and friends,
Of pets, music, and the delights of life,
There are the struggles—
Ones that may strengthen our spirit,
The turbulence of life, the cares and sorrows
That hang heavy over our heart,
the grief and sorrow of death.
But we remember at certain times
the love and perfection,
Times when we gaze into the eyes of loved ones,
The closeness of family and friends,
The sounds of laughter, the playful glee of children, the innocence of a baby.
Freshly falling snow may bring remembrance,
As may the first blossom of spring,
A visit by hummingbird, the beauty of butterfly,
The first star of night,
The mystery and beauty of nature.
Our remembrance is of our heart and soul,
Of the starlight eternal.
Remember, remember, remember.
Then it is time, the heavens call.
A time to return,
Return to the purity of heavenly love,
To the perfection and oneness of heaven.
In the heavens a star shines brighter.
To the ones we leave behind,
Know that you are loved,
And know...you are never alone.
Rev. Dr. J. C. Husfelt, 2014

Foreword

"Then you will know the truth, and the truth will set you free."[1]

This book is not based on faith or belief. This book is based on truth and knowing. How do I know? Let's just say I do and leave it at that. As a truth seeker, I have traveled for more than thirty years to different parts of the world, ever seeking wisdom and the myth, magic, and lore of elders and indigenous people. I have self-sacrificed and sacrificed self to self. My experience of "listening, looking, and learning" flows from indigenous elders, healers, and shamans from all over the world. It also comes from my interactions with the young and old of other races and cultures and emanates deeply from my own soul's wisdom. This knowledge is what I refer to as the "first knowledge."[2] It is knowledge that is woven throughout and found in all the "first people" (i.e., indigenous) spiritual and religious traditions on this earth. This "first knowledge" has been referred to as primordial knowledge or the Primordial Tradition (perennial philosophy). As such it portrays universal themes, principles, and truths. In other words, "the term Primordial Tradition is utilized to describe a system of spiritual thought and metaphysical truths that overarches all the other religions and esoteric traditions of humanity."[3] Furthermore, "the perennial philosophy proposes that reality, in the ultimate sense, is One, Whole, and undivided—the omnipresent source of all knowledge and power. We do not perceive this reality because the field of human cognition is restricted by the senses. But the perennial philosophy claims that these limitations can be transcended."[4]

It stands to reason that the knowledge contained within this book comes from my firsthand experience and from my soul. I have experienced a descending spirit, a vision and voice from heaven, and been in the presence of angels who appeared as messengers due to my prayer. I discovered my modern-day John the Dipper in the person of the late Salish elder, Vince Stogan, who passed on his knowledge to my wife and me, which included the power and authority to put people in the stream—submersion bathing—as it has been done for thousands of years.

In other words, my firsthand experience has been of the type that William James documented in *The Varieties of Religious Experience*. In this classic study, he "finds the origin of belief in an 'unseen' world in the experience of 'religious geniuses' who experience firsthand the realities of which religion speaks, and carefully distinguishes this primal experience from what he calls 'secondhand' religion, the beliefs that people acquire through tradition."[5]

Here is a fact: the majority of religious writers, scholars, priests, ministers, rabbis, and other religious leaders of our day are secondhand mouthpieces and not teachers or students of the Primordial Tradition, or what I would call nature's truths of God's reflection; sanctification practices; or indigenous shamanic teachings and practices, such as the death-and-rebirth ceremonial ritual of bathing. But Jesus was, and I am.

⚜

I do not believe but know that Christianity is based on a lie. I call it "the greatest lie ever told." What if I told you that "the greatest story ever told" was in reality the greatest lie? Would you immediately tense up and close your mind to what I know is the truth? Or would you choose to read through this book and then decide if it was the "greatest story" or the "greatest lie"?

The world is a mess—socially, culturally, economically, and environmentally. We live in a dominator society, male-dominated, not a partnership society. Inequality rules the day, ever reinforced by the dogma of organized religion and the siren's song of wealth. Christianity as a religion does not put forth or encourage an altruistic, egalitarian message but only a message of sin, separation, and second-class citizenship for women. Its dogma deems Christianity the only true religion and the only one with God's son—Jesus Christ—in material form born of a virgin.

Christianity's primary dogma states that Jesus was God's son, who was incarnated on earth and, as the Savior, gave up his life to cleanse all others of sin—original sin. According to the church, Jesus (the Son) along with his Father (God) and the Holy Spirit unite in form as the Trinitarian Godhead of Christianity.

Christianity was born, and the die was cast in fool's gold, when the Nicaea Council declared Jesus God:

> We believe in one only God, Father Almighty, Creator of things visible and invisible; and in the Lord Jesus Christ, for he is the Word of God, God of God, Light of Light, life of life, his only Son, the firstborn of all creatures, begotten of the Father before all time, by whom also every-thing was created, who became flesh for our redemption, who lived and suffered amongst men, rose again the third day, returned to the Father, and will come again one day in his glory to judge the quick and the dead. We believe also in the Holy Ghost. We believe that each of these three is and subsists; the Father truly as Father, the Son truly as Son, the Holy Ghost truly as Holy Ghost; as our Lord also said, when he sent his disciples to preach: Go and teach all nations, and baptize them in the name of the Father, and of the Son, and of the Holy Ghost.[6]

⚜

This is Christianity's lie, pure and simple: the propaganda that Jesus was exclu-sively divine—the actual Son of God. This lie of Christianity has existed and grown in the fears and doubts of its followers, a lie created to hide the truth. But now, the lie is exposed and the truth revealed.[7]

⚜

The church[8] will not want you to read this book. Additionally, I include in this statement the plutocrats, the 2 percent elites of the world. They do not want the 98 percent of us to demand equality and an egalitarian way of life.[9] Accordingly, it is important to note that equality and egalitarianism were two of the primary teachings of Jesus.

A Revolution Is Needed!

The doctrine of the divinity of Jesus is made
a convenient cover for absurdity.
—US PRESIDENT JOHN ADAMS

There is a multitude of reasons for a revolution to occur, not only in religion but in its equally "evil" twin, capitalism. The most important one is that the world as we know it is on the verge of collapse. The biodiversity catastrophe humanity is facing has been brought about by two destructive paradigms: institutionalized religion and capitalism.

The big three institutionalized religions have promoted humanity's—or, as they would put it, "man's"—superiority over nature and its creatures. And as "stewards" of the earth, man knows what is best for the earth. This has given free rein and moral license to the lords of capitalism to do whatever is needed to increase profit, even if it means indiscriminately destroying rainforests, habitats, and indigenous tribes while arbitrarily polluting the environment. This is all in the name of progress and profit.

Only revolutionary thought and action can overcome the ingrained corruption and outdatedness of these institutions and paradigms of organized religion and capitalism. The problems created by these two paradigms cannot be solved or overcome by the same type of thinking that established them in the first place.

It has been proven that "throughout history, the orthodox, the past-oriented, have feared any degree of spiritual rebellion. Not a single founder of any of today's socially acceptable religions has come from an established priesthood or hierarchy."[10] I, as well, do not come from an established priesthood or hierarchy. And there is an important reason for this. Only a person with the inner fires of rebellion and revolution burning within, and without any ties or loyalties to the established orthodox theologies, can bring a new message and a new light to the world. Many of the established scholars writing about Jesus have come from established religions, and thus their assumptions and conclusions concerning Jesus have been filtered through their religious beliefs and a consciousness wrapped around dualism. Additionally, many lack my knowledge and experience of hands-on healing and sanctification practices, such as submersion bathing, all of which Jesus knew and practiced.

⚜

From a very young age, I've always seen things differently and felt a revolution-ary seed within the core of my being. This has always been an urging and need of my soul that is connected with issues of justice and injustice and the righting of the wrongs of life.

During college I was not at a crossroad of life but on a path that branched out into three different directions: marrying the love of my life; serving in Vietnam; or abandoning my life as I knew it and joining up with the leftist revo-lutionary Ernesto "Che" Guevara, who dreamed of a new consciousness driven by altruism rather than materialistic greed and power. Joining Che was more of a whimsical dream than a reality, while serving in Vietnam was not a dream, but I was willing to go. I had been reclassified from my college deferment and reported for my preinduction physical. Of course, I passed with flying colors. I returned to college and waited to be called up. But a mystery occurred: I never received any papers to report for basic training, just a notice that I had been reclassified again and my college deferment was back in place (however, my grades had not improved, and I was still on academic probation). This took place in 1966, when things really began heating up in Vietnam, and the military was taking any breathing, warm-bodied male—except me!

Instead, as you might have guessed, I married my soul mate, Sherry (still married, close to fifty years), while in college and never did join Che, who was executed in 1967 in Bolivia, or serve in Vietnam. I only mention this in passing to give you a little insight into myself. It was more what Che stood for and was attempting to do than actually joining him in his quest for an equalitarian type of society as opposed to one based on the insidious greed and corruption of capitalism. His theme of righting the wrongs of economic injustice resonated within my inner core, even though I came from what you would call a blue-collar, middle-class family. I was not buying into the great American dream, but I was still too young to realize my purpose and destiny.

Revolution may be defined as "a drastic and far-reaching change in ways of thinking and behaving."[11] It seems to me that at this point in humanity's history, there needs to be a drastic shift in both thought and behavior, not only at the individual level but, more importantly, at the level of the so-called sacred cows of society and culture—organized, institutionalized religion and capitalism.

⚜

Countering established thought is difficult. The only way to achieve a new level of thinking, a new consciousness, is through "shock and awe." Love works, but only revolutionary action can achieve the necessary disruption of the conservative mode that most people sense as reality. Even liberals have a tendency to resist change. People as a whole are more comfortable with the status quo. This is based on their fear of change, which is rooted in the fear of the unknown. Even people in abusive relationships will stay in the known, painful as it is, instead of leaving the relationship and walking through the doorway of change and into the unknown.

A new consciousness is desperately needed within humanity. I believe this is possible to achieve, but only through a radical revolution in religious belief, philosophy, and thought. This will bring human consciousness to a new level of being and awareness. This religious revolution will expose institutionalized religion for what it truly is: corrupt and outdated. In fact, was there ever a need for dogmatic, hierarchical religion in the first place? As I mentioned before, I am not the first to propose a revolution in religion. Jesus, who was a pioneer of democratic thinking, brought a revolutionary message and philosophy to all who had ears to hear and eyes to see: "There can be little doubt that Jesus was a revolutionary, and that the message he promoted was so highly altruistic that its full acceptance in any hierarchical society would prove impossible because the very hierarchy would be undermined. His fine and egalitarian ideals suffered the moment they were extended into the community...Christianity could claim success, but did it reflect the true message of Jesus?"[12]

No—only its lie fueled its success, as "the true message had died with the election of the first pope of Rome, and the real tragedy of the life of Jesus was the manner in which his words had been distorted."[13]

⚜

You never know when you may be in the presence of an angel. The light is dimming in the late afternoon, but a sheep has wandered off the path. What do you do? Out of awareness and compassion for the well-being of a lost sheep,

Moses wandered off the beaten path seeking one thing, but discovered an-other—the reality of the "burning bush."

I would ask each of you to seek the truth from your heart and mind. Step off the path of Christian dogma and discover the truth of Jesus and his message.

Rev. Dr. J. C. Husfelt, August 29, 2012—sixty-sixth birthday

Preface

But to those who have understood that Love is the key, the
White Owl will appear, and lead them into another time. One
cycle ends, but another commences—and a seed group will
go forward into the Age of Aquarius, the Age of Holy Spirit.[14]

Our life[15] has been magical, metaphorically and in reality. It was in this tradition of magic and for esoteric and spiritual reasons that I began this book in the sixty-sixth year of my life. Two years later, the heavens arranged themselves in a very powerful way. The winter solstice and the new moon happened on the same date: December 21, 2014. Uranus,[16] the revolutionary planet, turned direct only minutes before the Capricorn solstice, and supposedly, this solstice's period of darkness was the longest ever recorded on earth.

After the greatest period of darkness, the prophesied light returns. I determined that the perfect date for birthing *Do You Like Jesus—Not the Church?* would be December 22, 2014, as the first book of Snowy Owl Publications. On the night of the winter solstice, Sunday, December 21, with the return of light and the new moon, my wife and I conducted a ceremony around our apple tree. The description of the ceremony is not necessary, except for my wife's final words of blessing and honor for my book: "May your words of light shatter the darkness of ignorance." One second, two seconds, and...an otherworldly cry erupted through the dark of the night, maybe thirty or forty feet away, at the beginning of our driveway. Our view of the source of the cry was blocked by trees and shrubs.

I looked at my wife as she looked at me.

"What was that?" she asked.

"It sounded almost like a coyote but not quite," I replied. "I don't know."

At this point, I didn't know if I was going to have to face down some type of wild beast.

My wife said it might have been a bird. We did have a small flashlight, and we crept to the area of the cry. After we had passed through our front arbor—a portal, so to speak—I felt the need to raise our light up into our Gaia tree, a tall burl maple. And there on an outstretched branch was a large owl staring at us. Even with the light focused on the branch for a long time, it did not move or fly away. To be respectful, I turned the light off as we spoke our prayers and blessings to it as the witness to our ceremony and our words (the branch was in a direct line of sight to our apple tree). Finished, we retraced our steps to our apple tree and then into our home.

As I relate in chapter 7, be comforted—I know the truth of our heavenly partners. The visitation also occurred on a Sunday, the night of a new moon, August 3, 1997. Add to this my close relationship with the owl, especially a snowy owl,[17] a reflection of my soul, and once again magic happened—on the new-moon winter solstice of 2014.

"I cannot teach anybody anything; I can only make them think."
—SOCRATES

Introduction

Christianity is based on deliberate untruths and false premises...Far from being a religion of love, Pauline Christianity is selfishness in the extreme.[18]

Over the past few years, there has been an upsurge in people coming out of the Christian closet declaring they like Jesus but dislike the church. This is understandable since the church (Christianity) does not follow the teachings or the message of Jesus. As people have discovered, Jesus is not the problem. As a hierarchical, patriarchal religion, the lies of the church and Christianity are the problem.

Christianity is to Jesus as oil is to water. Jesus's life was dedicated to exposing the corruption and falsehoods of the hierarchical structure of Judaism that was ruled over by the Jewish priestly power elite—the Sanhedrin. He was no different than other religious revolutionaries and heretics and in good company with the Hindu heretic Buddha. Furthermore, many of Jesus's teachings were Buddhist in nature.

Today, it is eerily the same as it was two thousand years ago. Judaism has improved somewhat but still feels entitled with the mind-set that Jews are the "chosen ones." But the new religious paradigm that needs to be exposed and toppled is Christianity.

It is very evident that Jesus would not have preached, taught, or promoted an institutional, hierarchical religious philosophy, especially one based on inequality, such as Christianity. Instead, Jesus, who was a pioneer of democratic thinking, brought a revolutionary message and egalitarian philosophy of equality, unity, and love to all who had the silence of mind to hear.

It seems "there can be little doubt that Jesus was a revolutionary, and that the message he promoted was so highly altruistic that its full acceptance in any hierarchical society would prove impossible because the very hierarchy would be undermined. His fine and egalitarian ideals suffered the moment they were extended into the community."[19]

Additionally, it has been proven that "throughout history, the orthodox, the past-oriented, have feared any degree of spiritual rebellion. Not a single founder of any of today's socially acceptable religions has come from an established priesthood or hierarchy."[20] There is an obvious reason for this. Only a person with the inner fires of rebellion and revolution burning within, and without any ties or loyalties to the established orthodox theologies, can bring a new message and a new light to the world.

⚜

There is "one common fact: the amount of available historical information concerning Jesus and the sum of his recorded sayings is astoundingly little. Indeed, so little is known of the one in whom billions of Christians have placed their faith that scholars and others have interpreted what there is to mean almost anything, according to their own beliefs and bent of mind."[21] Additionally, "if we try to penetrate to the heart of the events of Christianity we meet great problems, as the events surrounding the historical personality of Jesus Christ, and the unfolding of Christianity during its first century, are so incompletely documented as to allow theologians an enormous field for their speculations and disputes. However impossible it might be to see these events clearly, one point I think is certain, that Christianity arose as a reaction against the prevailing rigidly codified Jewish religion of that time that killed the spirit."[22]

Furthermore, "Jesus Christ seems to have felt himself to have a mission to transform the polarized, distorted patriarchal religion of his fathers and bring about a new means for humanity to relate to the spirit. Thus we note the soft, forgiving side of Christianity as an antithesis of the hard, unyielding masculine codes of the Patriarchs. Christianity attempted at its inception a balancing of the feminine and the masculine components of the soul. Initially, the impulse was toward the integration of these two polarities, and not to their separation, nor the further stage of denying or repressing the feminine component."[23]

In other words, "Christianity would in all probability have remained a religion devoted to the balancing of these opposites, had not the Pauline impulse worked to change its direction. This led eventually to Christianity becoming a largely state religion, and ultimately it had to sacrifice its inner spiritual balance as it became the agent of social control in a patriarchal society."[24]

Egalitarianism

Equality for all! One of the core beliefs and visions of Jesus was egalitarianism. "Elizabeth Fiorenza and some other biblical scholars have plausibly argued that Jesus is responsible for the egalitarianism in early Christianity. He countered a custom that Jews shared with most traditional cultures, namely that a woman's fulfillment is inseparable from her homemaking role. He alarmed his friend Martha by encouraging her sister to learn from a rabbi, properly a male role, rather than serve food. Some female learners were included in his traveling band, and women were later sent out as agents to convey his message."[25]

Christianity is based on inequality. It is male dominated, and women are considered second-class citizens. On the other hand, inequality is not limited to Christianity and other organized religions—economically, it is found throughout the width and breadth of our planet. Greed is rampant on our earth, and this was *not* Jesus's vision for humanity.

The Golden Age Before and Yet to Come

As it was two thousand years ago, a change of ages, so it is today.

During the dawn of humanity's awakening in the paradise called earth, religion was simple. Each individual enjoyed the blessings of nature as a child of wonder in a garden of delights. There was no need for formalized prayer, as each word and thought carried gratitude, love, and respect for all things. A religious hierarchy did not exist, as each person was a priest or a priestess unto himself or herself. People did not see any reason to build magnificent temples of worship, as the sky was the roof of their church and the earth its foundation. They did not worship; they honored. Theirs was a religion of simplicity. It was a religion of, by, and for the people. This age of humanity was known as a Golden

Age. It was a primordial time of peace, equality, and love—a true community of egalitarianism. This *was* Jesus's vision for humanity and the earth—a return to Lost Eden.

Heretic

Today, as they have been throughout history, people are still complacent to religious knowledge. They willingly but blindly follow tradition. In the twenty-first century, the majority of people in the United States are more interested in money and consuming than they are in asking questions and delving into the workings of organized religion and the mysteries of self and life. For many, life is based on accumulating wealth and a feeling of security. They accept at face value, as faith and as truth, what their religious leaders tell them or what they read in the Bible. This is especially true of Christians. I call Christianity the lazy, sleepwalking religion. At least in Islam, you're required to pray five times a day. And what about the historical Jesus, whose image and name Christians use for their corrupt religion? Christianity goes totally against his original teachings and message:

> That Jesus gave the Pharisees and Sadducees a hard time cannot be denied, and that he probably gave the Essenes just as hard a time is only just beginning to be realized. This was a man of passionate belief, a man of action, a man who believed himself fully qualified and positioned to challenge the religious leaders of his time…This was no half-baked revolutionary with a rabble behind him: it was an individual of clear mind and strong heart who wished to inaugurate a revolution on both the religious and social levels of his culture and time. This is what is so attractive about him—one senses the passion in him boiling away as he tries to make his often doltish disciples understand his insights and long-term plans. He is special, and he knows he is special. He can see only too clearly that his religious peers have become bogged down in narrow-minded, nit-picking practices, and as a Galilean with a deep sense of space and freedom he wants to reveal what he has personally found out about God—that He does not live in a box labeled Religion.[26]

In today's world the Church of Rome will look at the words within this book as heretical because the author views Jesus as the perfect (divine) and imperfect (human) man, but not fully one or the other and surely not the "living" God or the redeemer. And the church would deem sacrilegious Jesus's belief in the divineness of the earth and all its creatures (kingdom of God[27] spread before you).

⚜

There is also a belief that Jesus's first followers viewed him not as the risen God but as a philosopher, prophet, and teacher. To the Sanhedrin, the council that defined Hebraic law, Jesus was in all likelihood viewed as a heretic. According to Douglas Lockhart, "Jesus is by definition a heretic. And this is not to do Jesus an injustice, for in the light of his nonconformist teachings and behaviour, he was without doubt a heretical figure in Jewish eyes. And if he returned today, he would, likewise, be a heretic in the eyes of the Christian Church."[28]

What beliefs would make Jesus such a heretic? Was it his egalitarianism? Was it just his message of love and forgiveness? Or was it something more? Could it have been a message about one's inner spiritual sun—the spirit of the Creator—God (*Alaha*[29]) the Divine within? And when it was combined with his sharp words and criticism of the prevailing religious thought and attitude, it caused such an uproar and discomfort among others, as well as the religious and civil authorities, that he was branded heretical and a danger to the ruling elite:

> The question is, if Jesus himself was not the message, then what exactly was the message? Is it possible to identify what it may have been? Are there still traces of it around? As a sentiment "love one another" may appear to be an important ingredient of the message, but as each of us knows only too well, love, like hate, cannot be conjured out of thin air—it has to spring up inside of us due to a profound connection between *"self"* and *"other"* [my italics]. We seldom hate for the same reason that we seldom love—lack of a profound connection.
>
> I think Jesus understood the dynamics of "connectedness," the meaning of love, and hate, but that what he had to tell us has been

changed into an exercise in self-propaganda, a narcissism which we have each taken up in our own way.[30]

Without a doubt, the key to Jesus's message is the connection between *self* and *other* based on "natural law."[31] It is an awakening[32] of a new consciousness—a "new" way to see one's self and others, perfection not only within but perfection outside of us—an inner kingdom and an outer kingdom spread throughout the earth. This would change our attitude and treatment of fellow human beings and all other things, such as the earth and all its creatures. This would "awaken" us to the divineness of others and ourselves as well as the humanness of life. When we have a knowing within our hearts that we have starlight, a "spark of creation—a sun of God," within us and a knowing that others do also, we are then able to truly "love our neighbor," to forgive, and to have compassion for others. This is the heart knowledge of the oneness of life and the heart knowledge of the humanness, the joy, the struggles and the suffering of life. We understand our own selves, and we understand others. This is true empathy and compassion.

With this knowledge, the need for any organized religion as "gatekeeper" between God and us becomes nonexistent.

Pagan[33]

As I explain in chapter 6, Jesus had all the qualities, works, and words that would identify him as a shaman—a pagan, an outsider to the Orthodox Jews. It makes common sense that Jesus's "mission began with a vision from the other world and the descent of the Spirit upon him."[34] This didn't occur in the temple of Jerusalem but out in nature after his immersion in living waters.

In Jesus's time, a pagan was considered nothing more than a rural person. The etymology of pagan is *paganus*, meaning a person who lives in a rural area. Jesus's home base, Galilee, was such a place.

Today, Jesus's teachings would be viewed as earth based—in other words, pagan. He loved nature and could be labeled "green" for his beliefs and practices. He knew within his heart that the kingdom was not only within us but also outside of us in all things of nature. In other words, the vibrational love and light of God, which is infinite, is within each person and is outside of each person, reflected in nature and the earth of our birth. This kingdom has the potential to be a paradise: a state of spirit, mind, and body where an atmosphere of love and peace extends outward to our families and to our physical surroundings. The kingdom is ever present, if only we have the eyes to see it and quiet minds and hearts. It is *not* a future event of apocalyptic proportions or an earthly kingdom of God, a heaven on earth of only the select ones.

Furthermore, it will only be revealed when people open their eyes and ears to true empathy and a radical (in any millennium and location on earth) egalitarianism!

The reality is that few people know or acknowledge the kingdom and instead focus on external kingdoms of power, status, and wealth, ever seeking a feeling of security. Religious structures are outward signs of their finite, earthly wealth and power. These so-called structures of God only separate the clergy and worshippers from God's paradise: the earth, the sky, and nature. Pure hypocrisy: hidden within many of these luxurious buildings of religious piety lies a stagnant swamp of sexual perversion on one hand and corruption and falsehoods on the other. For them the kingdom is the sole property of the clergy, not to be questioned and always to be obeyed.

Jesus's teachings, besides being earth based, were also heaven based and primarily centered on the "original way" of Moses. He learned this from John; the goddess tradition of King Solomon; the Egyptians; his own studies in Egypt; and various other teachers, such as "Buddhist missionaries who had overrun Egypt, Greece, and even Judea."[35] It is important to note that "the original religion of the Hebrews was, like that of all other ancient cultures, polytheistic— venerating both gods and goddesses."[36]

These teachings of the "original way" also viewed nature and the earth as divine. Many of these teachings could be traced all the way back to the Egyptian mystery-school tradition. "Morton Smith, in his *Jesus the Magician*, states unequivocally that Jesus's own beliefs and practices were those of Egypt—and, significantly, he based this assertion on material from certain Egyptian magical texts."[37] Additionally, according to Lynn Picknett and Clive Prince in *The Templar Revelation*, Jesus's crime "was that he tried to introduce *pagan ideas and pagan gods* into the Jewish lands."[38] In other words, Jesus knew radical nonduality in his heart from his experience of the descending spirit and thus knew that the unseen kingdom of the otherworld was composed of a multitude of energetic beings, whether they are called angels or gods or goddesses—an understandability pagan worldview.

Philosopher

It is reliable knowledge that "except a handful of self-styled Christians who subsequently won the day, all the civilized portion of the Pagans who knew of Jesus honored him as a philosopher, an *adept* whom they placed on the same level with Pythagoras and Apollonius. Whence such a veneration on their part for a man, were he simply, as represented by the Synoptics, a poor, unknown Jewish carpenter from Nazareth?"[39]

Hypocrisy[40]

> *Woe to you, teachers of the law and Pharisees, you hypocrites! You are like whitewashed tombs, which look beautiful on the outside but on the inside are full of the bones of the dead and everything unclean. In the same way, on the outside you appear to people as righteous but on the inside you are full of hypocrisy and wickedness.*[41]

Jesus loathed hypocrisy,[42] feeling that it was one of the most abhorrent of human behaviors. Today, if you evoke the name of Jesus, you'd better believe in and promote social justice and a culture and society of unity, freedom, equality, choice, and an egalitarian way of life. If you do not, then you are a hypocrite. The pope likes to spout the words people want to hear, but there is little action to match his words—all talk, no walk.

Let me restate the words where action needs to be taken—unity, freedom, equality, choice, and an egalitarian way of life—for all. If your religion preaches a moral philosophy of helping the poor and downtrodden on one hand and on the other hand advocates a religious doctrine of inequality and restriction of choice, such as a woman's right to an abortion, then it is a religion of hypocrisy. How hypocritical is it for a male minister, priest, bishop, or so forth to condemn homosexuality and gay marriage as an affront to God while sexually abusing other males or looking the other way while his "brothers" sexually abuse men?[43] And many times the abused are children and teenagers. In February of 2014, a United Nations panel on "the rights of a child" put light on this issue:

An independent United Nations panel on children's rights accused the Roman Catholic Church...of shielding priests who have sexually abused tens of thousands of children worldwide and called on the Vatican to dismiss the perpetrators and refer them to civil authorities for prosecution.

The panel also urged the Vatican to review the church's doctrine on abortion, saying its position forbidding abortion in any circumstances "places obvious risks on the life and health of pregnant girls," and to revise its stance on homosexuality, saying its condemnation of same-sex relationships had led to harassment and violence against children.

The panel accused the church of covering up incidents of child abuse...The Vatican has yet to sanction any bishop for having covered up for an abusive priest, even though more than a decade has passed since the scandal exploded in the US and countless law-enforcement investigations around the world made it clear the role bishops played.[44]

The secret of happiness, you see, is not found in seeking more,
but in developing the capacity to enjoy less – Socrates

Another hypocrisy of the church is wealth. It is evident that Jesus was contemptuous of wealth and its accumulation: "Don't worry about tomorrow. Don't accumulate savings. It is easier for a camel to go through a needle's eye than a rich man to enter the kingdom of God."[45] Accordingly, he taught that you can't have two masters—money *and* God. Spouting the Bible and attending church while casting a blind eye to poverty and hoarding millions or billions of dollars[46] while homelessness and hunger are rampant and the chasm between the "haves" and the "have-nots" is great and ever widening is hypocritical. As "such hoarding of treasure—or in current speech, the 'amassing of wealth'—is in itself productive of many evils, e.g. greed, avarice, covetousness, leading to all manner of temptations and crime; for 'where your treasure is, there will be your heart also.'"[47]

Today, the church is more concerned about who marries whom and controlling women's bodies through their opposition to abortion and birth control than focusing on the plight of the poor and homeless. Only hypocrites would hoard wealth[48] as the church does while giving the illusion that they care about the poor. Even their hoarding is secret and seemingly illegal. The Institute for the Works of Religion, known as the Vatican Bank, has been accused over the decades of shady dealings and money laundering:

> Whereas Benedict XVI and his predecessors have preached humility and ethical financial dealings from the window overlooking St. Peter's Square, his confidants working directly beneath the papal windows have continued to pursue shady financial transactions.
>
> The Vatican has yet to divulge the business practices its bank has been using for decades. "There is fear that, owing to the transparency necessary today, one will find something in the past that one doesn't want to," says Marco Politi, a Rome-based Vatican expert.
>
> Such things could include a complex system of ghost accounts and shell companies like the bank had when Archbishop Paul Casimir Marcinkus was its head in the 1980s. At the time, the bank did business involving foreign currency and weapons with the Milanese banker Robert Calvi and the mafia financier Michele Sidona—and helped launder illegal proceeds the mafia earned from drug-trafficking as well as bribes paid to Christian-conservative Italian politicians.[49]

Despite the atrocities, tragedies, sufferings, and deaths occurring daily around the world, the church focuses on denying the God-given right of freedom for women and the love of two human beings who just happen to be of the same sex. These dogmatic crusades against any form of equality, contraception, abortion, and same-sex relationships are basically conducted by men. Tragically, these equality issues have been a political and institutionalized religious travesty that has extended back, at the very least, more than two thousand years. Ironically, it is still occurring even within our technologically advanced but philosophically, spiritually, and religiously debased twenty-first century.

Hypocrisy is clearly as rampant today as it was two thousand years ago, with the church and the moneylenders marching at the head of the parade. It was Jesus who declared that the temple had become a "den of robbers." The same is true today. One word of caution: beware of the present pope.[50] The current pope is great at PR and saying the words people want to hear, but as far as action and deeds go—nothing. But by far, he is not the first "PR scheme"—enter Mother Teresa. "Researchers today have called Mother Teresa an empty "PR ploy" by the Vatican to rehabilitate their tarnished image."[51]

By early summer of 2014, Francis has been pope for over a year, and nothing has changed outside of appointing a council to investigate the sexual-abuse scandal. Of course, any institution's stalling tactic is to form a commission to investigate the problem: "The Vatican on Friday (May 23, 2014) faced criticism from a U.N. panel for the second time this year over failures to report priests accused of sexually abusing children to civil authorities or to ensure redress for victims."[52] Additionally, the pope wants couples to raise children, not pets, which means more "sheep followers" and more money for the church. "Pope Francis said that staying childless will ultimately bring married couples nothing but 'the bitterness of loneliness'…four-legged friends don't offer the same opportunities for love and godliness as raising a child."[53]

Finally, "Pope Francis has affirmed Catholic doctrine on abortion, contraception, and homosexuality. Whilst maintaining the church's teaching against homosexual acts, he has said that gay people should not be marginalized. As a Cardinal, the Pontiff opposed gay marriage in Argentina. In addition, he maintains that he is a 'Son of the Church' regarding loyalty to Church doctrine, and has spoken against abortion as 'horrific,' insisted that women be valued, not clericized. Summarily, Pope Francis reiterates that 'It is absurd to say you follow Jesus Christ, but reject the Church.'"[54] That's exactly what I am saying—reject the hypocritical church!

A Hypocritical Religion and Their Conversion Methods

I have examined all the known superstitions of the world, and I do not find in our particular superstition of Christianity one redeeming feature. They are all alike founded on fables and mythology. Millions of innocent men, women and children, since the introduction of Christianity, have been burnt, tortured, fined and imprisoned. What has been the effect of this coercion? To make one half the world fools and the other half hypocrites; to support roguery and error all over the earth.
—THOMAS JEFFERSON

Basically, Christianity as a religion of hypocrites has utilized two methods of conversion. The first was the brutal forced conversion of indigenous people,[55] such as that used by Charlemagne against the heathen Saxons. While preaching a gospel of love, Charlemagne massacred some forty-five hundred Saxon prisoners, destroyed heathen places of worship, and decreed the death penalty for all those who refused to be baptized or those who continued to practice the pagan faith.

The second may be loosely termed conversion by *syncretization*. The Jesuits were masters at this form of conversion by subtly converting indigenous people through their establishment of schools, universities, and hospitals.[56] In the twenty-first century, this is still ongoing, with the merger of many secular hospitals with Catholic-run institutions, and with the new PR pope, who just happens to be a Jesuit.

Pope Francis speaks to what people want to hear even though there will be no change in dogma and doctrine. He is the front man now for the church's conversion by *syncretization*. Outside of the examples above, another hypocritical statement concerns one of his "10 Tips for Becoming a Happier Person." His number seven is "Respect and take care of nature." With the ongoing effects of climate change, this is something many people would accept and possibly agree with, further establishing within these people's minds the trueness of the church—*maybe we need to return to church, as the pope is concerned about nature* (i.e., climate change). People want to hear these types of statements, but the bottom line is that there will be no change in the doctrine of the church concerning nature and its subservient position to "man." A change in doctrine to match the pope's statement would be to declare as doctrine the sacredness or divinity and consciousness of nature (please see chapter 6, "Mother Nature and Women"), which will never happen, as it is in opposition to Christianity's lie. As I said before, be wary of the PR pope.

As It Was Then, It Is Now Even More So

We are living in very interesting times. As a species, we are facing catastrophic consequences caused by the actions of the ruling male-dominated systems of capitalism; capitalist democracy; institutionalized religion; and corrupt, political systems of governance.

The established paradigms on this earth are corrupt and broken. These patriarchal economic, governmental, and religious systems have based their existence on spreading fear and separatism while accumulating excessive amounts of wealth and power for their controlling elite at the expense of the rest of humanity and the earth. Sadly, this problem is not unique in the annals of history, but it is potentially the most destructive of all time—not only to the human race but to all the creatures of the earth.

Jesus did not—as theologians would have us believe—descant on the blessings of poverty or the sinfulness of sowing and gathering into barns—none but a fool could do so—but discoursed on the evils of a system which was based on wrong conceptions and false assumptions.

His theme...was the eternal problem of the oppression of the many by the few: a problem which was hoary with age already in those far-off times, and which, nevertheless, is still the most burning question of the present day. "The poor ye have always with you," and the question to which Jesus tried to find an answer was not—as is the case with most *soi-disant* reformers—what to do with them, but *how to eliminate from the social organization the conditions which produce them.*

For let it be noted that Jesus never prescribed remedies—so-called—but always sought to find the *cause* of the evil, and then proposed to choke it off at its source. With his postulates ever present in his mind that "Every good tree bringeth forth good fruit, but a corrupt tree bringeth forth evil fruit," he did not fall into the error, so common among students of social problems, of mistaking the *symptoms* for the *malady*, and then try to combat the evil by palliating the effects which result from it. His contention was for *preventives*, and not for palliatives. There can be no "remedy" to correct the evil of the fruit which is brought forth by a corrupt tree. You cannot gather figs of thorns, nor grapes of thistles. Therefore the only way of combating an evil is to destroy the source whence it springs; or, in the metaphor of the Teacher, "Every tree which bringeth not forth good fruit is hewn down, and cast into the fire."[57]

A Synopsis of Jesus's Teachings

Jesus believed in direct experience of the otherworld; the divine; the kingdom of God—the outward kingdom being nature. In Greek, direct experience or experiential knowledge is called *gnosis*. His teachings came from his soul's knowledge and his direct experience, or *gnosis*, of the kingdom. This is *knowing* God—the seen and unseen aspects of creation.

This is what Jesus taught: his teachings emphasized love, which unites, over fear, which separates. He saw no cosmic battle between God and the devil or a duel between good and evil.[58] He only saw the evil deeds that people are capable of doing to others as well as the lack of regard people have for the poor and the outcast.

Jesus walked his talk as an example to his students—both male and female. Deeds were more important than words. He made mistakes and got angry—his human side. He talked and walked his truth, forgave, and healed—his divine side.

He lived the importance of self and other. He felt more comfortable in the presence of the "outcasts," as they were more authentic, whereas the rich and the temple elite were greedy and hypocritical—false faced.

He embraced life in all its shades of light and dark and asked others to do so as well.

The True Message

"I and the Father are One."[59]

Jesus's worldview was based on radical nonduality—as is mine. During my vision the voice from heaven declared, "This star is you; you are this star. The purification is of the people; all are one." Even though the knowledge of oneness was part of my soul, the heavenly voice reinforced it. *All* are *one* is the core of the seed of the kingdom[60] of God. This is the core of Jesus's true message—oneness. Not just Jesus, but *all* things are divine with the spark—the starlight of God within them. In other words, the divine is within *all* things (seen and unseen), and *all* things are within the divine. This is radical nonduality or oneness where spirit and matter interpenetrate.

Jesus's kingdom paradigm was a revolutionary worldview then, as it is now. The kingdom of God is within us and outside us. It is a kingdom of consciousness of heart and mind (oneness), love, compassion, kindness, and equality. This revolutionary worldview I call Divine Humanity—humanity refers to "all" things of the universe. In the following pages, the lie of Christianity and the true message of Jesus will be clearly presented: the truth is revealed—freedom awaits you.

Do not ask why, but only experience from the depths of your soul the mystery, and you will know; but will you ever know?

Raven, creator to some, evil to others,
Earthbound, injured wing, can't you fly?
Why, if divine where comes the suffering?
Do you remember flying high, voice of power—black,
or was it white?
Why maimed, earthbound, separate from heaven?

"Black to some is life while white is death.
Experience the mystery for yourself," Raven shouts.
"Why do you refuse to see the mystery within me?
Always looking, judging, separating, but never seeing the light of the mystery.
You do not know me; I am Raven
The majestic one that suffers and weeps
For the ones I have left behind.

"What is life to one as me?
Surprise will be my answer to you.
I am not what I appear;
I am you, and you are me.
We are one."[61]

Part 1

THE LIE

The only good is knowledge and the only evil ignorance.
—Socrates

Then you will know the truth, and the truth will set you free.
—John 8:32

CHAPTER 1

Oral Teachings of the Messengers—Do They Turn into Written Truths?

The biblical writers may have indulged in a good bit of "spin."[62]

I would ask you, do you believe that the gospel truth is taught and preached in the church? Is it the truth of Jesus's teachings and message? Are Moses's commandments, known today as the Ten Commandments, the actual ones Moses brought to his people? Is the Bible the true word of God? Does this mean God is multilingual?

The simple answer to these questions and others is not an absolute no, but close to it! The prime purpose of this revelation is what we know today is not the total truth or a clear picture of the messages or, most importantly, the hearts and minds of the messengers. To take written accounts from oral teachings[63] and stories years or even decades after the events have happened, and after the messengers have passed over, is the height of folly, egotism, and laziness—the laziness of the ones that accept and blindly follow the dogma and doctrine of institutionalized religions.

Judaism does assume that the stories and teachings that stand behind the written texts were transmitted orally for many generations, in some cases hundreds of years, before they were written down. Accordingly, they do not attempt to cover up this fact.

However, in deference to factual history and the truth that the books of the New Testament were written decades or more after Jesus had passed over, Christianity still insists and promotes as absolute truth that the New

Testament is the "Word of God" (i.e., the "Word of Jesus"). But is the New Testament truly "the Word" of Jesus? Furthermore, who was Jesus, and how could he be described?

Pure and simple, Jesus was an enigma, not only to the ones he encountered daily but, most importantly, to his own apprentices:

> Jesus is the Jewish Socrates. He confronts us, nonbelievers and believ-ers alike, with an array of enigmas. Yet how could it be otherwise? Islam accepts Muhammad as the Seal of the Prophets, but grants Jesus a unique status among the precursors of the ultimate, definitive proph-et in a line that stems from Abraham. Jews have a negative relationship to Christ, but not necessarily to Jesus, who is scarcely responsible for what supposed Christianity has done in his name...Albert Schweitzer, preaching in 1905, said, "The glorified body of Jesus is to be found in his sayings." But there is a difficulty Jesus never intended: which are his authentic sayings?[64]

What then are Jesus's authentic and often enigmatic teachings after the spin doctors and liars have hidden and corrupted the truth of them? It is easy to understand if your mind is quiet that "Jesus' words are frequently enigmatic. What is an enigma? It can be a verbal riddle, or a puzzling thing, or an inex-plicable person. Jesus speaks the first almost invariably, his actions give us the second, and he himself is the third."[65]

How can any person ever replicate the exact words of an enigmatic per-son and come up with his or her authentic sayings and teachings? In addition, Jesus was bringing to his students radical, mystical ideas—not radical, mun-dane stuff but something far more difficult to understand—a revolutionary spiritual philosophy clothed in symbolic metaphor.

Symbolism is the language of mysticism and philosophy that may help us transcend the limitation of words. Symbolic metaphor may open vis-tas of meaning within our minds but also may hide truths that we may not understand without having the speaker or writer to give us further clarification.

We may readily see the quicksand bog that magically appears under our feet once we transverse any type of landscape dotted with radical, symbolic religious metaphors: "The value of a metaphor is in the meaning that it can create. Meaning happens inside the mind and as such is an individual experience."[66]

Even more troubling in determining truth is the translation from oral teachings to written words—especially when the words were spoken in symbolic metaphor. When oral teachings are written down, they have the potential to open up a Pandora's box of manipulation and corruption. The original meaning of the words, which in all accounts may not be known, may be twisted to suit the writer's or the institution's own egotistical mind. Additionally, we must not forget the problem of translating one language into another, especially ancient Hebrew, which consisted solely of consonants, or "common" Greek, where there were no spaces between words.

⚜

Once we look to the past to evaluate sayings or events, we must understand that the past, especially one that extends back two millennia, can never be empirically proven—only reconstructed. This truth can be revealed with the following experiment: Find a teacher who will work with you privately for just one hour. During that hour have the teacher orally lecture you on a subject of his or her choosing. No notes are to be taken. Seven days after the presentation, write down what your teacher said. Be as specific as you can about the exact quotes. Present for feedback. Just for fun, repeat this experiment using an interval of ten years; try fifty years.

I think we all know the results. This experiment can be made even more difficult by having your teacher present new and particularly difficult concepts. Try finding a teacher who has radical views and teaches esoteric, metaphysical, or religious subject matter. How much would you retain and really understand, much less be able to replicate in the future? Yet the sacred teachings many use to guide their lives (for some, fanatically) came from a technique not too different from the parameters of our experiment.

Even if the orally transmitted knowledge is close to the original sayings and teachings, what will stop a person from consciously changing it? The person or group, such as the Jewish scribes or the Christian Gospel writers, that commits to writing the oral teachings of prophets, such as Moses and Jesus, may still change, omit, and further dilute or adapt the stories, sayings, and teachings in a way to serve their own personal ambitions.

⚜

The best tools available to determine our truth are intuition and reason (as well as common sense). Truth resulting from intuition and reason is not new knowledge. In fact, it dates as far back as the Greek mystery schools and Greek mythology, where intuition and reason were the two torches the goddess Ceres carried as she wandered the world searching for her abducted daughter—Persephone.

In figurative terms intuition may be viewed as centered in the heart and reason as originating in the mind. In metaphysical teachings the sun symbolizes our hearts and the moon our minds. The moon has no intrinsic light of its own but relies on the sun for its illumination and, most importantly, its reflection. With this being true, and considering that light is the most common symbol for knowledge, solar light (the heart) represents direct knowledge, which may be termed "heart knowledge," while lunar light (the mind) corresponds to reflective knowledge. Our hearts intuitively know divine truth, while our minds can only find reason through discursive knowledge and cannot function properly except through the guidance of the higher intellect of our hearts. In other words, our hearts and our minds must work together to determine truth.

Always keep in mind truth is very personal. My truth may very well not be your truth. It is up to each individual to determine his or her own truth. But personal truth based on a "book," and not on one's own heart and mind, is the height of folly.

Of course, following the Bible literally or the dogma and doctrine of the church is easier than listening to our own hearts and minds when our past woundings prevent us from trusting ourselves—guilt and doubt are ever present. Thus, in our stress-filled and fast-paced lives, the Bible and the church are an easy alternative to our other option—seeking truth within ourselves, within our hearts.

The Heart

> For as he thinketh in his heart, so is he. (Proverbs 23:7a [KJV])
> '...that you may know the thoughts of
> your heart. (Daniel 2:30b [NKJV])

Wondrous and magical is the heart physically and spiritually. It is the center of our consciousness of oneness, while the brain is the center of our dualistic consciousness. Amazingly, the heart possesses its own nervous system. A key to the wonderful quotes above is the Hebrew word *leb* with the meaning of heart, feelings, will, and intellect. The heart thinks! It is an intelligence system. In fact, the brain receives more orders from the heart than the heart receives from the brain. In Biblical usage, the word *heart* has meant mind, knowledge, thinking, reflection, and memory.

Furthermore, our indigenous ancestors "understood the heart's ability to intelligently perceive and decipher the world around them, and acknowledged the limitations and reductionist nature of living in a manner in which one relies primarily on the mind.

"They went beyond the thoughts in their heads, using the heart as an organ of perception to connect with the energy fields of other organisms – not just other humans, but the earth as well – in order to fully immerse themselves in the deeper meanings embodying their thoughts."[67]

Moreover, new research has discovered that the heart has a sense of smell. Even more amazing is the hormone it secretes—oxytocin.[68] This is the bonding or love hormone that brings things together. In this bonding we experience feelings of compassion, harmony, love, and peace. In other words, the heart is the key to our awakening of radical nondualistic consciousness.

The Bible[69]

Those who believe in the infallibility of the Bible are blindly stuck in an elusive, dogmatic quagmire of mistranslation, misinterpretations, and misinformation.
—REV. DR. J. C. HUSFELT (1997)

The truth is here in the "book." Let me read to you from the "book." Let me preach to you from the "book." The justification for my actions is in the "book." Let us pray from the "book." Let us "bow down" to the "book," as it is the Word of God. *Sounds to me like "idol" worship.*

Of course, the "book" is the Bible[70]—a book that, in my estimation, has brought more chaos, destruction, separateness, pain, and suffering than it has unity, love, and forgiveness. I've always wondered what would happen if, in the moment, a Christian priest, minister, or preacher was asked to put aside his or her Bible and prepared sermon and ceremony and conduct a service totally from the heart and mind without quoting, reading, or "praying" from the Bible or conducting some preset ritual.

I remember the story that Vince Stogan, modern-day John the Baptist, told my wife and me many years ago. Vince and his wife, Mom Stogan, were teachers to us and the primary elders of the First People of British Columbia. They were instrumental in bringing back their people's spirit dancing in the smokehouses. If you needed heavy-duty healing, it was Mom and Vince you sought out. They were true shamans through and through; however, Vince didn't like to use that term, and when pushed for a label, he would just say, "Call me an Indian doctor." Both he and Mom were the spiritual and religious leaders of their people. Both are no longer on this earth. Vince would probably object to my use of the term "religious" leader, as organized religion was not his thing.

Vince decided one time that he needed to see what this "church" stuff was all about. So he went to a Sunday church service. This was the story that he shared with us about his experience and feelings of church: "I wanted to give church a chance to see what it was like. I only lasted a short time before I left the service. When the person up front said, 'Let's bow our heads and pray' and started reading from a book, that was enough for me. You do not pray from a book; you pray from your heart—the words come from your heart, not from something written in a book."

The "book" seemingly overrides common sense and experience. Add to this the realization that the Bible is a translated copy of words and teachings spoken ages ago. According to *Newsweek*, "No television preacher has ever read the Bible. Neither has any evangelical politician. Neither has the pope... At best, we've all read a bad translation—a translation of translations of translations of hand-copied copies of copies of copies of copies, and on and on, hundreds of times." [71]

Not only do we have inaccurate translations, but we have something even more sinister—manipulation for agendas of power and control. "In Philippians, the King James Version translates some words to designate Jesus as 'being in the form of God.' The Greek word for form could simply mean Jesus was in the image of God. But the publishers of some Bibles decided to insert their beliefs into translations that had nothing to do with the Greek. The Living Bible, for example, says Jesus 'was God'—even though modern translators pretty much just invented the words."[72]

Drumroll—in the fourth century CE, the emperor Constantine enters the picture of Biblical duplicity. According to Kurt Eichenwald in the *Newsweek* article:

> Christianity was in chaos in its early days, with some sects declaring the others heretics. And then, in the early 300s, Emperor Constantine of Rome declared he had become follower of Jesus, ended his empire's persecution of Christians and set out to reconcile the disputes among the sects. Constantine was a brutal sociopath who murdered his eldest son, decapitated his brother-in-law and killed his wife by boiling her alive, and that was after he proclaimed that he had converted from worshipping the sun god to being a Christian. Yet he also changed the course of Christian history, ultimately influencing which books made it into the New Testament.[73]

So various gospels, such as the gospel of Mary Magdalene, which was closer to Jesus's true message and teachings, never made the cut!

And then there is Constantine's creation of the Nicene Creed, which sealed the lie in fool's gold and set a standard of wealth over spirit. At the lakeside town of Nicaea, "Constantine arrived wearing jewels and gold on his scarlet robe and pearls on his crown, eager to discuss the true essence of a poor carpenter who had died 300 years before."[74]

As a reflection of the ignorance of the majority of churchgoers, "things that are today accepted without much thought were adopted or reinforced at Nicaea. For example, the Old Testament was clear in declaring that God rested on the seventh day, making it the Sabbath. The seventh day of the week is Saturday, the day of Jewish worship and rest. (Jesus himself invoked the holiness of the Jewish Sabbath.) The word Sunday does not appear in the Bible, either as the Sabbath or anything else. But four years before Nicaea, Constantine declared Sunday as a day of rest in honor of the sun god."[75] If we use common sense, Sunday would not be the perfect day to rest or to be the Sabbat. On the contrary, it would be the best day to begin the workweek, as the sun symbolizes outer expression and energy. Beginning the workweek on Monday doesn't make sense, as the moon symbolizes inner expression and energy.

With the question of the Sabbath already settled, discussions at Nicaea took the form of whether Jesus was a man who was the son of God or was God himself. Of course, this argument didn't occur a few years after Jesus had passed over but some three hundred years later. True to form:

> Constantine sided with those who believed Jesus was both God and man, so a statement of belief, called the Nicene Creed, was composed to proclaim that. Those who refused to sign the statement were banished. Others were slaughtered. After they had returned home and were far from Rome, some who signed the document later sent letters to Constantine saying they had only done so out of fear for their lives.
>
> About 50 years later, in A.D. 381, the Romans held another meeting, this time in Constantinople. There, a new agreement was reached—Jesus wasn't two, he was now three—Father, Son and Holy Ghost. The Nicene Creed was rewritten, and those who refused to sign the statement were banished, and another wholesale slaughter began, this time of those who rejected the Trinity, a concept that is nowhere in the original Greek manuscripts and is often contradicted by it.
>
> To this day, congregants in Christian churches at Sunday services worldwide recite the Nicene Creed, which serves as affirmation of their belief in the Trinity. It is doubtful many of them know the words they utter are not from the Bible, and were the cause of so much bloodshed.[76]

⚜

Written words, especially words thousands of years old and not in the original language, can lead to various interpretations. Add to this the manipulators of word and fact. As we have seen, wrong translations, personal agendas, lies, and manipulations of truth have caused much suffering and bloodshed over the centuries—a fact still true today. What then is the truth?

✣

I believe our truth comes from knowledge, the experience of that knowledge, and our connection to and experience of nature as revealed by heaven and earth. It does not solely evolve from what someone else has written, whether it is supposedly God inspired or not.

Jesus felt this way. It's very evident Jesus looked to nature, the "kingdom outside us," for truth. He did not stop people in the street or gather them by the seashore and quote from the Torah. He asked people to look within themselves and to look to nature. "Unlike the teachers of conventional wisdom of his day, Jesus was not a 'Torah sage.' His teaching ordinarily did not take the form of elaborating or commenting upon the Torah, even though he obviously knew it and sometimes referred to it. Rather than appealing to sacred text or citing opinions of earlier teachers, he most often appealed to the world of human experience or made observations about nature."[77] Accordingly, let your Bible as literal truth collect dust. Let us turn to nature and our heart for truth:

> Seek not the law in your scriptures, for the law is life, whereas the scripture is dead. I tell you truly, Moses received not his laws from God in writing, but through the living word. The law is living word of living God to living prophets for living men. In everything that is life is the law written. You find it in the grass, in the tree, in the river, in the mountain, in the birds of heaven, in the fishes of the sea; but seek it chiefly in yourselves. For I tell you truly, all living things are nearer to God than the scripture which is without life. God so made life and all living things that they might by the everlasting word teach the laws of the true God to man. God wrote not the laws in the pages of books, but in your heart and in your spirit. They are in your breath, your blood, your bone; in your flesh, your bowels, your eyes, your ears, and in every little part of your body. They are present in the air, in the water, in the earth, in the plants, in the sunbeams, in the depths and in the heights. They all speak to you that you may understand the tongue and the will of the living God. But you shut your eyes that you may not see, and you shut your ears that you may not hear. I tell you truly, that the scripture

is the work of man, but life and all its hosts are the work of our God. Wherefore do you not listen to the words of God which are written in His works? And wherefore do you study the dead scriptures which are the work of the hands of men?[78]

This law, the living vibration of living God, is the divine spark and starlight and divine consciousness that is within all things of creation. This is the true message of Jesus.

⚜

One last point, we must ask ourselves this question: What keeps human beings seeking power, either for themselves or for their religions, from taking oral teachings, sayings, and stories and twisting and changing them to fit their own egocentric, materialistic religious needs? It is established fact that the Old Testament section of the Christian Bible was changed from the Hebrew original to one that better matched their lie.

The Hebrew Tanakh ends with 2 Chronicles, while the Christian Old Testament purposely reorders the sequence of books of the Tanakh and ends not with Chronicles but with Malachi, one of the Twelve Minor Prophets. According to Harold Bloom's *Jesus and Yahweh*, "In order to lead into the three opening chapters of the Gospel of Matthew, the Christian Old Testament concludes with Malachi, 'the Messenger,' proclaiming Elijah's return (as John the Baptist)."[79] Ironically enough, this would point to a belief in reincarnation and not a one-way trip to heaven or hell.

God as Book

The dawn of a new age is upon us. As a human race, we are walking out of the darkness of the past thousands of years and approaching the light timidly, as only one can after being imprisoned for so long in a shadowy, corrupt world ruled by fear and materialism. These past millennia have been a time of religious darkness that witnessed gatekeepers, in the form of priests, popes, rabbis, and mullahs, between the people and God. Why keep following these religions of the dead? If it is fear, let it go, and instead, embrace a message of life—Jesus's true message.

⚜

As we examine our spiritual history, the true message of Jesus needs to be heard: Each and every person comes from a divine lineage, previous incarnations, as well as a human one. Each person is both divine and human.

Each person, as divine, has direct access to God and the mystical without going through an intermediary. Because each person is also human, in accessing the divine, a person may filter the knowledge through his or her own ego, such as his or her biases and expectations, with the result that the objective divine truth becomes the subjective human opinion.

This concept, applied to religious texts, brings us insight into sacred writings. Sacred scripts are both the "Word" of God (divine) as well as the word of man (human). Every text may be sacred as well as profane. Because some texts may be more sacred than others, it is up to each individual to determine which words have been divinely inspired or humanly filtered. For this reason, all writings contain the seeds of divinity as well as humanity—there can be no sacred text innately superior to any other.

If you accept this premise, then the Bible simply morphs into just another sacred/mundane book that can possibly provide us with some guidance, but it is not "the sole Word" of God. However, we must ask ourselves these questions: what are authentic teachings, what has been manipulated for control and power, and where may truth be found within the Bible?

Commentary

To base a religion solely on the contents of a book is the height of ignorance, madness, recklessness, and folly. Even though the book is based on the supposed teachings of a prophet, it still opens the "gates" to metaphoric hell. This is not the hell preached by certain religions as an eternal punishment after death. This hell is the one that we may experience while alive on earth.

The maddness is that these are foundational religious books whose interpretations people fiercely contest. Interpretations of these so-called holy words have the potential to lead to horrendous and unspeakable acts of depravity as witnessed by the current actions of ISIS.

Tanakh
Genesis, the Foundation of Dualism

Christianity, beginning with Saul, was and still is based on lies and half-truths. Moreover, the manipulation of truth extends further back in time, possibly to the scribes of Judaism. We will never know for sure if the beginning section (Genesis) of the Hebrew Tanakh was accurately recorded by the Jewish scribes based on the oral teachings of Moses through King David and Solomon.

The fact is, the commonly accepted translation of Genesis establishes a foundation and justification for religious dualism.

> In the beginning when God created the heavens and the earth, the earth was a formless void and darkness covered the face of the deep, while a wind from God swept over the face of the waters. Then God said, "Let there be light"; and there was light. *And God saw that the light was good; and God separated the light from the darkness.* God called the light Day, and the darkness he called Night.[80]

In this beginning passage, we discover the roots of the male-dominated religion of Christianity, the dualism of separation, light (male) being good, with a subtle indication that in the separation of light (good) from darkness (female) that darkness is not good. This sets in place and in play the dualistic conflict of light and dark, right and wrong, good and evil, God and the devil.

In contrast to this Western religion creation myth, we have the beautiful Polynesian myth of creation called *Kumulipo*. This saga was passed on through the magic vocalization power of chant. Considering the vibrational aspect of creation, it is very appropriate to "chant the universe" into existence.

In direct opposition to the Bible, the Kumulipo emphasizes, not just once but over and over again, the process of *He po uhe'e i ka wawa*—"darkness slips into light." According to a translation of Kumulipo by Martha Warren Beckwith, *He po uhe'e i ka wawa* is repeated forty-three times during the first four chants (forty-three reduces down to seven; ponder this). This is significant and demonstrates the importance of darkness slipping into light. There is no separation, only the gradual, interpenetrative aspects as darkness slips into light. We are faced with two different teachings on humanity's foundational myth of creation. Which one is correct?

If we turn to nature for the answer, I think it is obvious. Using the concept of "nature's truths of Gods reflection," we realize that every day and night on this planet, darkness slips into light, and light slips into darkness. I have yet to observe a day when one moment it is light, and in the next moment there is the separate state of darkness. Even though this truth, the truth of the inter-penetrative aspects of dark and light, is very evident every dawn and dusk, millions and millions of people still look to the Bible and the separation of light and dark, and all the ramifications of such, as the absolute truth of life. How about you?

Genesis Translated from the Ancient Hebrew

> In the summit "Elohiym [Powers]" fattened the sky and the land, and the land had existed in confusion and was unfilled and darkness was upon the face of the deep sea and the wind of "Elohiym [Powers]" was much fluttering upon the face of the water and "Elohiym [Powers]" said, light exist and light existed, and "Elohiym [Powers]" saw the light given that it was functional and "Elohiym [Powers]" made a separation between the light and the darkness, and "Elohiym [Powers]" called out to the light day and to the darkness he called out night and evening existed and morning existed one day.[81]

Can you see the small but gigantic difference between the two translations? Common sense tells us that a slight change in the translation of a word can turn a mountain upside down to the meaning it conveys. The religious and philosophical impact of the difference in meaning between the accepted translation of Genesis and the ancient Hebrew translation is earth-shattering.

Forcefully, and for impact, the commonly accepted reading of Genesis states, "Then God said, Let there be light; and there was light." The alternative translation from the ancient Hebrew states, "Elohiym [Powers] said, light exist and light existed." Without worrying about the difference in meaning between God and Elohiym [Powers], the next few words are very important. The accepted translation states, "And God saw that the light was good; and God separated the light from the darkness."

And the ancient Hebrew states, "Elohiym [Powers] saw the light given that it was functional and Elohiym [Powers] made a separation between the light and the darkness."

On the one hand, we are served the word "good," and on the other hand, the word is "functional." They are very different in meaning and implication. Good is subjective, a word of judgment, and purely dualistic in its implication—good or bad. Good utilized in this way sets up a paradigm of separation, just as during the Iraq War, a commonly used term when referring to the opposition was "bad guys," with an implicit connotation that we were the "good guys." If you accept the Bible as the literal Word of God, Genesis is stating light is good. This would be the absolute truth, with the inference that the darkness is bad. In dualistic terms light equates to heaven, father, male, and so forth, whereas dark equates to earth, mother, and female. We can see the conclusions from this dogmatic reading of Genesis.

Alternatively, in the ancient Hebrew translation, the word is "functional," which indicates performance and is descriptive of something that operates in a manner congruent with its purpose. It asserts that "Powers" saw the light as being functional and thus "made a separation between the light and the darkness." Additionally, it indicates that the light was a part of and within the dark. In contrast to the accepted translation in the Tanakh and the Christian Bible, there is no implication here that the light is "good" and the dark is the opposite, "bad."

Furthermore, there is a subtle influence on a person's understanding of the issue of separation. When I asked the question on separation to our apprentices, one replied that "the first implies light and darkness as distinct and unconnected. The second implies a connection via an intermediate something that is a separation." The first is pure and simply dualistic, while the second implies nonduality and connectedness. This makes sense since this translation is probably closer to the actual teachings of Moses, who experienced firsthand God and nonduality. This otherworldly, nondualistic event Moses experienced was the burning bush.

The New Testament
In the fourth century of the Common Era, the Roman Empire was in decline, stretched to its limits through its materialistic conquests. As we have seen,

the Roman emperor Constantine I had an inspiration—a way to consolidate power and hold the empire together. His idea was to make Christianity the religion of Rome. As a worshipper of Sol Invictus, the sun god, it was a simple step to take—make Jesus God—and keep the control and money in Rome.

His idea was a great success. In 325 CE he summoned the First Council of Nicaea, and by vote Jesus was declared God—even though at the time, this ridiculous proclamation went against the current belief of the majority of Christian churches. And then the final iron seal on the truth occurred in 367 CE, when it was locked into place by the censorship and editing of the bishop of Alexandria and other church officials.

> The New Testament came together gradually over a period of 400 years, and it took its final form as a result of a Church Council, not, as some seem to think, as a result of divine intervention.
>
> Bishop Athanasius of Alexandria finally compiled a list of works to be included in the New Testament in 367 CE, and the Church Council of Hippo ratified this list in 393 and again in 397. The New Testament which we know today was agreed upon by those Councils, and many books with just as much historical validity and holy purpose were rejected...
>
> Each and every book, all 27 of them, have undergone multiple additions and deletions, and the corpus contains material which often points to early sources of information about Jesus and his Mission which do not properly gel with what the compilers, as opposed to the original writers, wished to say, or the Church Fathers wished to know. The early Church, with a stroke of its magisterial pen, had consolidated its doctrinal position and initiated the process of scholarly reification which would more and more stunt Christian intelligence concerning New Testament makeup and composition. Necessary it may have been for the sake of continuity and coherence, for the sake of social control and the eradication of ideas already deemed heretical by the ruling elite—but it would eventually lead to a massive distortion of historical and spiritual reality.[82]

Firsthand Knowledge—the Prophet; Secondhand Information—the Priest and the Church

According to Max Weber's *Sociology of Religion*, a prophet is "a purely individual bearer of charisma,[83] who by one's mission proclaims religious teaching or divine commandment."[84] Furthermore, "the 'personal' call is the decisive element distinguishing the prophet from the priest. First of all, the prophet declares new revelations by charisma, whereas the priest serves to a sacred tradition. It is no accident that almost no prophet has come from the priesthood."[85]

⚜

We are living in a technological age of information. Want to know something? Then just Google or Bing. In an instant these search engines make information available to the masses. But as Ogden Nash once said, "The masses are asses, but Nietzsche is peachy." Information is just that—information. It is not knowledge, nor is it anywhere close to wisdom. For information to become knowledge, there needs to be the experience of the information. And for knowledge to become wisdom, we need the experience of the knowledge. In our culture and society, firsthand experience is fleeting, as most people rely on secondhand information and, in a religious sense, tradition and faith.

Contrary to relying on tradition and faith for one's truth, a prophet is a person who has had firsthand experience of the otherworld or the unseen world—truth through personal experience. In *The Varieties of Religious Experience*, William James documented this type of experience. In this classic study, he "finds the origin of belief in an 'unseen' world in the experience of 'religious geniuses' who experience firsthand the realities of which religion speaks, and carefully distinguishes this primal experience from what he calls 'secondhand' religion, the beliefs that people acquire through tradition."[86] According to William James, the church is a secondhand religion.

This firsthand knowledge is also referred to as gnosis. This knowing is directly experienced. I know angels based not on faith but on my own direct, physical experience, gnosis, of them. Faith is of the church; gnosis is of the prophet. From my knowing or knowledge comes wisdom or Sophia.[87] The experience of knowledge is wisdom, which we discover within ourselves when we directly experience the kingdom inside and outside us.

I would ask each of you to use common sense in considering the following question. How precise and accurate can a person be in writing about religious practices and truths concerning sanctification practices without ever having "walked" the teachings and practices he or she is writing or preaching about? Here is a fact: the majority of religious writers, scholars, priests, ministers, rabbis, and other religious leaders of our day practice, preach, and promote secondhand religion. I realize Pauline Christianity is based solely on "faith." However, there remains one most important truth. Jesus practiced and believed in sanctification practices and teachings, not ones of salvation based on "faith." Following in the footsteps of Moses, Jesus didn't believe in God—he knew God, just as Moses knew God and I know God.

Exemplary Prophet

A prophet who brings a message and leads by example is known as an exemplary prophet. This was Jesus. He emphasized deeds over faith. By his personal example, he "showed the way" to the kingdom. This was not by faith but by deeds. His teachings were based on love (unity), not fear (separation). Through our deeds we may perfect ourselves. There was no original sin. Accordingly, a priest, who might absolve sins, was unnecessary. Furthermore, there was no need for temple obedience as an ethical duty. It was one's deeds based on one's heart that mattered and led to the awakening of the kingdom.

The Otherworld and Sanctification

To be elected pope, bishop, or any other religious leader, otherworldly experiences are not required, not even one! I am not talking about personal dreams, near-death experiences, or manifestations of one's own unhealthy ego where supposed angels in human form come to you, or you go to heaven and talk to Jesus. What I do mean is actually experiencing the physical manifestation of the otherworld as it was experienced by Moses, Jesus, and me.

The church is based on salvation, not sanctification. Conversely to the doctrine of the church, Jesus's whole life was focused on the philosophy and practices of sanctification, many times as a sacrifice of self to self.[88] He spent the majority of his time out in nature in the blessed lands of the Galilee, not in

Jerusalem. The beauty of the Galilee was an inspiration for his teachings—the sea, the stars, and all of God's creatures.

Jesus loved nature while recognizing the divine in nature and the sacredness of all living things. One of the ways he referred to himself was as a "son of man." In Hebrew it is *ben 'Adam* or "son of Adam." Originally, Adam meant humanity and was linked with the word for "earth"—*Adamah*. Jesus was referring to himself as a "son of humanity and the earth." If people embraced this mind-set that we are citizens or "sons and daughters of the earth" first and foremost, not of a country, this alone would help break down barriers of separation between people.

As one "sown from the earth," he understood nature as being both sacred and profane (earthly). How much more connected to the earth can you get? Furthermore, how much closer to the earth can you get than conducting your sanctification practices out in nature and not in the temple area? His bathing practice and his baptism of others were always conducted in a flowing river or stream, never in the temple's artificial bathing pools.

Imagine standing before first light on the edge of a flowing river while listening to the sounds of the rushing waters as if they are the heavenly chariot of God. And further imagine your bare feet on the sacred ground of the earth, your naked body feeling the winds of the earth, while your uncovered head and eyes observe the dimming night sky—one embedded with hundreds of sparkling jewels. And then you voice prayers to your earthly mother, the spirits of the land, and your heavenly father before entering alone and submerging yourself by fully squatting underwater and then coming straight up to stand once again in the rushing waters—not once but three times.[89]

Would not this form of spiritual or sanctification practice make you feel one with nature, with the earth, and with the heavens? The answer is obvious. I know firsthand the feeling and power of this experience, as this is a description of my own spiritual practice as well as Jesus's.

The Burning Bush

Jesus and Moses experienced the otherworld firsthand. It is recorded in the Torah that Moses was tending sheep for his father-in-law, Jethro—the priest or shaman of Midian. While Moses was herding his flock, he wandered off the path searching for a lost sheep. It was through his concern and compassion for a lost animal that he discovered the truth of existence: "The angel of the Lord appeared to him in a blazing fire from the midst of a bush; and he looked, and behold, the bush was burning with fire, yet the bush was not consumed" (Exod. 3:2). This was a bush that defied the logic of physics. This was his experience of interpenetrative radical nonduality or oneness on Mount Horeb.

Moses's "eyes had been trained to see beyond the obvious, to look for allusion in all illusion, to discover meaning in all subtlety, mystery in all conspicuousness, sacredness in all mundaneness. And so he looked not at a bush engulfed in flames but at a bush and at a fire dancing their separateness in unison. He saw both their distinctiveness and their oneness. And in that way of perceiving, the Spirit that harmonizes all opposites spoke to all of him, to Moses the finite person and to Moses the infinite spirit: 'And the Creator called to him from within the bush, and said 'Moses, Moses!'"[90]

This is the earliest recorded religious verification of the divine spark within and of nondualistic interpenetration reality—radical nonduality. Over a millennium later, as far as it is known, the next Jewish person to experience this otherworld reality was Jesus. With the morning star shining in the east as first light broke through the darkness of night, Jesus experienced his spiritual awakening with a vision of the otherworld and the descent of spirit (the dove representative of the morning-star aspect of Venus) into his body. This was his experience of interpenetrative radical nonduality or oneness.

Moses and Jesus were mystics, and each had a firsthand experience of radical nonduality. Why then are both religions, which were supposedly birthed by them, dualistic?

⚜

Moses and Jesus did their own spiritual work not in some building but out in nature. Both knew in their hearts that immersion in nature was the only way to be able to grasp an understanding of the mysteries of heaven and earth.

They were exemplary prophets who guided their people in a natural "way"—a process of experiential and initiatory experience where the "mystery" could very well reveal itself. They worked against fear, bringing a message of inclusive love. This was a love based on oneness and connectedness of the self to all other things of the earth and the heavens. This would reveal the spirit and otherworldly aspects of life.

Contrary to this, Christianity is based on dogma, doctrine, faith, fear, and guilt but not love. There is no oneness or connectedness except to the church and its sham Christ. So where is the direct experience of the other-world and the love, oneness, loving-kindness, and connectedness taught by Jesus?

CHAPTER 2

The Greatest Lie Ever Told

There is not a sentence concerning Jesus in the entire New Testament composed by anyone who ever had met the unwilling King of the Jews.[91]

Christianity is based on a lie.[92] "The simple truth is that the creation of Christianity was no more than a fantasy gone wrong. Moreover, it was concocted by a bunch of rather sick but ambitious individuals who not only lied through their teeth, but also sent millions of people to their death with the sole purpose of dying, so they thought, in the name of 'the Lord.' The history of Christianity is bloody, savage and cruel."[93] The illusion they spread basically alluded to the following mind-set: "All is 'right' when you have faith and follow 'the Lord.'"

How ironic that the lies were a cover-up for Jesus's true message, which was about self and other, about compassion and love, not blood and cruelty. One brief example is Jesus's teaching to do unto others as you would have them do unto you ("natural law"). Christianity's lie was totally opposite of what Jesus stood for and what he taught and, yes, even lived. The lie made him the only divine one, the Son of God, and corrupted his true message that the angelic spark (divineness) or spirit of God was within all things, which comes down to us today as the teaching of the "kingdom within."

There has been evidence unearthed by Michael Baigent called the "Jesus papers." Baigent was one of the authors of *Holy Blood, Holy Grail*, and in his newest book, *The Jesus Papers, Exposing the Greatest Cover-Up in History*, he relates his meeting with an Israeli he didn't name but referred to as "my friend." It seems that this Israeli was in the possession of papyrus texts, the so-called Jesus papers:

The papyryus texts were two Aramaic letters written to the Jewish court, the Sanhedrin. The writer...called himself bani meshiha—the Messiah of the Children of Israel. This figure, the Messiah of the Children of Israel, was defending himself against a charge made by the Sanhedrin—he had obviously been accused of calling himself "son of God" and had been challenged to defend himself against this charge. In the first letter, the messiah explained that what he meant was not that he was "God" but that the "Spirit of God" was in him—not that he was *physically* the son of God but rather that he was spiritually an adopted son of God. And he added that everyone who felt similarly filled with the "spirit" was also a "son of God."

In other words, the messiah—who must be the teacher we know as Jesus—explicitly states in these letters that he is not divine—or at any rate, no more than anyone else. This, we can be sure, is something the Vatican would not like to be made public.[94]

Knowledge is power. In addition, I believe that knowledge and experience result in wisdom and truth: "know the truth and the truth will set you free" (John 8:32). Blindly believing, in my opinion, does not set you free but only imprisons you in a fortress of lies. Knowledge is freedom, choice, and movement, while ignorance is imprisonment and stagnation. Rev. Dr. J. Clifford profoundly put it this way: "It is not the truth that suffers from the most searching investigation; they suffer who will not undertake it; and who would hinder others from seeking it."[95]

Religious ignorance propagates a religion such as Christianity, which is solely based on faith. To believe and not to question or to turn a blind eye because you are too busy working and consuming allows destructive paradigms to flourish. Unjust wars, dictatorships, and destructive religions are just some of the results of this ignorance.

Seek and question, and truth may be revealed. With a little research, we may discover a glimpse of Jesus's true message. Partially, this is revealed in various writings that were concealed and thus never saw the light of day in what became known as the New Testament of Christianity. The following is excerpted from a sermon by United Methodist Minister Toni Cook:

Matthew, Mark, Luke and John weren't the only Gospels used by the ancient church. It is estimated that there were hundreds of other gospels and accounts of Jesus's life and teachings.

One of those is the Gospel of Thomas, which was written around 90 C.E. It is one of the oldest gospels in existence. It is a collection of Jesus's sayings probably used by Jewish Christians living in Eastern Syria...Thomas provides us with new ways of hearing some of the familiar sayings of Jesus, and gives us other sayings and parables with radically different slants than those in the Bible. Thomas says we have come from the Light, that divinity shines within us all...

Professor Elaine Pagels, in her wonderful new book *Beyond Belief*, asserts that the Gospel of Thomas was a direct threat to the exclusive divinity of Jesus proclaimed by the Gospel of John. "John says that we can experience God only through the divine light embodied in Jesus. But...Thomas' gospel (says)...that the divine light Jesus embodied is shared by humanity...that the image of God is hidden within everyone."

And the Western Church, with its headquarters in Rome...felt compelled to set the canon of Scripture, and decided which of the many Christian Gospels to include as official Christian Scripture and which to throw out. And the Gospel of Thomas, a gospel used more in the Eastern Church—a gospel which challenged the exclusive divinity of Jesus while urging us to realize our own divinity—was discarded along with many other ancient gospels. And the official canon of the New Testament was set in the year 367.[96]

In addition, there were many tentacles to support and justify the original lie. For example, the virgin birth of Jesus was another lie promoted by the church. This supposedly occurred at the time of the winter solstice (by the Julian calendar, December 25), which was the indigenous Roman celebration and rite of Saturnian. The Church of Rome not only wanted the people to spend money on their celebration and not on the pagan Saturnian, but also wanted to convert people to their "new religion."

To this day a virgin birth, a birth not mythological or symbolic, still defies reason, logic, and the natural laws of creation. But the lie of the virgin birth of Jesus helped recruit new converts to the "one and only" true religion, promoting "Jesus as God."

If we probe even further, we discover the Roman Catholic Church's adoption of legends that pertained to various other religions' mythic saviors to Jesus's life. The church, however, claimed these happenings of birth and life not in mythical terms but solely as truth and reality.

The bottom line is that the greatest lie in the history of humanity has been the one voiced by Paul and Christianity (birthed by the Roman Catholic Church) that transformed Jesus's social, spiritual, and religious teachings and practices into a religion that was exclusively one of "faith" and worship. This resulted in his exclusive divinity and the "redeeming faith and worship" of the Lord Jesus Christ—Son of God, as revealed by the following belief:

> We have all sinned and deserve God's judgment. God, the Father, sent His only Son to satisfy that judgment for those who believe in Him. Jesus, the creator and eternal Son of God, who lived a sinless life, loves us so much that He died for our sins, taking the punishment that we deserve, was buried, and rose from the dead according to the Bible. If you truly believe and trust this in your heart, receiving Jesus alone as your Savior, declaring, "Jesus is Lord," you will be saved from judgment and spend eternity with God in heaven.[97]

If all I have to do is declare that Jesus is Savior and Lord, and then I will be spared punishment and spend eternity with God in heaven (even though I have caused many people pain and suffering), then sign me up. This also means that I can cause more pain and suffering, and it doesn't really matter as long as I believe Jesus is Savior and Lord while receiving Jesus in my heart. For a fearful person filled with guilt and shame with little personal power, or for a selfish, greedy person only concerned about himself or herself and not others or the greater well-being of the earth, this is a perfect religion.

Saul (Paul of Tarsus), "the Spouter of Wickedness and Lies and the Distorter of the True Teachings of Jesus"[98]

Paul was the first corrupter of the doctrines of Jesus.
—THOMAS JEFFERSON

As often as Jesus's name is invoked and chatted about by Christians and the church, it is easy to understand why the majority of people believe that Christianity is Jesus's Christianity. But this is not the case; Christianity is, pure and simple, Pauline Christianity:

> Who was it who declared Jesus to be "both Lord and Christ"?
> That it was not Jesus himself we may safely conclude from the few relics of his teaching that have been preserved for us. Nor is it possible to believe that he would have tolerated any such distinction to be conferred on himself by others. That would have meant the negation of all that he taught and strove and died for...
> Paul...the author of the Christ-myth and the founder of Christianity. It is he...who first conceived the idea that Jesus was Christ, and who built so vast a superstructure on so weak a foundation.[99]

According to *The Hiram Key* by Christopher Knight and Robert Lomas, "Doctrines which Paul invented were totally different from the revolutionary egalitarian ideas of Jesus. Jesus had been a revolutionary and a pioneer of democratic thinking. Thanks to Paul and the non-Jewish hierarchical cult that he developed, Jesus's teachings were buried and forgotten."[100]

To further his lie, Paul used "Christ" as a proper name, implying that Jesus had a double nature as fully human and fully divine. But this is an oxymoron—an impossibility. We are human, and we do have a divine spark within us that needs to be awakened,[101] but that does not make us fully divine.

What resulted from this lie was an incarnation doctrine where "the Two Natures were so intrinsically fused that Jesus was simultaneously all human and all divine—an utterly impossible combination of opposites quite beyond anyone's capacity to understand or explain. And yet this incomprehensible notion continues to be voiced from pulpits, and congregations and men of the cloth take it for granted."[102]

Can you see the very slight difference, but totally different meaning, between this incarnation doctrine and one where human and divine interpenetrate, resulting in not being fully one or the other? Paul promoted the lie that Jesus was the Son of God—fully human, fully divine. This was directly opposite to Jesus's true message that each one of us is human (son of man) and each one of us has the spirit of God within (son of God). Think for a moment how different the world would have been over the past two thousand years if Jesus's true message had been spread and not the lie of Saul's.

There is one last point that magnifies Paul's duplicity, deceit, and, at the same time, brilliance. Saul would have known about the "dying-and-rising god" myths of the ancient Near East, such as the Egyptian death-and-resurrection myth of Osiris. These gods are too numerous to list, but here are a few: Adonis, a Greek symbol of the seasonality of vegetable life; Baal, a Canaanite weather and fertility god; and Dionysus, the Greek god of wine and of all liquid elements in nature, such as the sap in trees. It was not too much of a stretch for Paul to spread the message that a "myth" had walked the earth in human form. This was the first time ever that a "dying-and-rising god" had lived, breathed, died, and, of course, resurrected—Jesus Christ.

Paul's Corruption of Jesus's Message

Jesus taught that we are all divine as well as human, and the way to our divinity is through love, which is discovered within ourselves, within the kingdom of God. This is exactly opposite to Paul's message of the "Risen Christ" and his religion of salvation with the finite church being the kingdom of God.

> The Christian idea of the relation of the Risen Christ to the Kingdom of God, considered simply as the rule of God in human hearts and human affairs, carries with it many of the ideas of Jesus, to be sure, but in the main as expressed in theology and institutions, Christianity is far more of Paul than it is of Jesus.
>
> Concerning the conception of the kingdom of God, which Jesus made so prominent, there is almost no evidence of an understanding of it, or interest in it, by the Christian Church. In a general way it was considered to be synonomous [sic] with the Church, visible and invisible. Paul showed but slight knowledge or interest in it. The great councils, in formulating the creeds tell us nothing about it. Modern catechisms only say that baptised [sic] believers become members of it. In the modern emphasis on ethical idealism, and the common fear of mysticism, men see the Kingdom in some vague way as the idealized social community. Only to the great mystics of the Church has the vision of Jesus in this particular been preserved. And Jesus's faith in

the supremacy of Love, while held in theory, is often forgotten in the Christian's larger interest in theistic dogmas, competitive economics and private profit, nationalism and war.[103]

Most Christians, being in the dark about the origins of their faith, do not even realize that Christianity is not based on Jesus's message and teachings but on Paul's. It is not widely known by the masses that attend church that Paul's egocentric revelation on his way to Qumran, also known as Damascus, was nothing more than an idea about a new kind of Christianity. He would transform Jesus's original message and teachings into one of his own making. At this time, in 60 CE, Jesus's thought and philosophy was still being followed by a group at Qumran under the leadership of James the Just, the brother of Jesus. They were at first mystified but then pleased that one of their chief critics, Paul, was calling himself a Christian. "But their relief would later turn to rage when they heard the kind of 'Christianity' Paul was preaching—that Jesus had died on the cross as a scapegoat for the sins of mankind, and that anyone could become free of original sin by accepting Jesus as the Son of God."[104]

While Paul was aboard preaching and "selling" his brand of Christianity to the Gentiles, James was murdered by the Hebrew priests. This resulted in the Jewish revolt of 66 CE, wherein the majority of Qumran Christians were killed and the true teachings and religion of Jesus died along with the failed revolt. In the sometimes unfair mysteries of life, a twist of fate resulted in the survival of Paul's church of lies.

By AD 300 the Roman Empire was falling to pieces, overstretched by its conquests and its need for huge armies. The emperor Constantine had an inspiration. About one in ten of his subjects were Christians. If he made Christianity the religion of the Roman Empire, he would have a supporter in every town and village, and a fellow emperor in every city large enough to have a bishop. (Constantine himself never became a Christian—he remained a worshipper of the sun god Sol Invictus.)

His solution worked, and Christianity held together the Roman Empire for another two centuries. But by now the Christian Church had taken over the reins of power.[105]

As a commentary on history, Pope Leo X, a contemporary of Henry VIII, remarked on his church's power and success, supposedly stating, "It has served us well, this myth of Christ."[106]

The Origin of the Lie

> *This All, which you see, which encompasses divine and*
> *human, is One, and we are but members of a great body.*
> —SENECA, 4 BCE–65 CE

This statement of Seneca's verifies that there was knowledge of the oneness of all things during the time of Jesus. There is no evidence at all to support the contention that Jesus believed himself to be the one and only fully divine one. But his sole divinity is one of the pillars of Christianity. The whole liar's game of Saul's began with the story of Jesus's anointment.

Jesus was anointed by one Mary of Bethany—the Magdalene. In the Jewish faith, "both king and high priest were anointed and were thus a meshiha, a messiah."[107] Messiah in Greek is Christ or Christos. Thus we end up with Jesus Christ and the term Christianity. Not Jesus the anointed or Jesus the Christ, but Jesus Christ—"a purely functional title distorted into a proper name."[108]

The claim by Saul that Jesus was fully divine was a lie. But why the anointment? Could Jesus's anointment by the Magdalene have had a deeper meaning? Could it have been an acknowledgment of his unique humanness and role as prophet and messenger? And could it have been a statement of his divine mission and an outward sign of his divinity within—the divine spark?[109] In addition, why was the anointing done by a woman and not by one of his male disciples? Could it have been a symbolization of the sacred marriage, which signified oneness?

Anointing with oil generally meant a person or object was "set aside" for divine service. This was a form of sanctification identifying a person as a priest or king—a messiah. This sanctifying practice extends back to the goddess tradition of the Near Eastern religions, where "anointing the head of the king with oil was a ritual performed by the heiress or royal priestess who represented the Goddess. In Greek, this rite was called the *hieros gamos* or 'Sacred Marriage.' The anointing of the head had erotic significance, the head being symbolic of the phallus 'anointed' by the woman for penetration during the physical consummation of marriage…Through his union with the priestess, the king/consort received royal status, he became known as the 'Anointed One'—in Hebrew, the 'Messiah.'"[110]

"Early Christian texts describe Mary Magdalene as 'the woman who knew the All'; she was the one whom 'Christ loved more than all the disciples'. She was the apostle 'endowed with knowledge, vision and insight far exceeding Peter's'; and she was the beloved bride who anointed Jesus at the Sacred Marriage (the *Hieros Gamos*) at Bethany."[111]

It would appear Jesus and the Magdalene had a special relationship for her to have anointed him. This special relationship was as husband and wife. Jesus being referred to as Rabbi indicates he was married. And the Magdalene would have been the most likely candidate.

By what authority could Mary Magdalene anoint Jesus? By all accounts it would seem she was of a royal lineage of the Tribe of Benjamin and possibly a priestess in the manner of the Egyptian cult of Isis.[112] Being of a royal lineage and a priestess meant that Mary had the authority to anoint Jesus.

But there is more to the anointment than it seems. Jewish by birth, Jesus was bringing a different message and interpretation of the Law of Moses, contrary to the temple priests. "Many of Jesus's actions and teachings, as portrayed in the gospels, are strongly critical of contemporary Judaism. Jesus is pictured as preaching a message of spiritual love rather than one based in the Mosaic Law; he breaks the observance of the Sabbath and criticizes religious officials for blind adherence to custom while ignoring the reality of the spirit; like a rebel reformer, he casts the money lenders out of the Temple; he accuses the Pharisees of taking the keys of knowledge and hiding them; and he teaches the mysteries of "the kingdom within," the mysteries of transformed consciousness, rather than expounding teachings to be upheld by a priestly class."[113]

Being outside the acceptable framework of Judaism, Jesus needed acknowledgment of his divine mission and message. He needed a legitimacy of his authority as a prophet; he needed to be anointed. However, as a symbolic priest-king and prophet, he was bringing something unexpected—a message of equality and freedom of the mind and spirit not based on human laws but on holy or "natural law."

Jesus was not bringing a physical revolution to restore the Jewish kingdom from the yoke and the oppression of the Romans. This was what the Jewish people wanted and expected of their messiah. They wanted a liberating monarch, a warrior-king messiah riding a white horse to lead them, not a messiah spouting philosophy and riding on an ass. But Jesus knew in his heart that the purest, and in some ways the most radical, means to a revolution is to transform the consciousness of people—a freedom that no tyrannical state can suppress.

Tilting at windmills when they are real is always difficult and dangerous. His altruistic and "'libertarian' message apparently did not go over well with the authorities in charge."[114] And it seems that in one way or another, Jesus's plan didn't work out as he thought it would, and the rest is history—a history that is not an account of truth, but a history based on a lie—the greatest lie ever told.

⚜

I know the power of anointment. During the fall of 2008, we were in France, once again leading a spiritual group to the Rennes-le-Château area. Staying at the bishop's palace in Alet-les-Bain, we were shut off to any news from the outside world. We had last brought a group of our students here in 1999. Nine years later, it was refreshing to see few changes in the spiritual and physical landscape compared to the influx of greed and capitalism that has happened at various other sacred sites around the world—one such site being Machu Picchu in Peru.

The Rennes-le-Château area of Southern France is very special to my wife, Sherry, and me. There are many prophecies and legends connected with this area, such as the Holy Grail and the site of the New Jerusalem. This sacred land has also been known as a place that has survived previous earth changes. Ever since The Da Vinci Code, Rennes-le-Château has experienced an astounding increase in tourism. Most visitors focus on the hilltop site, its church, and the graveyard but miss the real spiritual power, which lies in the valleys and mountains surrounding Rennes.

We only spent a few hours at Rennes-le-Château, as our real focus was on the spa town of Rennes-les-Bains, the saltwater and freshwater streams that feed into it, and a local sacred site known as the "devil's chair." Named by the Catholic Church, it is a stone chair on the side of a mountain that looks toward the rising sun in the east. A pre-Christian site, this pagan stone throne commands an imposing place on the mountainside. Due to its location, a church could not be built over it. Whenever this was the case, the church would demonize the spot in various ways—one being identifying it as a site sacred to Satan. In opposition to the Christians, I renamed the stone seat the Morning Star Seat.

This stone seat has a power that is hard to describe. Right next to it is a spring in a circular shape that is further proof of the power of this site. At this spot, while seated in the chair, Sherry performed an ancient anointing ceremony on me, witnessed by three of our apprentices. The details are not necessary to share, but the stone seat was honored in a manner that possibly had not been done for thousands of years.

Rennes-le-Château

> But to those who have understood that Love is the key, the White Owl will appear, and will lead them into another time. One cycle ends, but another commences—and a seed group will go forward into the Age of Aquarius, the Age of the Holy Spirit.[115]
> —ELIZABETH VAN BUREN

How did we discover Rennes-le-Château before the publication of *The Da Vinci Code*? Was it from a dream? On the contrary, the knowledge came from a book and a soul need. During the spring of 1998, while conducting a spiritual journey to various sacred sites in England and Wales, I stumbled upon Elizabeth Van Buren's book *Refuge of the Apocalypse*. I was awestruck with the book and determined that Sherry and I needed to visit Elizabeth and the focus of her book—the Rennes-le-Château area of Southern France. I had already read *Holy Blood, Holy Grail*, the original bestselling book about Rennes and the bloodline of Jesus and Mary, and had planned on visiting this area, but Elizabeth's book spurred me into action. And within six months, we arrived in the Languedoc-Roussillon region of France.

Flying into Montpellier, we drove to the medieval city of Carcassonne to spend the night. We arrived at our hotel late in the afternoon. Since it was situated right outside the medieval city, I decided to explore Carcassonne while

Sherry stayed in the room and rested. I have a vivid imagination and am a romantic at heart. Entering over the drawbridge and through the castle gates, I was transported back to a time of the Knights Templar and the troubadours. As I wandered the streets like a kid in a fantasy world, I heard music and singing coming my way. The full moon had just risen over the city, providing some natural light.

I decided to wait on the battlements to discover what merriment was approaching me. As I closed my eyes, I could almost sense the shades of the defenders of these stone walls. I wondered how much laughter these stones had seen and how many tears had been shed over the centuries. In the next moment, I was drawn out of my reverie by five medieval-clothed figures who were now personally serenading me. And they say magic doesn't happen!

⚜

Over the next few days we were able to track down Elizabeth and became fast friends with her. An eccentric and rebel much like us, she graciously shared her knowledge and experience of the mysteries surrounding Rennes-le-Château and its sacred landscape. What had intrigued me about Elizabeth's book were her discussions of the relationships that Rennes-le-Château has with alchemy, the Holy Grail, Archangel Mikael, and Venus. But there was still something more about Elizabeth's book, and it had to do with the theories surrounding Jesus and Mary Magdalene.

The theory of the marriage between Jesus and Mary was initially made popular by the book *Holy Blood, Holy Grail*. However, Elizabeth's book speaks more to the esoteric aspects of Rennes-le-Château and the hidden teachings of Jesus and Mary rather than simply to a bloodline of relatives flowing from Jesus and the Magdalene. One of the keys to understanding this region is symbology. Scattered throughout the landscape and churches are symbols not found (or rarely found) in any other Christian churches, such as pentagrams and the Jewish six-pointed star.

One of our first stops with Elizabeth was the church at Esperanza dedicated to Saint Michel. There are two extremely important images here. One is a statue of the archangel with his or her spear tip inside the mouth of a dragon. This is the true esoteric meaning of transmuting the base dualistic energy within us, symbolically represented by a serpent or dragon, into the nondualistic energy of creation. Throughout history the church has led us to believe that it is the devil being slain, not a dragon or serpent being transmuted.

The second image is of a large painting hanging over the main altar. Again it is of the archangel, this time posed with a sword, standing on what appears to be the devil. But closer scrutiny reveals that the figure has the head and body of an old man. This is Father Time or Saturn conveying the teaching that we must learn to "press down" linear time so our lives are not controlled by the fear of aging and death. Both of these are not the dogmatic teachings of Christianity. In fact, they counter the dualistic-fear-induced propaganda of the church.

Our next stop was the hilltop site of Rennes-le-Château and its church, which overlooks the valleys of the Aude and Sals. The church, with its Tower Magdala, is quite unique. As we entered the church, we were greeted by a stooped, squatting figure holding a water stoup on its shoulders, and above the stoup were four angels. Some people have identified this hideous figure as the devil, while others have said it represents Asmodeus—a demon guardian of treasure of the Temple of Solomon.

Since the release of *The Da Vinci Code* in May of 2002, more people are aware of the various mysteries that shroud Rennes-le-Château like a dreary mist in a good, old-fashioned Dracula movie. The main mystery has to do with treasure. What is the true treasure here? Is it that of the heretic Cathars, decimated by the church through the Albigensian Crusades? Is it Solomon's treasure discovered beneath Jerusalem by the Knights Templar and subsequently brought to and hidden in the mountains surrounding Rennes-le-Château? Or is it Jesus and Mary's (Magdalene) gravesite? Of course, any physical evidence that Jesus survived the cross and died at a later time would destroy the church and would have to have been well hidden.

On the other hand, if the priceless treasure is the hidden knowledge of Jesus's true message and teachings, would it be possible to prove this by using common sense, logical thinking, and intuition? The clues could possibly be found within a parchment, but most certainly in the many symbolic images scattered throughout the region. This knowledge of Jesus's true teachings and beliefs would be easier to discover than the physical evidence proving his survival of crucifixion.

The decade-ago controversy surrounding *The Da Vinci Code* and any possible bloodline would pale in comparison to revealed truth about Jesus and his message. Yes, he was married to his special Mary of Bethany, but the "greatest lie ever told" is not about his marital status. The fact is that his being married or not does not really collapse the foundation of Christianity. The truth about him and his message does.

One important point remains to be made. There is one painting of Jesus with his students that really stands out and reveals truth. Out of the dozen or so students, only three are male, and the rest are female. The truth is, when Jesus taught, there were many times more female students than males. Of course, Christianity wants us to believe that there were only male disciples to justify their patriarchal rule. I pose a question: why do men fear women's power and equality?

Son of God and Son of Man

Jesus taught that there is nothing covered that will not be uncovered, or hidden that will not be revealed. But sometimes the obvious is not so apparent. The "son of man" and the "Son of God" sayings of Jesus have perplexed scholars for centuries. A multitude of explanations have been presented.

However, Jesus was speaking from personal experience as well as from oral teachings handed down since the time of Moses. His "son of man" and "son of God" personal statements were based on his own firsthand spiritual experience—his descending-spirit experience while bathing in the Jordan. The descent of the dove into Jesus, symbolic of the Holy Spirit, was a reference to nondualistic interpenetration—spirit interpenetrating matter[116] (and the voice from heaven verified the divine within as a son of God). This was Jesus's awakening and the formal beginning of his quest to bring his message of the divine in all things to all people of the world.

But without firsthand experience of the interpenetration of the divine and human, how would you truly know the meaning of these statements? You could only base your explanation for his seemingly contradictory pronouncements on secondhand knowledge.

Common sense, my knowing, and my firsthand experience of nondualistic interpenetration and vision give me an understanding of their meanings: "son (daughter) of God"—divine, "son (daughter) of man"—humanity. This was the original message of Jesus handed down from the time of Moses—we are each a "son (daughter) of God" and a "son (daughter) of man." We are *divine humans*.

We each have a direct connection to the otherworld and to God—no need for a priest or any other religious person to be a barrier between us and God. This thunderous, earth-shattering knowledge and belief alone crumbles the foundations of any Western institutionalized religion.

CHAPTER 3

The Lie of Salvation

Salvation: the belief that human beings require deliverance.[117]

Common sense dictates to us that the concept of salvation requires no self-responsibility, self-reflection, or "work," whereas sanctification requires personal responsibility as well as "work." The "work" I refer to is both spiritual and mundane (i.e., forgiveness [spiritual] and right actions, such as speaking our truth [mundane]). Salvation as religious dogma and doctrine negates personal responsibility for our words, thoughts, and actions. A person's mind may harbor thoughts of anger, resentment, and greed, but as long as the person professes "belief in Jesus Christ," it doesn't matter. He or she is still "saved."

This type of religion, a religion that is totally one of salvation, is destructive to a person's true spirit and the spirit of the earth—this is Christianity. Christianity is a religion of salvation—pure and simple—due to the actions of Paul and eventually sealed in stone with the proceedings of the Council of Nicaea. This council "created the literally fantastic Jesus of faith and adopted the pretense that this was a historically accurate rendering."[118] This redeeming faith created by the council anchored, once and for all, the lie of Paul and established Christianity as a religion of salvation.

Guilt by Proxy

Walk into the majority of Christian churches, and what do you see—a crucified man on a cross or an empty cross. Where is the love in the crucified image? It is dark and depressing but serves a very important point. It keeps the symbolic "sheep" in line through guilt. If we leave the realm of ignorance and do a little research, we discover that Jesus did not believe in original sin. In fact, it was not a belief of Judaism or of the pre-Gnostic Mediterranean mystery cults.

If you want to be depressed, then go to a Christian church. The atmosphere is one of doom and gloom where sinners get absolved of sin. Where is the beauty, and where is the love of the kingdom of God—the kingdom of heaven and the realm of earth—in these churches?

Christianity's kingdom is the patriarchal church and its lie of salvation. But the kingdom in Jesus's message is revealed through the Gnostic Gospel of Thomas: "The Kingdom is inside you and outside you."[119] This refers to the sacredness of the earth and to the divineness that we each have within us—our divine spark. The key to the kingdom is our hearts—not religious institution's dogma and doctrine.

We do not need the lie of salvation preached by Christianity; the earth does not need its salvation. What we do need and what the earth needs is love. Love of self, love of all others, love of the earth and all its creatures, love of the sun and the moon, love of the stars and the heavens—this is the love of God.

How then do we discover and awaken this love of God? Not through salvation but through a nondualistic consciousness where spirit and matter interpenetrate. This is achieved through experiential and initiatory sanctification practices (oneness through spiritual work). Jesus revealed this to his students when he taught: "When you make the two one, and when you make the inside like the outside and the outside like the inside, and the above like the below, and when you make the male and the female one and the same...then will you enter [the Kingdom]."[120]

Christianity's establishment of a religion of salvation was based on a lie and was a direct assault against Jesus's true message, belief, and practice of sanctification. He taught a pathway that resulted in a transformation of consciousness. This was not through salvation but through the process of initiation and sanctification. One of his primary initiatory and sanctification practices was bathing. This was taught and passed on to him by John the Dipper.

Sanctification

Sanctification is "the ritual process of purification, the procedure for making a person, place, or thing sacred."[121] It is based on "natural law" and *participation mystique*, which is a "knowing" of the things of life and their inherent mysteries through the experience of the mundane as well as the spiritual. It is an immersion in the mysteries of nature and the seeking of knowledge through mystical participation. This results in a transformation of consciousness. It is a "doing" and an awakening of the heart and mind. It is not a stagnation of the spirit that results from a belief in Christianity's lie of salvation and the supposed resurrection of the body after physical death.

Sanctification embraces purification, illumination, and unity, which are so essential to our own awakening and love. A belief in salvation contains none of these necessary items and requires no self-transformation. Salvation as your faith requires no "turning the other cheek," which is based on our own personal ability to forgive.

Forgiveness is essential for a transformation of consciousness, but the church has once again taken the power from the people and empowered itself by being the "gatekeeper" for the forgiveness of sins. "The sinner, having gone through the ritual of confession and penance according to Church doctrine, is now quite literally at liberty to commit the same sin again and again. At no stage in this process is there any recognition in canon law or practice that the sinner has to seek the forgiveness of those he has sinned against or make amends to them."[122]

On the other hand, a belief in sanctification puts the responsibility for forgiveness and our life and the brightness of our soul in our hands. Salvation as a belief takes our soul, our forgiveness, and keeps it locked away within the church's prison of power and control. And they let you know that they have the say on whether your soul goes to heaven or to hell. Salvation as a belief matches the inside of a church—all doom and gloom—whereas sanctification practices honor the love and beauty of nature. Which one would you choose?

Bathing—the Initiatory Rite of Death and Rebirth[123]

Ritualistic immersion in running water (stream or river) or the ocean is one of the oldest forms of initiation and symbolic death and rebirth. It is one of the essential steps in awakening. It is frightening but necessary. We need to physically symbolically "die" to the old to be "born again"—our second birth. It is not membership in an earthly or religious institution. It is the beginning of an awakening to the truth—of the world and one's authentic self.

Few in the world still practice and teach this form of purification. Even in Jesus's time, baptism in the River Jordan was a "unique event that even Catholic editors of the Jerusalem Bible consider to be an initiation."[124] Outside of the Mandeans of the Middle East, the greatest concentration of "dawn bathers" is to be found within the indigenous communities that still practice and adhere to the old ways. But even here, there are few still alive that can "initiate" and put people into the "living waters" of the earth.

I am blessed to be one of those who still practice and "initiate" people into bathing. This "initiation" is not one of membership, but one of "death and re-birth." After I put a person into the stream, he or she is free to revisit any stream and repeat the ritualistic immersion. Going bathing will help a person release the stress and hurt that comes from living in today's chaotic and fear-filled world. And quite possibly, it may be a preventative for Alzheimer's.[125]

After the "initiation," there are multiple reasons for a person to revisit a stream and bathe. Bathings will increase a person's spiritual power and his or her inner vitality; the living waters will also help release anger, guilt, resentment, fear, and uncertainty, as well as the other emotional baggage that we seem to carry and refuse to release. In addition, I use it as a method of healing others.

How is it that I came to the knowledge and the practice of bathing? How did I find my modern-day John the Baptist? In 1990 my wife, Sherry, and I sponsored a conference in Maine on Native American spirituality and shamanism. We were encouraged to invite as presenters two native elders, a husband and wife, Vince and Mom Stogan, from Vancouver, British Columbia. As soon as Sherry and I met them at the Portland airport, we were struck by their unassuming authenticity. It was as though we were meeting our long-lost grandparents.

During the conference we were unaware that Mom Stogan was watching Sherry do her spirit work and Vince was watching me. After the conference and back at our home, Vince and Mom asked to speak to both of us in private. They told us they saw us in them and asked if we would like to learn their medicine ways. Of course, we were privileged and honored to be asked and willingly accepted.

Our apprenticeship with Vince and Mom was of the "old school," where you learned by listening, watching, and doing and not writing anything down. Many of our experiences and learnings we cannot tell you about or share in print. This is typical with any oral and initiatory traditions, such as the Nazarenes—a branch of the Essenes. However, I can tell you some things about bathing and our experiences.

The Northwest Coast First People have three primary ceremonial practices: winter spirit dancing, bathing, and burnings or "feeding the spirits," as well as the traditional methods of shamanic healing. Bathing is their primary sanctification or purification rite. Sher and I, and sometimes our daughter, Jess, would travel to Vancouver and stay with Mom and Vince 24-7. Many of the stories and teachings we heard were learned around the kitchen table. These informal sessions would sometimes last late into the night, with Vince smoking cigarette after cigarette and drinking glass after glass of Pepsi.

Many times we would not get to bed until two o'clock in the morning, and then we would have to get back up at three o'clock to go bathing. It was about an hour's drive north of Vancouver to the bathing spot. Bathing as a symbolic death and then rebirth from the great mother, Mother Earth, replicates our human birthing experience as we leave the waters of the earth mother and transition from the dark to the light on a physical as well as a metaphoric and spiritual levels. Timing is always touchy, as you must enter the waters in the dark but then leave the stream or river in the first light, which is approximately an hour before sunrise.

Bathing as spirit training was not easy, especially when you consider that the training period was during the winter, which was esoterically considered the summer in the otherworld. Standing barefoot and naked on the riverbank with the stars as the ceiling of my church and the roar of the river as the gateway to eternity always put me not only in the now, but in a state of timelessness where I was one with all things. When I entered the river with my first step, there would be an explosion of my senses, and the illusion of dualistic reality would dissolve into a oneness of truth. With my first squatting submersion, I would die once again, only to be reborn as I exploded straight up out of the "mother's" waters into the air, with my primal scream escaping from my lips. And for a split second, my mind would shift into the realization that I must do this again and again and again.

After the last submersion, how long I would remain in the freezing but not freezing waters was always a mystery. The siren's song was always to stay in the power, to stay in the true oneness of life where all the human worries and fears do not exist. It is only you and the mystery of God—the realm of the earth and the kingdom of heaven: the kingdom of God.

Bathing or Baptism

It is well known that baptism is one of the major sacraments of Christianity. In fact, baptism may be thought of as the first sacrament as the "early apologist Tertullian (d. ca. 200) first used the term to refer to baptismal rites in which Christians pledged their faithfulness to Christ."[126] Pure and simple, baptism is a Christian initiation—a granting of grace, entrance into the holy arms of the church, and thus one's salvation. But baptism for salvation is not bathing. Baptism has nothing to do with sanctification. However, if you are to believe the church, baptism was one of the major teachings of Jesus, thus the justification, so-called truth, and the reason it is a major sacrament of Christianity. But is it the truth? Is it fact?

The original form of baptism was full-water immersion that is called "bathing." It was usually conducted in living waters (running stream or river). "Baptism is one of the oldest rites and was practiced by all nations in their Mysteries, as sacred ablutions."[127] Bathing was not a Christian baptism performed for salvation. It was full-water immersion conducted for initiation and sanctification and did not invoke the ritualistic saying of "Father, Son, and Holy Ghost":

> The baptism was changed from water to that of the Holy Ghost, undoubtedly in consequence of the ever-dominant idea of the Fathers to institute a reform, and make the Christians distinct from St. John's Nazarenes, the Nabatheans and Ebionites, in order to make room for new dogmas, Not only do the Synoptics tell us that Jesus was baptizing the same as John, but John's own disciples complained of it...
>
> Apollos, a Jew of Alexandria, belonged to the sect of St. John's disciples; he had been baptized, and instructed others in the doctrines of the Baptist. And yet when Paul [the liar Saul] cleverly profiting by

his absence at Corinth, finds certain disciples of Apollos' at Ephesus, and asks them whether they received the Holy Ghost, he is naively answered, "We have not so much as heard whether there be any Holy Ghost!" "Unto what then were you baptized?" he inquires. "Unto John's baptism," they say.[128]

We can see the duplicity of the Christian fathers in their changing of Jesus's rite of sanctification to one of salvation. Even though "baptism, the early church's ritual of initiation, was understood as a death of an old self and a resurrection of a new self,"[129] it is important to know that true baptism is ritualistic immersion in "living waters" for sacred purification of body, mind, and spirit, not for salvation or membership in a corrupt, false religion. Bathing allows us to experience in our body-mind continuum a transformation of consciousness through a symbolic experience of the death of the old self and the rebirth of the new self.

⚜

Everything known about Jesus leads us to know that a onetime ticket to heaven, granted by an institution, was not his spiritual philosophy. On the contrary, he taught, practiced, and believed in practices of sanctification—one of the foremost being bathing:

> Based on the indications we get from the gospel of John, the baptizing campaign of Jesus and his disciples in the countryside of Judea must have lasted throughout the summer and fall and into the winter of A.D. 27...That Jesus was baptizing at all was clearly a problem.... He is not administering a "Christian baptism" in the name of the "Father, Son and Holy Spirit." A later editor of John even added a parenthetical qualification: "although it was not Jesus himself who baptized but his disciples" (John 4:2). That type of interpolation is like a red flag telling us that someone is very uncomfortable here, even though the text plainly says that Jesus was baptizing and making disciples!...
>
> The shocking truth is that none of the apostles or disciples of Jesus ever had a proper "Christian baptism" as it came to be defined in

Christian dogma—that is "in the name of the Father, the Son, and the Holy spirit."[130]

✣

The Jewish religious purity laws required cleansing through immersion in water. If a person was polluted by childbirth, sexual activity, or various other sources of contamination, such as contact with the dead, the person needed ritualistic cleansing through immersion in water—mikveh.[131] "But how and in what should one immerse oneself? Priestly Zadokites (the 'Sadducees' of the Greek Gospels) could afford luxurious bathing pools, sometimes in their own private dwellings. The Pharisees built stepped tanks (*miqvaoth*) with a reserve of water the same size that served entire communities and were financed co-operatively. The Essenes of Qumran had larger reservoirs for the exclusive use of their community. All these pools were carved and built in rock, as were their cisterns, channels, steps, and enclosures. Many Jews, however, had no access to a pool."[132]

At any time and any place on this earth, there are always dissenters that provide an alternative to what is commonly accepted—religiously and socially. During Jesus's time it was various rabbis that were known to cleanse through immersion in "living waters"—rivers and streams. These immersers "were successful because they tapped into popular discontent over attempts by factional elites to control how Israelites made themselves clean. They insisted that the Lord of Israel cleansed people in his own 'living waters' (water flowing or collected naturally), so that the artificial pool of the sects were superfluous."[133]

Jesus discovered one of these "dippers" on the banks of the Jordan River in the person of John the Baptist, whose "message resonated with Jesus, who, as a Galilean, resented the elaborate bathing required by the Judean priesthood as a condition of entering the Temple,"[134] where, of course, a payment was required.

John took Jesus on as a student and, after a period of time, initiated him into the esoteric teachings and inner wisdom of bathing as well as the Merkavah, Chariot or Throne of God meditation, and many other equally mystical practices. During the act of bathing, John would tell the ones in the water, prior to immersion, to repent, which "meant a 'return' (*shuv* in Hebrew, *tuv* in

Aramaic) to God. By repenting, one acknowledged being headed in the wrong direction; by changing course, one was realigned with the divine. Repentance did not emphasize sin or depravity; the notion of original sin as a hopeless condition was a later motif in Christianity, developed by Augustine of Hippo during the fifth century C.E. John, far from preaching hopelessness, offered in repentance a pragmatic alternative to being estranged from God. In both Hebrew and Greek 'to sin' (*chata, hamartano*) originally meant to miss the mark, as in archery. A rabbi's teaching showed how one could go right again, and only implied where one had gone wrong."[135]

Jesus listened and watched John and eventually learned to conduct the sacred rites of immersion himself. During this period, a spiritual philosophy developed within him that would stay with him throughout the rest of his life. His intense spiritual practice of predawn bathing and Chariot visualizations brought the world of spirit and a knowing of oneness closer and closer to Jesus. The Chariot, as the moving Throne of God, was one of the primary esoteric visualizations within Jewish mysticism. With its wheels of fire rolling through the heavens, accompanied by the sound of mighty waters, the Chariot meditation brought the divineness of creation intimately alive within the body, mind, senses, and soul of Jesus.

His spiritual powers increased, until early one morning, while standing waist-deep in the chilly stream with the morning star in the east and the first light of dawn breaking through the darkness of the night, he had his vision. As recorded in the Bible, it was the vision of a "dove." In esoteric teachings the dove not only symbolized the holy spirit of divine love but also represented Venus, the morning star. The dove or the star descended into him, and for Jesus this symbolized the divine spirit or the light of divinity within him and within all things. Keep in mind that Jesus, as a student of the original kabbala, believed in the sacred knowledge that we all have the "holy spark" of God within. This was Jesus's experience of interpenetrative nonduality (the Holy Spirit descending on him like a dove[136]), the interpenetration of spirit (dove) into his body (matter), or the oneness of existence.

During this otherworldly experience, Jesus heard a voice from heaven declaring him a Son of God. This was an awakening of the divine within, the Holy Spirit within, and became the foundation of his kingdom teachings.

⚜

Your world and life will change after you consciously experience the descent of spirit into matter and hear a voice from heaven. You no longer *believe* in the kingdom of God within and without—you *know*, as I know, as I have experienced firsthand the descent of spirit into my body and heard a voice from heaven.[137] This was a descending-spirit exorcism. Commonly, exorcism is known as a "spirit" being taken off or out of a person who is supposedly possessed. A descending-spirit exorcism is where "spirit" merges or blends, interpenetrates, with a person. As recorded in the Bible, this was the experience of Jesus with the descent of "spirit" in the form of a dove.

⚜

The vision of the morning star and the descent of spirit was the moment of awakening and enlightenment for Jesus, just as it was for Gautama, the historical Buddha, and Kōbō Daishi, founder of Shingon Esoteric Buddhism.[138] This awakening and enlightenment for all three was not the completion of a path but the beginning of a "way"—bringing a message of light to a darkened world.

Driven into the Wilderness

"And immediately the Spirit driveth him into the wilderness. And he was there in the wilderness forty days."[139] According to one Gospel writer, this supposedly occurred right after Jesus's descending-spirit visionary experience. During this time he was allegedly tempted by the devil, spent time with the wild beasts, and was ministered by angels. After being in the wilderness for forty days, Jesus then ended up back in Galilee. This is an interesting story but not true.

Jesus never left Galilee. He didn't spend forty days in the wilderness but spent his time developing his version of the "Way of the Wilderness,"[140] which was simply known as the "Way." What better manner in which to solidify the lie of Paul than to have Jesus "driven" into the wilderness, where he is tempted by Satan and ends up hanging out with angels. Of course, let us not forget the special and often repeated number in the Bible close to one hundred times, from the flood's forty days and nights of rain to wandering in the wilderness for forty years. Moses's life was even marked by three forty-year segments. Why is the number forty special and sacred? One reason—forty is one Venus cycle. Another reason, a Venus retrograde period is usually about forty days and forty nights. Myths describe Venus in retrograde as a journey to the under-world followed by a triumphant reemergence. "Besides visually passing from her Evening Star, through the underworld, and into her Morning Star phase, Venus' retrograde establishes a new 'seed moment,' where the foundation or wellspring of Venusian energies for the next 19 months is established."[141] Appropriately, Venus is the planet of love.

Venus, the brightest object in our sky outside of the sun and moon, is still visible in the dawn sky as the sun rises. It is the herald of the light out of the dark of the night. Venus and the sun are intertwined in an immortal dance of rebirth. As the morning star, or the light coming out of the dark of the night, Venus announces the arrival of the sun. It is the harbinger of the day to come. It stands at the breaking of dawn as the last star to disappear into the glory of the sun. And in the darkest of times, hope will light the way—this is Venus as the morning star, the star of hope.

The morning star was seen as "God's eye," positioned between darkness (ignorance) and light (knowledge) but always the way-shower to understanding and wisdom. The great Lakota Black Elk spoke of the importance of the morning star as follows:

> Morning Star, there at the place where the sun comes up, you, who have the wisdom which we seek, help us in cleansing ourselves and all the people, that our generations to come will have light as they walk the sacred path. You lead the dawn as it walks forth, and also the day which follows with its light, which is knowledge. This you do for us and for all the people of the world that they may see clearly in walking the holy path, that they may know all that is holy, and that they may increase in a sacred manner.[142]

Since Venus is the brightest heavenly body apart from the sun and the moon, it's understandable that its brilliance has always symbolized knowledge and enlightenment as well as the journey to bring this light to the world. Venus spends its time as either the morning star or the evening star. This perception of Venus as "twins" and the significance of its luminosity underscores the mythological religious ideals of many cultures. The "twins" designation symbolizes the dual forces manifested in humans and the dualities of life, the light and the dark, male and female, which contain the potentiality for a unified balance of wholeness or oneness—nondual interpenetration. For that reason, Venus is viewed as the bridge builder between pairs of opposites, specifically spirit and matter. This is also the role of the religious revolutionary who teaches that equality and balance are of the utmost importance in achieving spiritual transformation.

There is no greater external sign of the Holy Spirit of God than the morning star, the star that symbolizes rebirth in Judaism. Even the historical geographical location of Judaism, Jerusalem, is connected with Venus. Its name "effectively means the place dedicated to Venus in its evening setting."[143]

After his vision of the dove of Venus, Jesus didn't disappear into the wilderness but began developing teachings and practices based on his "Way"—divine transformation through oneness and love.

The laws of nature are but the mathematical thoughts of God.
—EUCLID

There is another hidden meaning to the number forty and its repeated use in the Bible. There are twenty-two basic letters in the Hebrew alphabet (or aleph-bet). Each letter in the Hebrew alphabet has a numerical value. The letter mem is the thirteenth letter, with a value of forty.[144] The totality of the knowledge of mem is one of the keys to understanding the overwhelming use of the number forty within the Bible.

This is a complete study in itself. But briefly, I will point out the highlights of the reasoning behind forty. Mem is the symbol of water and is one of the three mother or primary letters of the alphabet, the other two being aleph and shin. Looking below the surface, mem symbolizes "womb" and as "Mother" holds within itself the potential for new life. Mem is divine transformation. The Hebrew words for "one" (*echad*, implying a unity in diversity) and "love" (*ahavah*) both have the numerical value of thirteen. Furthermore, during our study we must not lose sight of the power of thirteen. Thirteen is the number that purifies, cleanses, and bonds multiplicity into oneness. From thirteen comes the birth of spirit.

Within the letter mem, the secret knowledge of oneness and love is to be found. Therefore, wherever you find forty in the Bible, such as "forty days in the wilderness," understand that the hidden meaning refers to an unknown period where the death of the unhealthy ego occurs, resulting in a victory of spirit. It is "divine transformation through purification (sanctification), oneness, and love."

Any discussion of mem is incomplete without the additional knowledge of the next Hebrew letter—*nūn*. "The word nūn means 'seed,' but also represents the idea of 'continuing.' In the original pictographic script the nūn is an image of a seed."[145]

Mem is the death of the unhealthy ego. This is the ego state of mind, which focuses solely on self and materialism. With death, there is rebirth. Our resurrection of spirit is to be found in nūn, the fourteenth letter of the Hebrew alphabet, with a numerical value of fifty. Nūn signifies a fish, a whale, which leads us to the tale of Jonah and the whale. "Jonah's emergence from the belly of the whale has always been regarded as a symbol of resurrection and therefore of passage to a new state and this must be compared, on the other hand, with the idea of 'birth' which, in the Hebrew Kabbala especially, is attached to the letter nūn and which must be understood spiritually as a 'new birth', that is, a regeneration of the being, individual or cosmic."[146]

Additionally, "the new birth necessarily presupposes death to the former state, whether it be an individual or a world that is in question. Death and birth or resurrection—here we have two aspects that are inseparable one from another, for they are in reality nothing other than the two opposite faces of one same change of state."[147]

There is further knowledge connected with mem and nūn revealed within the mysteries of the original tarot—known as Philosophical Medicine.[148] The fourteenth card of the tarot is Balance.[149] The Hebrew letter for this card is nūn. In ancient Hebrew, nūn is a picture of a seed sprout—new generation. In Aramaic, the meaning of nūn is fish. The letter before nūn is mem, which means water and sea. Mem and nūn are esoterically connected, where mem refers to the "waters of life" (water) within us, and nūn is not a physical fish but the life-force (fire) swimming within our sacred blood.

This card's numerical value is fifty. It is a card of blending of the metaphoric fire and water—a place of balance. It is the card of Aquarius, and it reveals knowledge of the coming Age of Aquarius.

With the value of fifty, it is the divine power of five on a higher plane of consciousness—ten times five equals fifty. This tarot card portrays the angelic queen of heaven holding an urn in each hand. One urn is golden, and the other urn is silver, symbolizing the spiritual and physical energies within us. The spirit energies reside in the pineal gland, and the physical energies within the sacrum or coccyx.

The angelic queen is blending the energies together. This card represents the interpenetration of spirit and matter—divine and human. Symbolically, this is where we cleanse "our faulty perceptions, connecting us in a divine yet human way with the immutable world beyond the reach of time's scythe."[150]

In conclusion, Jesus ascended from the great, watery womb of Mother Nature reborn in spirit. With his primal cry, his vision of the descending spirit of the dove was his moment of awakening. After his visionary experience, Jesus needed a period of integration of his new, awakened state of being. In other words, the "seed" of his awakening eventually led to his message of oneness—the kingdom of God.

Developing His Message—the Path and the Way

After his vision and awakening, and during the assimilation of his awakened state, Jesus began formulating his "original way" while continuing his own ascetic spiritual training and development. The result was that he became known as a Chasid—a Jewish shaman, faith healer, and sorcerer. During this "strengthening of spirit" period and directly related to his vision and repeated predawn immersion practice as well as his own visionary and prophetic gifts, Jesus came to know firsthand, within his heart and mind, that all people were already clean or pure with the divine spirit within them.

To Jesus, purity became one of the most important issues in his spiritual mission. But it was not the outward purity that mattered. What was necessary in the eyes of God was one's inner purity. To Jesus, the brightness and the lightness of a person's heart were more important than money and one's social and economic status. Jewish ritual immersions to cleanse away one's outward pollutions were not only ridiculous but unnecessary. However, bathing to cleanse one of the inner pollutions of fear, anger, and guilt was not only necessary but also one of the ways to increase God's Spirit within—a resurrection in life. And increasing the divinity within each person could change the world.

Jesus had been passed the inner knowledge and mysteries of bathing by John. John also saw the power within Jesus and thus gave him the authority and the power to conduct predawn immersion bathing. Jesus's bathing of others has always caused a problem for the "lie-makers" of the church. I must give it to them, however, as they have done a good job of keeping this knowledge twisted and hidden from the metaphoric masses of "sheep."

> Based on the indications we get from the gospel of John, the baptizing campaign of Jesus and his disciples in the countryside of Judea must have lasted throughout the summer and fall and into the winter of A.D. 27...That Jesus was baptizing at all was clearly a problem...He is not administering a "Christian baptism" in the name of the "Father, Son and Holy Spirit." A later editor of John even added a parenthetical qualification: "although it was not Jesus himself who baptized but his disciples" (John 4:2). That type of interpolation is like a red flag telling us that someone is very uncomfortable here, even though the text plainly says that Jesus was baptizing and making disciples!...
>
> The shocking truth is that none of the apostles or disciples of Jesus ever had a proper "Christian baptism" as it came to be defined in Christian dogma—that is "in the name of the Father, the Son, and the Holy spirit."[151]

You have to wonder about the baptismal rites of some Christian sects, not only the sprinkling of some water on the head of a baby but also the "born-again rites." In the "born-again rites," during the light of day,[152] two people hold each shoulder of the inductee, whose arms are crossed over his or her chest, and bend him or her back into the water (not a squatting immersion) as if he or she is in a coffin. The two helpers then pull the person back to an upright position, and he or she is "born again." The baptism or bathing posture as recorded in the Bible (KJV) is "straightway coming up out of the water."[153] This highlights the ignorance of the ones conducting this form of so-called baptism. Coming straight up out of the mother's waters also indicates that the person is following the straight and narrow path and is realigned with the divine.

Additionally, there is a very important part to initiatory baptism or bathing that differentiates it from a purely mundane submersion in water. This is the "seal of spirit"—the sign of life marked on the initiate before he or she enters the living waters to experience his or her second birth—awakening from spiritual sleep with the death of the old self. This is a secret symbol I paint on the initiate with red ochre. Without the seal there is no power of transformation.

This is the mystery of blood and spirit, both of which may be symbolized by the color red. Our red blood is the source of all that is life-giving. The religious and spiritual use of blood in the form of red paint or pigment or red ochre dates back far into the mists of time—250,000 years ago![154]

⚜

As we can see, the corruption of the original teachings and practices of Jesus is reprehensible. I've yet to hear of any pope immersing or dunking himself in a stream or ocean; much less any other bishop, priest, or clergyman. There is no seal of spirit marked on the ones blindly accepting the sham baptismal rites of the church. No Christian clergy knows it, or they would use it! If the church changed and corrupted these most basic teachings and practices of Jesus, we must ask ourselves, what else have they changed and corrupted?

Capernaum or Nazareth

Jesus's heart was centered on the breath and beauty of the mountains, the hills, and the rivers of Galilee and its blessed sea. He loved Capernaum. It was not only the center of his activities; it was also his home. Jesus's home was not Nazareth; he was not Jesus of Nazareth but Jesus the Nazarene. It doesn't take much research to discover that the village or town of "Nazareth is not mentioned in the Old Testament, the Talmud (the Jewish law code), nor in the Apocrypha and it does not appear in any early rabbinic literature. Nazareth was not included in the list of settlements of the tribes of Zebulon (Joshua 19:10–16) which mentions twelve towns and six villages, and Nazareth is not included among the forty-five cities of Galilee that were mentioned by Josephus (37AD–100AD), a widely traveled historian who never missed anything and who voluminously describes the region. The name is also missing from the sixty-three towns of Galilee mentioned in the Talmud."[155]

I am always suspect of the accuracy of travel writers and historians pertaining to their conclusions on manners of spiritual and religious practices. But Josephus is not describing ritualistic practices but purely mundane counting the towns in Galilee. Under these circumstances we would have to accept his accounting as truth.

Jesus the Nazarene

*"The Nazarene" is he who reveals what
is hidden. (Gospel of Philip)*[156]

Jesus was not from Nazareth but was a Nazarene. Nazarene comes from the root word *nazar* and refers to sanctifying one's self to the service of God (how better to begin than bathing?). As a verb *nazar* means "to consecrate or to separate things into their proper place or to make them kadosh. Nazar as a noun has been translated to mean crown."[157] What is *kadosh*? *Kadosh* may be translated as "holy," but it means more than this. "The Hebrew root KDS (kef, dalet, shin) ties together separateness and sacredness."[158] There are two ways to look at this aspect of separateness and sacredness. Dualistically, it would indicate something holy being set apart from other things. But nondualistically, it indicates the binding or tying together of separateness and sacredness, which would result in a oneness of the sacred and mundane (e.g., Moses's experience of the burning bush).

It is also interesting to refer to the original tarot. The Major Arcane of the tarot begins with the Magician's card, number one, and completes with the World card, number twenty-two. Each of the tarot cards is connected to one of the letters of the Hebrew alphabet. Kef is connected to Power, card eleven; dalet is the King, card four; and shin is the God-Man or Divine Human who has attained enlightenment, card twenty-one. From nazar to kadosh to KDS to the tarot, and what do we have? The power of the king as a divine, enlightened human.

⚜

According to the authors of *The Templar Revelation*, Jesus was a member of the Nazoreans (slightly different spelling of Nazarene). The name "derives from the Hebrew *Notsrim* signifying 'Keepers or Preservers...those who maintained the true teaching and tradition, or who cherished certain secrets which they did not divulge to others...'"[159] In other words, an esoteric tradition. Common sense dictates that Jesus was an esoteric teacher, a hierophant, revealing the mysteries of the kingdom of God. In this vein the raising of Lazarus would seem "to have been part of some kind of initiatory rite in which the initiate undergoes a symbolic death and rebirth before being given the secret teachings. Such a rite is a common part of many of the mystery religions that were widely practiced in the Greek and Roman worlds.[160]

⚜

Continuing on the esoteric track, Nazarenes could be referred to as the "sanctifying ones" with no inference at all to any concept of salvation. Nazar is also closely rendered etymologically to *nahash*, Hebrew for "serpent," and *nashamah*, or "soul" in Hebrew. The Nazarenes were an esoteric[161] sect connected or closely aligned with the Essenes. During this time, there were three primary philosophical sects of Judaism: the exoteric Pharisees, the Sadducees, and the esoteric Essenes.[162]

As is usually the case, any esoteric belief system is a threat to the primary and more commonly accepted exoteric systems. It is easy to see why. In exoteric paradigms, materialistic consciousness is given total validity as the only true state of mind. Higher states of consciousness or intuition are not considered valid or real.

Furthermore, in esoteric systems, people question. They question dogma, doctrine and anything written that is supposedly literal truth. But exoteric paradigms do not want questions, only blind obedience to their system of belief.

Esoteric followers are usually branded as cultist[163] (in a derogatory way), heretics, and revolutionaries. In first-century Judea, the Essenes were not the only esoteric cult or sect. There were the Nazars or Nazarenes—a branch of the Essenes, and even offshoots of the Nazars, Gnostics,[164] and others that "were more or less kabalistic."[165] In the eyes of the Jewish ruling elite, these sects were heretical and troublesome.

We might think that Judea was isolated and only teeming with Romans. But that was not the case. There were many others from varying cultures and belief systems, such as "Buddhist missionaries who had overrun Egypt, Greece, and even Judea"[166] and who influenced the Essenes. In addition there was a Babylonian and Chaldean influence: "The Jewish Scriptures indicate two distinct worships and religions among the Israelites; that of Bacchus-worship under the mask of Jehovah, and that of the Chaldean initiates to whom belonged some of the nazars, the theurgists,[167] and a few of the prophets."[168]

We have now arrived at a point in our investigation of truth where things begin to get interesting. One of the physical traits of the Nazars was their long hair. Supposedly, this identifying mark extended as far back as the long-haired Nazar Samson and the prophet Elijah. Jesus was also long-haired, but he was not what you would call a strict Essene or Nazarene, as he ate all kinds of food,[169] often drank wine, and enjoyed life.

Dogmatic doctrine, whether it is from an exoteric or esoteric tradition, is still dogmatic and doctrinal. In other words, neither is a paradigm of equality open to all people. Sometimes the esoteric sects are as close-minded and prohibitive as the exoteric ones. And this is what Jesus discovered and rebelled against. Not only were the Orthodox sects more concerned with rules and regulations than with "natural law," so were the esoteric sects.

Jesus was a Nazar and had been initiated through immersion bathing in the Jordan by John the Baptist, "known as the 'Great Nazar.'"[170] But he recognized the limitations and inequality of not only the Pharisees and the Sadducees but also the esoteric sects, and he saw the need for a "new way"—a new consciousness.

John being a descendent of the scripture Nazars was tolerated by the scribes and Pharisees of Jerusalem, "but the followers of Jesus evidently adhered to a sect which became a still more exasperating thorn in their side. It appeared as a heresy *within* another heresy; for while the nazars of the olden times, the 'Sons of the Prophets,' were Chaldean kabalists, the adepts of the new dissenting sect showed themselves reformers and innovators from the first."[171]

And furthermore, Jesus, a student of John and the Essenes, "cannot strictly be called an Essene...neither was he a nazar, or Nazaria of the older sect. What Jesus *was*, may be found in the *Codex Nazaraeus*...[172]

"'Jesu is *Nebu*,[173] the false Messiah, the destroyer of the old orthodox religion,' says the *Codex*. He is the founder of the sect of the new nazars and...a follower of the Buddhist doctrine."[174]

In the eyes of the Nazarenes, John the Baptist was the only acceptable prophet, not Jesus. Because Jesus had broken away from John's Nazars and had established his own sect countering the other esoteric sects, he would be accused of being a false prophet, or as stated in the *Codex*, a false messiah. So it's clear that Jesus upset not only the Orthodox Pharisees and the Sadducees but also the esoteric sects.

In her seminal work *Isis Unveiled*, H. P. Blavatsky states that "the motive of Jesus was evidently like that of Gautama-Buddha, to benefit humanity at large by producing a religious reform which should give it a religion of pure ethics; the true knowledge of God and nature having remained until then solely in the hands of the esoteric sects, and their adepts."[175] She later writes, "In his immense and unselfish love for humanity, he considers it unjust to deprive the many of the results of the knowledge acquired by the few. This result he accordingly preaches—the unity of a spiritual God, whose temple is within each of us, and in whom we live as He lives in us—in spirit."[176]

After approximately two thousand years, Sherry and I can vouch to the animosity and the grudge still held by the followers of John the "Nazar" against Jesus. It was November of 1998 when I was approached by a stranger in the medieval city of Carcassonne in the south of France. He asked me if I was going to visit Rennes-le-Château (later popularized by the publication of *The Da Vinci Code*), and I replied in the affirmative. He then went on to say there were many mysteries connected with Rennes-le-Château and this part of France. Again I replied that I realized that fact. And then as he walked away, he turned and with a stern look said, "John is the true messiah!"

Jesus as Cultural Hero

The cultural hero, and his return, is one of the most enduring as well as important cross-cultural archetypal prophetic themes known to humankind. Its importance is due to its message of hope and renewal. The meaning stays the same; only the names of the hero change. The Mesoamerican prophet or cultural hero was known as Quetzalcoatl—the morning star. The Hopi prophecies speak of their spiritual hero Pahana, the purifier or the elder white brother, while the early Hawaiians worshipped Lono as their savior and lord of peace. In our case, Jesus as the morning star carrying a message of the kingdom of God (equality, love, and forgiveness) was in all manners a cultural hero. Furthermore, Jesus was destined to return.

Symbolically, the return of the hero represents the spiritual concept of the infinite cycle of death and rebirth. But it as well represents the return of light or enlightenment to a world void of love and a humanity that has darkened once again. The religious histories of many cultures also portray the morning star, the planet Venus, in this same emblematic role of representing the returning hero.

The spirit, the teaching, and the message of the cultural hero endure for a period of time, true to their original form. But as the sands of time seep through the hourglass of life, people's minds and hearts become lazy. And a lazy heart and mind is one ripe for corruption. Enter the Christianity of Paul overshadowing Jesus's true message.

Cultural heroes were never "redeemers" saving people from original sin but were "revealers" of love and forgiveness. They were always role models, "walking their talk," as witnessed by the Egyptians' mythic hero, Horus.

> The Egyptians, who were the authors of the mysteries and mythical representation, did not pervert the meaning by an ignorant liberalization of mystical matters, and had no fall of man to encounter in the fallacious Christian sense. Consequently they had no need of a redeemer from the effects of that which had never occurred. They did not rejoice over the death of their suffering saviour because his agony and shame and bloody sweat were falsely supposed to rescue them from the consequences of broken laws; on the contrary, they taught that everyone created his own karma here, and that the past deeds made the future fate. The morality was a thousandfold loftier and nobler than that of Christianity, with its delusive doctrine of vicarious atonement and propitiation by proxy. Horus did such or such things for the glory of his father, but not to save the souls of men from having to do them. There was no vicarious salvation or imputed righteousness. Horus was the justifier of the righteous, not of the wicked. He did not come to save sinners from taking the trouble to save themselves. He was an exemplar, a model of the divine sonship; but his followers must conform to his example, and do in life as he had done before they could claim any fellowship with him in death. Except ye do these things yourselves, there is no passage, no opening of the gate, to the land of life everlasting.[177]

⚜

Christianity has been the source of wars, atrocities, and destructiveness since its inception in 325 CE. This not only took the form of "killing in the name of Christ," but in eradicating the "spirit" and beliefs of indigenous people while substituting their own. One example is Charlemagne's destruction of pagan sites and his massacre of thousands of pagan men, women, and children. His ultimatum was to be baptized or to die. Christianity is nothing more than a forced religion, not by choice but by fear.

This is in direct opposition to Jesus's message and teachings. In *The Hero with a Thousand Faces*, Joseph Campbell writes the following:

> Jesus, for example, can be regarded as a man who by dint of austerities and meditation attained wisdom; or on the other hand, one may believe that a god descended and took upon himself the enactment of a human career. The first view would lead one to imitate the master literally, in order to break through, in the same way as he, to the transcendent, redemptive experience.[178]

This is an example of the "messenger" being the "message." He continues:

> But the second states that the hero is rather a symbol to be contemplated than an example to be literally followed...Though Jesus is reported to have declared that 'the kingdom of God is within you,' the churches maintain that, since man is created only 'in the image' of God, the distinction between the soul and its creator is absolute—thus retaining, as the final reach of their wisdom, the dualistic distinction between man's 'eternal soul' and the divinity. The transcending of this pair of opposites is not encouraged (indeed, is rejected as 'pantheism' and has sometimes been rewarded with the stake).[179]

There is one pure and simple truth. If you manufacture a religion based on faith, exclusiveness, fear, and blind obedience, then your "savior," or God, will be so otherworldly that no one could ever be able to achieve the same ability. This religion is Christianity. But if your vision is to bring a change of heart and mind that others can do what you can do spiritually, then you would bring a message of unity—one of forgiveness, loving-kindness, choice, love, and hope. This was the teaching and message that Jesus attempted to spread—a pure, nonhierarchical religion open to all, an inclusive kingdom within and without.

This religion would not be based on salvation or on faith but on experience—the initiatory and transformational experience of the mysteries of heaven and earth—the very same mysteries that Jesus experienced and knew were open to all other human beings as well. I refer to his spiritual philosophy and pure religion of the kingdom within and without as Divine Humanity.

CHAPTER 4

Faith

God is the All, the Unknown, the One, the Great Mystery, the Sun behind the sun beyond human's consciousness to know— no group or religion can claim God, the All, solely as its own.
—REV. DR. J. C. HUSFELT

n Jesus's mind, faith was purely a manner of the heart. It was faith in the kingdom of God, within us and outside us. It was not in a religious or secular institution's dogma and doctrine and certainly not in one individual. To awaken faith through firsthand knowledge and experience, Jesus performed initiation and the sanctification rites of submersion bathing, "but after Saint Augustine's pronouncement that faith in the Established Church should take the place of everything else, the principle of initiation was suppressed, and blind faith superseded true knowledge...The proclamation of the dogma of papal infallibility may be considered the last stage of religious agnosticism, spiritual tyranny, and materialism...When Jesus said to his followers: 'The kingdom of heaven is within you,' he was promising the conquest of heaven through the inner life. We have seen how the Church succeeded in veiling the heaven of the Cosmos and the heaven of the soul by intellectual narrowness and the idea of spiritual domination."[180]

The church based on Paul "taught a doctrine that opposed teachings attributed to Jesus on several fronts, replacing Jesus's alleged teaching of universal, compassionate, selfless action with a selfish teaching of desire to gain a 'free gift' of salvation based only on faith and completely devoid of any behavioral requirement or obedience to law, and distracting us from the selfless teachings attributed to Jesus."[181]

If we turn to common sense, it tells us that doctrinal faith as the foundation of our religious belief means that we do not need to concern ourselves with our actions, our words, or our thoughts as to their impact and effect on others or to involve ourselves with the issues of forgiveness, compassion, and love. Any forgiveness or compassion given by a Christian is not from his or her heart but from his or her faith—a hollow obligation and not a heartfelt action. In other words, there is no need or desire to transform our consciousness to one that sees no separation between us and others and allows us to truly understand the teaching of "love thy neighbor."

Additionally, we can only "believe" what is told to us as truth but never really "know" or have the freedom to discover our own truth. Here is a simple example: When we were told as children that the stove top was hot when it was turned on, and not to touch it or we would be burned, we believed what was told to us; but, still, we did not truly know the truth until we accidentally, or to "see for ourselves," touched the hot stove. This is knowing through physical experience.

Basing a religion on doctrinal faith is an easy way to attract followers. People following a faith-based religion have little responsibility for their spiritual growth—it's been done for them. There is no sacrifice on their part, for they are following a broad path, an easy way that leads to an illusionary security and a materialistic egotism.

Followers of faith, for the most part, bask in an illusionary security of life and the "afterlife." They have accepted the ultimate "father" figure, and no matter what their actions in life, they will spend an eternity being taken care of in heaven. Faith is centered on an external consciousness. It is a consciousness of duality, of a discursive mind, and of discursive thinking; it is not a consciousness of the heart or one of radical nonduality. You can't have two masters: mammon *and* God. God is in the heart, while mammon is in the mind. Mammon means not only wealth but finding one's security[182] in the world. And the church provides this easy and illusionary faith-based security.

The church's faith is secondhand. There is no direct and personal knowledge of religious or mystical experience—no matter how much you jump around preaching the word while music is blaring in the background of an evangelical church. This type of faith is not based on reason or a knowing but on blind acceptance. Contrary to this, Jesus's faith was based on a firsthand knowing of the otherworld of spirit. This was his faith, the trust in God that was discovered within us and outside us, not a belief in an external institution. Jesus's faith was in this divineness that we needed to know and experience *firsthand*, not in what an institution such as the church tells us to believe as truth. This knowing is through sanctification practices, not through a belief in salvation.

Reason flies out the window with belief and faith. "The more absurd the belief, the greater the faith required,"[183] such as in the belief that the murder of abortion providers is "right in the eyes of Christ" even though there is that commandment of "thou shall not kill." With Rome's establishment of Pauline Christianity, "Latin theology triumphed; rational exegesis died. Faith overcame reason; philosophy languished. Dogma replaced revelation; wisdom, knowledge and understanding atrophied. Authority displaced individual responsibility; community vanished."[184]

Christian faith is also based on the belief of the Bible's verbal infallibility. It can be summed up by "this bumper sticker: 'God said it, I believe it, and that's that.' Slavery, patriarchy, and genocide can all be justified by this approach."[185] When a religion is based totally on faith and belief, not on the experience of self and others, or on the spirit and the "otherworld," then the religion only portrays a "smoke and mirror" illusion of security and spirit. In reality, Christianity is like the wick of a lighted candle that has been blown out—the religion's soul is black...the fire of Jesus's true message is gone, the true spirit of Jesus has been ripped out, and what is left is a religion devoid of the spark of life and spirit.

Power Within

Jesus's use of the word *faith* referred "not simply to trust in God but more specifically to confidence in his teaching as an authentic path to the divine Throne."[186] This is the divine Throne in Merkavah or Chariot mysticism. It is important to note that "the ultimate goal of the merkavah experience is transformative and deifying."[187] In other words, it is awakening to our innate divinity.

Faith to Jesus was the absence of doubt and the knowing of the interconnectedness and the oneness of life. It was confidence in the kingdom—within and without. In the teachings of his path and "original way," Jesus taught that the power is within each of us to transform and awaken our divine spark. It is this divine spark, this power of creation, that allows our kingdom within and kingdom without to flourish and to prosper. It makes sense that the source of our soul's prosperity is an understanding of our relationship to self and to all other things—and then doing the "right action" (e.g., love thy neighbor, forgive, turn the other cheek, and love thy enemy). Self-transformation was what Jesus taught. He taught an awakening of one's heart—one's divine spark and God's altruistic law. With this awakening comes happiness and love of self and love of others—humans and all of nature's creatures.

Christianity is far removed from these teachings of individual divinity, spiritual awakening, growth, natural law, self-responsibility, and love of nature. To the Christian dogma, the self is sinful, not divine. The "saving grace" for Christians is faith in Jesus. The only Christian responsibility is belief in the resurrection of Jesus, who "suffered and died on the cross to redeem our sins."

How ridiculous, irresponsible, and destructive. With this belief there is no need to directly experience anything—spirit, nature, or our relationships to self and others. It is in the "book" (the Bible). The church and the "book" are the guide. No experience necessary here.

There is no need to experience for ourselves the transformative mysteries of heaven and earth. Ironically enough, these are the very same mysteries of heaven and earth that guided the great ones throughout history: Abraham, Moses, Buddha, Jesus, and Mohammad. If you make Jesus the Son of God and not truly who he was—an extraordinary man (rebel, great teacher, exemplary prophet, and messenger who brought a new view of life)—then Jesus could explore and experience the mysteries of life and death, but you can't! Today, the church can, but you can't. This puts believers at the mercy of the church. This absolute lie about Jesus is so destructive.

I was once told about a T-shirt that conveyed the lie of the church in such simple terms: "His suffering; your gain!" How maddening and how destructive such a belief is to people's spirits and souls.

Original Divinity or Original Sin[188]

> *Jesus never spoke of original sin, only the evil of
> the world, which is completely different.*[189]

Jesus did not believe in original sin. He believed in original divinity, in purity, as each of us has the spark, the starlight of God, within us. We are born pure and "born in *love* and not in sin. There is no love greater or holier than that of mother and child. There is nothing more sinless—baptized or not—than the child in the mother's arms. Woe unto him who dare offend one of these little ones, *for of such is the kingdom of heaven.*"[190]

Judaism does not believe in original sin. Thus there is no need for a savior in Judaism as there is in Christianity. God's natural, altruistic law, stated in Jeremiah 31:33 that "it will be written on their hearts," means that as soon as the soul, the breath and light of God, enters the body at birth, God's divine mandate of love and compassion is written on the heart. The logical conclusion would be that the little one is thus born in divinity and not in sin.

Jesus was Jewish; as stated above, Judaism does not believe in the existence of original sin[191] but of original purity. Then did Jesus, out of the clear, blue sky, have an epiphany that babies are born sinful? Of course not; original sin is another lie of Christianity that, along with bodily resurrection, opened Pandora's box and let loose destructive beliefs on an unsuspecting populace. "The truth is that the Christian cult is the one and only religion in the world that was based upon the corpse instead of the resurrection in spirit. In no other religion is continuity in spirit made dependent on the resurrection of the earthly body."[192]

In other words, Christianity is a religious paradigm that is not based on the resurrection of spirit and soul but on a bodily resurrection—a religion that can only be called a worship of the "nailed god" or the "corpse." Additionally, we must not forget about one of the Church's sacraments—eating the body and drinking the blood of Christ. Symbolic as it is, it is still a manipulation of the faithful's consciousness reinforcing the church's lie of redemption, salvation, and original sin.

When we put our resurrection into the hands of another, as the church preaches, we achieve easy and illusionary salvation using the language of Christianity.

When we are not responsible for our own resurrection of self (spirit and soul), we are prevented from becoming authentic human beings. How tragic and destructive this is to each person who follows this lie and this travesty of truth.

Redemption—We Are Each Our Own Redeemers

The etymology of the word "redemption" comes from the Latin *redemptio*, which means a release or buyback. Our past may contain unpaid debt that needs to be repaid through forgiveness and possibly restitution.

True redemption results in our release from separateness. As human beings, with divine starlight within, our redemption is not obtained from a state of original sin but rather from a state of separateness. As divine humans we do not need a redeemer figure. We are each our own redeemers. Each of us knows this at a certain level of consciousness—a remembrance of paradise most commonly known as Eden. This memory of a lost paradise "lies within each of us. Its antiquity and its universality proclaim its archetypal nature; Eden is an essential human experience, whether it is called Dilmun of the Sumerians, the Elysian Fields of the Greeks, the Land of Eternal Youth of the Celts, Valhöll of the Norse, the Grail Castle of medieval legend,"[193] or Luz of the Hebrews.

Within all humans there is the longing for redemption. There is this need, possibly hidden but still influential, within each of us to resolve the guilt of the wrongs that each of us has done—a debt to be repaid. It is almost as if we struggle to acknowledge and accept our humanness and the mistakes and wrongdoings that originate in being human. But because we don't believe in ourselves or trust ourselves to redeem ourselves, we look outside of us for the answer. This is the current condition of humanity, but it is not new! "Throughout the long and turbulent history of religion as well as in social, political, emotional, and sexual spheres of life, we have, stubbornly and to our great cost, sought our salvation in someone or something other than ourselves."[194]

Common Sense

Professing your faith and belief in Jesus Christ as Lord—Son of God—guarantees your entrance into heaven. This even may occur right before you die, and no matter what your actions and their ramifications throughout your life, heaven is still open for you—no hell, just heaven.

In this context it seems reasonable to assume that Hitler is in heaven. He was raised as a Catholic and went to a monastery school. Interestingly enough, the school's coat of arms contained a swastika. It is very possible that right before he committed suicide, he reaffirmed and professed his faith and belief in Jesus. Common sense supports this, since "Hitler held many hysterical beliefs which not only include, God and Providence but also Fate, Social Darwinism, and ideological politics. He spoke, unashamedly, about God, fanaticism, idealism, dogma, and the power of propaganda. Hitler held strong faith in all his convictions. He justified his fight for the German people and against Jews by using Godly and Biblical reasoning. Indeed, one of his most revealing statements makes this quite clear: 'Hence today I believe that I am acting in accordance with the will of the Almighty Creator: by defending myself against the Jew, I am fighting for the work of the Lord.'"[195]

One step further, according to Christian dogma and doctrine, the six million Jews killed during Hitler's holocaust were barred from heaven (being Jewish) and, thus, in Christianity's paradigmatic thinking, hell was waiting for them. Using common sense, what do you think?

Accordingly, it's not what you do but what you believe that matters in Christianity. It's faith, not works (our actions, what we do, how we conduct our life, etc.). Common sense deems faith irrelevant, bordering on evil, and totally in opposition to the true message of Jesus.

Hollowness of Spirit

Jesus was a teacher of heavenly wisdom, which comes from his firsthand experience of the world of spirit. This wisdom flows from the transformational power within us and available to us. Contrary to this, Pauline Christianity took Jesus's teaching that the power was truly within each individual—the kingdom within—and transformed it into a power that was solely in the hands of the church through the province and name of Jesus Christ. The following is excerpted from a sermon at the Aspen Chapel in Aspen, Colorado, presented by United Methodist minister[196] Toni Cook:

> The church in the West—following years of theological warfare—made a wrong turn. The initial focus of Christians was a personal experience of God as love, a love that could transform the world. To them, scripture

was only meaningful if it led one into a deeper relationship with God. But the church decided to turn from an experiential focus to an ecclesiastical focus, from a focus on Spirit to a focus on structure; to a focus on church structure based on a strict and enforceable belief system. This meant the church became a spiritual power broker of right belief or official theology (orthodoxy). And the great irony of Christendom is that the man who preached a direct and un-brokered relationship with God was himself made into the ultimate power broker. The message of Jesus was obviously so volatile that it had to be contained at once and refocused onto the medium as the message, onto Jesus as God. Thus Jesus became the exclusive medium, the one and only way to God. And the church controlled access to Jesus. Thus Christianity turned from the Spirit written in the heart to the written letter of the law.

Jesus revealed to us our true selves: the divinity at the heart of each person...He lived as though there were no divisions between Jews and Gentiles, men and women, no divisions between those enslaved and those who were free. Everything and everyone is interconnected. This was a revolutionary social vision—fuelled by Divine Compassion—that swept across the Roman Empire. Jesus taught that everyone, no matter who, was a child of God, and could experience the love of God in their lives.[197]

Additionally, the church, from the very beginning, has made the dark (equivalent to the feminine) and the underworld—evil.

This in and of itself has perpetrated the lie of original sin and has allowed the followers of Christianity to embrace a separation paradigm of light versus dark—and it has allowed the continued expulsion of the feminine. The church encourages and supports dualism—the separation of opposites instead of a oneness of being where opposites interpenetrate...and what is the reason for this position?

It's what I would call a dualistic, one-sided religion. This type of religion controls its people through fear and guilt. In dualism there are two sides that are opposite from each other—the positive (the light, male) and the negative (the dark, female). Christianity's one-sided position is the positive side—viewed as the light and male dominated from a "male" god right on down to the earthly representative of this "male" god: Christianity's patriarchal churches.

This egotistic, controlling, one-sided view only validates the male, the light, the external, the sun, and all the things that they represent, such as a linear view of time and a literal interpretation of the Bible. Please keep in mind that I am not just talking about the Catholic Church but every church that considers itself Christian.

The light is the church, while the dark is evil, the lair of Satan, and something to be avoided at all risks. The dark is also symbolic of the unknown. And this is an unsettling territory for humans, as the unknown harbors their most deep-seated fears. Has this brain-washing subconsciously caused people to fear change—the unknown?

Isn't the dark where all growth begins and evolves? Symbolically, wouldn't the dark be recognized as being "within"? And did not Jesus teach about the kingdom of God within? "The kingdom of God is within you" (Luke 17:21), and "The Kingdom of Heaven is within you and whoever knows himself shall find it. Know your Self" (Jesus, *Oxyrhynchus Manuscript*[198]).

Know thyself: this was the primary maxim of the ancient Greek mystery schools. It was connected with Apollo, the Greek god of light, and was inscribed on a lintel at the Temple of Apollo in the holy city of Delphi. And, of course, this was one of Socrates's most famous sayings. Probably the greatest philosopher ever, Socrates's whole philosophical and teaching focus was on this guiding principle of self-knowledge overcoming one's ignorance: "One of the greatest thinkers and philosophers of antiquity. He devoted his life and work to moral philosophy and to search for moral good, virtue and justice. The main method he used was dialectics (the method of seeking knowledge by question and answer) by which he tried to teach men how ignorant they were and to help them know themselves."[199]

But this truth is not just limited to the Greeks. It possibly goes as far back as 2500 BCE as the guiding principle of the Egyptian mystery schools that explored the esoteric doctrines of Osiris. Interestingly enough, Moses was a student of the same Egyptian mystery school. And could not Jesus have been influenced by Socrates and the Greek mystery schools as well as the Egyptian mystery schools and the teachings of Moses?

If "know yourself" is attributed to a teaching of Jesus, how hypocritical is the dogma of Christianity? It is totally the opposite of "know yourself." But of course, without this guiding principle of "know yourself," just having faith and not questioning would be a sleazy but excellent manner in which to keep your followers as metaphoric sheep, only believing in their "shepherd's" dogmatic truth, not their own inner truth as Jesus wanted.

Without this principle and the symbolic dark, there is no searching, no seeking of the mysteries of life, no questioning…and the lack of these things is not only potentially destructive to others but is destructive to the soul! One of the very destructive aspects of Christianity's lie is that its followers do not have to look at their own dysfunctional darkness (e.g., inappropriate sexuality, abuse, etc.).

This lie of Christianity has been, and still is, so destructive to its followers' souls and spirits. What this lie means is that there is no need for a person to transform and to work on issues of inappropriate sex, security, safety, and fear—no need to do it, as it's been done.

Because of this, Christians have unenlightened, dull spirits. This dullness leads to arrogance and an ever-expanding, dysfunctional darkness within, which then affects every living thing on this planet—and I challenge anyone to deny this fact. If you're not working on cleaning up your "crap," then it's going to expand, pollute, and corrupt all that it comes in contact with. It's the height of stupidity to think that the work of spirit has already been done for you.

Weak Minds—Damaged Minds

> I am 30 years old and I am struggling to find sanity. Between the Christian schools, homeschooling, the Christian group home (indoctrinating work camp) and different churches in different cities, I am a psychological, emotional and spiritual mess.
> —A FORMER EVANGELICAL[200]

A philosophically weak mind, and I am not talking about intelligence, is one externally, dualistically focused on materialism and one's identity, safety, and security. A weak mind is a mind constantly chattering (mind-talk), nonempathic, and totally focused on one's unhealthy ego—it's all about the "I" of life. However, this does not mean that a person will not be successful and prosperous by the dictates and criteria of our present-day materialistic culture.

Even though a person may have a philosophically weak mind, it may not be a damaged mind. It seems that the combination of a weak and damaged mind as a concept is to be primarily found within the mind-control paradigm of institutionalized religions such as Christianity and Islam. According to Marlene Winell and Valerie Tarico, "in Bible-believing Christianity, psychological mind-control mechanisms are coupled with beliefs from the Iron Age, including the belief that women and children are possessions of men, that children who are not hit become spoiled, that each of us is born "utterly depraved," and that a supernatural being demands unquestioning obedience. In this view, the salvation and righteousness of believers is constantly under threat from outsiders and dark spiritual forces. Consequently, Christians need to separate themselves emotionally, spiritually, and socially from the world. These beliefs are fundamental to their overarching mental framework or "deep frame," as linguist George Lakoff would call it. Small wonder then, that many Christians emerge wounded."[201] One of Christianity's concepts that contribute to a weak and damaged mind is "grace."

Grace versus Compassion

Grace: a Christian theological term denoting divine gifts without which human salvation would be impossible.[202]

Compassion comes from within us. Grace comes from outside us as divine gifts, but, of course, only for the believers.
—REV. DR. J. C. HUSFELT

Christianity's concept of "grace" is the child of the two Fs: faith and fear. Pure and simple, "grace" is a paradigm of judgment flowing from a "father-figure de-ity"—the Christian God. Grace is an absurd, immature religious concept that is supposed to help explain the mysterious events of life, which many times are tragic happenings. In reality its prime purpose is to only keep the "faithful" in line and in fear.

Have you ever stood before a judge? I haven't, but I would have to think it is a little intimidating, with more than a touch of fear of the unknown thrown in. With "grace" we have the ultimate "judge and jury." Taking this one step further, and based on the dogma of Christianity, your priest or minister is God's representative—a very subtle and slimy way to generate respect and a bit of fear, either consciously or subconsciously.

Grace spreads a subconscious message of separation while scattering a veil of fear over a legitimate and, most importantly, religious concept—compassion.

Think for a moment about a scenario where children are trapped in a burning building—some survive by being rescued, and others aren't rescued and perish. And we hear a statement from the mother of the children who were saved: "By the grace of God, my children live."

How about the children who died? With "grace" as your belief, it means that your children who died were judged "not worthy" of life! How ludicrous a belief...but on the other hand, how dangerous a belief this is, as well as totally destructive, to a person's mind and sense of self—emotionally, mentally, and spiritually.

Let's now look at a real-life scenario. On Saturday, March 8, 2014, a Malaysia Airlines Boeing 777 disappeared off the radar screen. Presumably, all 239 people aboard perished. As another example of the destructive force of grace, "a Houston man whose heavy international travel schedule had him booked on Malaysia Airlines' ill-fated Flight 370 says his decision to cancel the trip was divine intervention...the fact that he's at home in Houston with his wife, Brooke, instead of missing in the Gulf of Thailand, is a gift from God, Greg Candelaria said Monday by phone. 'Some would call this luck,' he said. 'I would absolutely consider it one hundred percent the grace of God.'"[203] No words of compassion from him for the 239 and their loved ones, just arrogance. In other words, he was worthy of life, while the 239 people onboard were not worthy to receive the "gift of life" from the judgmental Christian God. What will be the impact for the surviving relatives if they hear about this statement? Along with their grief, it will just add another layer of pain, anxiety, and depression.

Ironically enough, but tellingly as well, Jesus didn't buy into a judgmental God who dispersed a "grace" based on salvation-condemnatory criteria. Jesus's God was compassionate. When Jesus spoke, it was about the compassion of God as it flowed to all people and to all things of the earth.

Compassion and forgiveness were some of the basic principles that Jesus taught and practiced. Jesus did not teach "grace" and never used the word "grace." He viewed compassion as a great, round mirror of the heart and mind that perceived self and others not as distinct but as merged identities. This was knowledge, wisdom, and the realities of life based on oneness, not an illusion of life centered on selective gifts from a "Man God." Flowing from this oneness of reality, empathy emerges for us as a motivating force for proper deeds or right action.

We must ask ourselves, then, why "grace" is one of the pillars of Christianity. In my heart and mind, the answer is obvious: power and control. Since Jesus never used the word "grace" or taught the "way of a judgmental God," we have another lie of the patriarchal church.

The Poor and Marginalized

The church is materially wealthy but poor in spirit. Its corruption and greed are widespread, reflected in its need for earthly power and abundant possessions—churches, buildings, and the golden items contained within. Contrary to this mind-set, Jesus warned to "be on your guard against all kinds of greed; a man's life does not consist in the abundance of his possessions."[204] Homelessness and hunger could be "wiped off the face of the earth" by selling the possessions of the Christian church (as well as by billionaires becoming millionaires). And where would the followers worship? Their churches or places of worship would be the same as Jesus's church. The hills, the valleys, the lakeshores—any place in nature where the ground is the foundation of the kingdom and the sky is the kingdom's roof.

Furthermore, in Jesus's mind the problems facing the poor and marginalized were not based solely on the lack of material wealth but on being outcast or on the outside of acceptable society. In some ways, doesn't this sound familiar? Today, the church deems same-sex marriage, same-sex physical and sexual relations, and women who have abortions as being, of course, sinful in the eyes of and outside the "grace" of God. Contraception for Catholics is a sin (more Catholic babies, more money for Rome). Furthermore, women are marginalized by being considered second-class citizens by the church. The marching orders in Rome suppress women and control their bodies. Where is the equality and compassion for all?

It is not to be found within the church. Its primary focus is the church with a single-minded attention on its theistic dogmas, earthly power, competitive economics, and private profit. The Catholic Church even has its own bank—not for the poor but for the rich and for itself, and possibly to use as a haven for money laundering!

⚜

"Although Jesus was born to a peasant family in Galilee, and the Buddha to a powerful ruler who held sway over northern India, both arrived at the same moral destination. Each felt not only that wealth was not the way to heaven and enlightenment, but that worldly riches interfered with an attempt to lead a good life."[205]

Do You Wear a False Face, or Do You Have a Heart That Sees?
(An Awakened Heart)

In the introduction I discussed hypocrisy. I would like to expand on that, as it is a hindrance to awakening and entering the kingdom of God. Being a hypocrite means wearing a false face. Presenting a false face is not the sole province of Christianity; it is rampant throughout the majority of capitalist and political institutions. The worst of the worst wearers of false faces are to be found on Wall Street and within the majority of bankers and politicians.

What is a false face? It is our outer mask we present to the world. It hides our true thoughts and feelings and is a reflection of our power-seeking minds, cut off and separate from our hearts. A person with a false face does not have a "heart that sees," which in the Mesoamerican tradition was called *Ollin*. This symbolized the "motion principle" in Mesoamerican thought, but in addition, it had the meaning of a purified heart or a "heart that sees" truth. It is a compassionate heart that sees everything in life as sacred and every action we take as hallowed. There is no stagnation in our lives, only movement. This movement is always toward destiny and away from the mediocrity of a life that has been lived in self-blindness.

With *Ollin* hearts, we bring our inner selves out into the world for all to see who we are. This is a concept that is foreign to our culture and society. Many live a lie, but few live their truth. We are taught to hide "who we truly are" from others, including our coworkers and neighbors. We present falsehoods and false faces to the world. And depending on the circumstance or the environment, we even wear different false faces—one face at work, another face at home, and yet another face alone. With the "heart that sees," there is only one face—our true heart face.

This cultural scourge is not just a modern fixture of life in the twenty-first century. Being a hypocrite and wearing a false face was one of the issues that Jesus dealt with concerning the Pharisees. During Jesus's time, actors wore masks, and the word for actor was hypocrite. In other words, a hypocrite wore an outer mask (i.e., a false face). The shedding of the mask or false face is needed before one can awaken, or in Jesus's terms—enter the kingdom of God. This is "the primary point of Jesus's teachings against Pharisaism. Jesus is opposed to the Pharisees primarily because the Pharisees wear masks—they conceal themselves—and so mislead men because they themselves are false."[206] We get a glimpse into Jesus's mind about his feelings toward the Pharisees and their inner corruption. "Woe to you, scribes and Pharisees, hypocrites! For you are like whitewashed tombs, which outwardly appear beautiful, but within are full of dead people's bones and all uncleanness" (Matt. 23:27 [ESV]).

Seeking the kingdom of God, we cannot put worldly goals ahead of spiritual goals.[207] And this is where seeking wealth, and the external power connected with it, comes into play. The focus is not on the inner self but on the outer; the making of one's own external kingdom, whether it be small or large. It seems that one's accumulation of wealth depends greatly on wearing an outer mask—a false face.

In conclusion, I would ask each of you to look within yourself and ask the following question: do you wear a false face, or do you have a heart that sees (an awakened heart)?

Inequality and Injustice

An earthly mystery—why after two millennia are social issues basically the same, corrupt and inequitable? Peace on earth is nowhere to be found. Jesus's message of love, equality, and forgiveness is just words. It is not an ongoing state of mind or consciousness for the majority of people. Jesus's belief in egalitarianism through thought and practice is not a reality in any church, culture, or society. In fact, the opposite is true. Jesus's egalitarianism on our beautiful earth is not a reality or even a partial reality. Greed and inequality rule the planet. In America, "inequality levels, which have risen and fallen across this country's history, are at historic highs now."[208] Additionally, "higher inequality has been linked to increased health and social problems."[209]

REV. DR. JC HUSFELT

There is hope in a paradigm Jesus would have embraced—intrinsic egalitarianism. This concept is too extensive to fully explain here. Briefly, there are three primary hindrances to social, economic, and religious egalitarianism: lust for wealth, lust for power, and lust for a feeling of security. In fact, lust for wealth, external power, and security is the beast that eats away at a person's heart and soul. And you don't need to lust after all three; even one feeds the beast. This beast rules the capitalist landscape. Our culture's economic, political, and religious rules and laws are based on wealth and power. On the contrary, Divine Humanity's belief in natural law, which serves the common and greater well-being, is nowhere in sight.

It is my belief that socialism, Marxism, communism, and capitalism have all been deficient, corrupt, and far from providing across-the-board equality for all humans and all things of the earth. The beast has served each of them in its own stead. On the other hand, the common and greater well-being and equality are the bane of this beast. But it seems that the belief in equality is just a musing of philosophers and not the underpinnings of society.

In my mind, capitalism has been the worst instigator and exploiter of this inequality of any of the isms above. Capitalism prays on people's endless quest for security. Constantly remaining in this unhealthy, dysfunctional, egocentric state of being results in insensitivity to the suffering of others and to the various inequalities of life. In addition, capitalism is the root cause of the biodiversity collapse of our planet. It needs to be destroyed before the planet is a dead zone. What is the solution, and what is the alternative to this destructive paradigm of inequality?

Intrinsic egalitarianism is the answer. Basically, it means there is a balance to a standard of living that is equal across the board. Philosophically, there would be no haves and have-nots in an intrinsic egalitarian society. This is a society that is not based on rules and regulations, especially ones that benefit the wealthy, but based on the principle of natural law.

Intrinsic egalitarianism is a social and cultural paradigm that deems the Reformation movement and John Calvin's doctrine (such as equating wealth with divine salvation) to be wrong and destructive to the spirit of humanity and to the biosphere of our planet.

For many people, the "Reformation movement considerably increased and manipulated fundamental existential fears and anxieties and channeled most of the resulting energy in the direction of work—the so-called Protestant work ethic. This initiated an unparalleled period of frantic activity that enabled the birth of capitalism as a doctrine of exploitation of people and natural resources...A massive increase in military operations ensued, carving huge colonialist empires that yielded an unprecedented accumulation of wealth and power concentrated in a few nations and families...The coupling of this ruthless exploitation with military power gave rise to the military-industrial complex that currently dominates the world, promoting fierce economic competition, arms races, and wars among nations. Native populations were either eliminated or brutally enslaved."[210]

Intrinsic egalitarianism sows a garden of earthly and heavenly benefits for all people. Egalitarian means there is across-the-board equality, just as all people are created equal with the divine spark within. Intrinsic means that compensation for services or work done is based on a fair and equal intrinsic scale. It is not about consuming excessive amounts of goods or accumulating excessive material things.

It focuses on the interconnectedness of all things on the earth and the effect that one person has on the many and the many on the one person. Intrinsic egalitarianism is based on circular time, the present moment, not linear time, which puts emphasis on the past and future but not on the present. Intrinsic egalitarianism establishes the principle of across-the-board equality that provides for the "greatest well-being" of all things of the earth.

Natural Law, and Then There Is Church Law

> *"Do not think that I have come to abolish*
> *the Law or the Prophets; I have not come to*
> *abolish them but to fulfill them."*[211]

There is human-designed law, there is the "natural law" of God, and then there is church law.

Once again, things are not much different than they were two thousand years ago. At that time the Sanhedrin, the council defining Hebraic law, controlled people's behavior through the external purity laws with no concern for the people's inner purity. This kept them in line and increased the wealth of the priests and the elites of Jewish society. Over the millennia there has been

improvement in this flaw. The Sanhedrin is no more. In its place is the new corrupter of truth. No matter what, it seems the materialistic void is always filled
with the same greed, power, and control, but in a different time with a different
name—the name this time is Christianity. (As an aside, Islam is as culpable as
Christianity with its sharia law. One example of its law requires women to be
covered fully or to wear a head covering, which in some countries is enforced
by religious police.)

Legal law and "natural law" interpenetrate. "Natural law" and church law
do not, as the church feels it is above the "natural law" of God. Additionally,
church law[212] seems to feel it is also above the legal laws of the land and furthermore makes every effort to be outside and not accountable to them.
Physical and sexual abuse of children leaves everlasting scars on a child's body
and mind. This is reprehensible. But sexual abuse of a child by a so-called representative of God (priest, minster, etc.) is an intrinsic reprehensible evil action
that scars a child's body, mind, spirit, and soul. On top of this priestly abuse,
there has been an across-the-board cover-up of it by the church.[213] Truth is in
actions, not words!

The Creed of Christianity—Dualism

> When the missionaries came to Africa they had
> the Bible and we had the land. They said, "Let us
> pray." We closed our eyes. When we opened them
> we had the Bible and they had the land.
> —DESMOND TUTU

Religion in its purest form unites people. At the other extreme is institutionalized religions, which through their dogmatic textual beliefs separate people
into the believers (I'm right) and the nonbelievers (you're wrong). Christians
believe in a divine Jesus. Muslims believe in a human Jesus who was a prophet.
Unity would come from acknowledging that conceivably he was divine as well
as human and was a prophet who brought a radical message that was contrary
to the message of the established Jewish religious authorities.

The I'm-right-you're-wrong mentality is not quite the worst case of dualism. With little effort it can morph into a dualism of "us" versus "them."

Wherever there is a consciousness of dualism, there is a mind-set of separation. Where there is separation, there is always the potentiality for fear and conflict. When we individually separate our hearts from our minds, there is conflict within our souls. When we feel separate from nature, our minds want to either conquer or control.

The Christian cancer of "us" versus "them" comes in various shades of arrogant superiority. At one end of the spectrum is the bland arrogance of a group of Texas high-school-football cheerleaders who displayed "banners with religious messages such as, 'If God is for us, who can be against us.'"[214] At the other end of the spectrum, and the worst case of "us" versus "them," is the type that can erupt into forms of conflict ranging from murder and lynchings rooted in racial issues to the violence of secular and religious wars.

Undoubtedly, over the past thousands of years, religion has been an underlying factor in many conflicts that have erupted on this earth. The same is true today. Of course, there is another very important factor. Where there is the church, there is power, gold, and land to be had (economic power)—all in the name of God; that is, the Christian God, not the Islamic God or the heathen or pagan gods and goddesses.

Past examples of Christianity's "missionary work" could fill a tome full of its atrocities. According to Bil Linzie, "The Christianization of northern Europe took place over a period of slightly more than a millennium with the first monks moving into the British Isles around 350–400 CE to the final declaration of Christianity as the official religion in Lithuania in 1387 CE. It was during this 1000 year time period that Christianity had time to refine its method of conversion."[215] This was not conversion through love and forgiveness, only extreme violence. Exemplifying this use of violence was the converted King of Norway St. Ólaf. In his mind he "taught them the right faith. And he laid such stress on it that if he found that someone did not want to abandon heathendom, he drove him out of the land. Some he maimed, having their hands or their feet lopped off, or their eyes gouged out, others he had hanged or beheaded, but left no one unchastised who refused to serve God."[216]

❧

The mind-set of "us" versus "them" is a fact of most people's unhealthy egos. It always stays in the recesses of one's dualistic consciousness. It seldom erupts into extreme behavior, such as murdering abortion providers, but it is still always there, and the church takes full advantage of this unhealthy mentality.

Additionally, Christian dualism encourages a battle between the dark and the light—good and evil: the devil[217] and God. The church loves to blame the devil for its wrongdoing and shortcomings. In an interview, "Hide-the-Pope" Benedict "acknowledged some of the church's failings, like in the sexual-abuse crisis, which he called 'a volcano of filth' sent by the devil."[218]

⚜

I wonder at the lack of common sense most people seem to use when it comes to religion, even sometimes to the point of "drinking the Kool-Aid."[219] Is it so difficult to consider and reflect on the mysteries of self, heaven, and earth? Are most people so disempowered that they blindly have faith and believe what someone else tells them as long as that person wears the priestly collar or blue jeans while flashing a Bible in the air?

I do understand that for millions on this earth, survival needs are foremost in their consciousness. For them the considerations of the mysteries of heaven and earth would definitely take a backseat to the needs of safety, shelter, food, and water. This fact alone is a tragedy. Could this be the reason the powers that be desire to keep the people symbolically "down"? If I have to spend the majority of my time "toiling the soil" to get the bare essentials, when am I going to have the strength or time to even consider the mysteries of heaven and earth, much less question established beliefs, religious or otherwise?

But how about the rest of us for whom shelter, food, and water are not survival issues (at least at the present time)? The sun shines on my face, and the rain falls on my head—as it does for every human being and creature of this earth. I can be of any faith and have any thought in my mind, and the sun will still shine on me as it will on you. The mystery of life and creation does not discriminate. Why then does the church force people through fear and righteousness to discriminate and to "see" others, creatures and humans alike, as different from and lesser than themselves? Where is the common sense of the "faithful"? If survival is not the issue, what is consistently more important: following blindly or seeking truth within one's heart?

⚜

One of our first steps to awaken to the divine within and without is to let go of our old ways of thinking, such as "us" versus "them." Let your consciousness see a oneness of reality, not separation. Instead of me and the tree, me and the bird, me and the star, shift and substitute in your consciousness a knowing that I am that tree, I am that bird, I am that star—I am nature.

Is There Heaven?

Yes, there is heaven—it is part of the unseen-reflective absolute that interpenetrates with the seen—relative of creation. But this is not the "once in, never out" heavenly realm of Christianity or Islam in opposition to the "once in, never out" of hell. Even though there is heaven, there is no hell.[220]

Today's dualistic religions' dogmas and doctrines say that hell[221] does in fact exist in a place that is separate from paradisiacal heaven. Christianity hangs a sword of fear over its followers' heads, threatening hell and its fires of punishment for disobedience. Believers, though, are then rewarded for their right belief with their promised spot in heaven. After death, we are sentenced to one or the other depending on our "faith" or lack thereof.

But is there any choice other than heaven for ones who are so fearful and spiritually ignorant that they willingly follow along so blindly? This carrot-and-stick approach is nothing more than a brilliant marketing method to keep churches filled and coffers overflowing. It is the pinnacle of bogeyman dualism.[222]

Common sense and heart logic fly out the window under such an illusionary reign of guaranteed heavenly paradise. The promise of a blissful experience in a heaven, a heaven of one religion's own fanciful creation, opens the doorway to a multitude of problematic and possibly terrifying behaviors.

It gives permission for terribly destructive acts. Within this framework it becomes not only OK but actually holy to think, "I'm going to blow myself up and others, whom I do not even know, because my religious leader, based on his interpretation of passages within a book, says that it's right." This is just one example of the destructive results of dualistic thinking and believing in such things as us and them, heaven/paradise and hell.

Part 2

THE TRUTH

*Jesus said, "It is to those who are worthy of
my Mysteries that I tell my Mysteries."*
—THE GOSPEL OF THOMAS

*A human being is part of the whole called by us universe, a
part limited in time and space. We experience ourselves, our
thoughts and feelings as something separate from the rest.
A kind of optical delusion of consciousness. This delusion is a
kind of prison for us, restricting us to our personal desires and
to affection for a few persons nearest to us. Our task must
be to free ourselves from the prison by widening our circle
of compassion to embrace all living creatures and the whole
of nature in its beauty. The true value of a human being is
determined primarily by the measure and the sense in which
they have obtained liberation from the self. We shall require a
substantially new manner of thinking if humanity is to survive.*
—ALBERT EINSTEIN

CHAPTER 5

The Message

Concerning the conception of the Kingdom of God, which Jesus made so prominent, there is almost no evidence of an understanding of it, or interest in it, by the Christian Church.[223]

Jesus was a Jewish peasant who was deeply compassionate and fought for equality and justice. He brought a new way of thinking, living, and being that was all-inclusive. As a mystic Jesus was deeply rooted in an experiential knowledge of God. This firsthand knowledge of the otherworld, the world of spirit, gave birth to Jesus's true message. In simple terms, this is the message: each of us is divine, and each of us is human. We are divine humans, not fully one or the other. This divineness or divine spark is blended with our humanness at birth. Imagine an egg that is blended or enfolded into cake batter.[224] You will not see the egg or taste the egg when the cake is baked and eaten. But, nonetheless, it is still there and part of the cake.

Jesus knew from his firsthand experience of the divine descending into him that each and every person has an immortal "spark" within him or her.[225] This is an indestructible seed of divine light: the divine immanence. This indestructible seed of divine light may be likened to a mustard seed within our hearts.[226] This divine seed of immortality or spark, which sometimes may be referred to as the divine golden dew, constitutes the soul—an eternal spark in its essence, since it is a fragment of God, and immortal.

This is our sacred self. This inner, indestructible seed of light settles over and interpenetrates our earthly DNA as "divine golden dew." It needs to be awakened, to grow in its brilliance, and to be brought to the surface until its radiance spreads to all others and to the world.[227] This is our luminous body that grows within and shines without. In so doing, our relationship to ourselves and to all other things of the world is transformed from being based on fear to being based on love.

This divine spark is the essence and foundation pearl of our kingdom within, and at birth it interpenetrated with the totality of our human being—spirit and divine and matter as a oneness of being. In different terms the absolute, father (divine), and relative, mother (matter), are one. Spirit and matter are not separate from each other but interpenetrate as a unity.

Father, Mother, and Christ

Symbolism is the preferred vehicle for esoteric knowledge. Esoteric or religious philosophical concepts, such as the divine or the absolute, are nearly impossible to understand by using language alone. This type of knowledge is best expressed not "by means of the written or spoken word, but through symbols."[228]

If we view the vertical realm of creation as the absolute, we may assign the term father to this vertical imagery. Accordingly, the relative of creation could be viewed as horizontal and called mother. This is one of the reasons why I refer to Mother Nature as not just an earthly concept but the essence of the totality of our universe.

From a mathematical and sacred geometric aspect, the father (Source, God) is phi (ϕ) and has no beginning and no end. The mother is the Fibonacci sequence, in which each number is the sum of the two previous ones (1, 1, 2, 3, 5, 8, 13, 21, 34, 55, etc.). This sequence of numbers is nature's numbering system (Mother Nature). It has a beginning and interpenetrates with phi (golden ratio). The further the progression of numbers goes, the closer it gets to the Source, becoming more divine.

In addition, there is a little-known fact that, at one time, the mystical science of numbers began with one, not with zero. This was an acknowledgment of the scientific theology that all came and comes from One. Sacred geometry has always believed in the metaphysical philosophy of the unity and the inexplicable oneness of existence.

The absolute or the reflection of the absolute, the father, interpenetrates the relative, or the mother. And the aspect of the father that interpenetrates the mother in the totality of the universe has been labeled the Christ. "The

Christ is within every person. The Christ is the innate divinity of everyone. There is a higher self within us; not separate from us. The higher self, the God self, the Christ, is the ultimate reality of us.

"If this reality is true, then why are we not aware of it? God is so marvelous that God gave us freedom of choice. We may choose to live from an awareness of this intrinsic God presence, or we may choose to live from an outer, sense-consciousness perspective."[229]

In other words, we must awaken to our innate divinity, our divine spark, our father, our Christ, and then awaken this divine light and bring it to the surface of our being. According to John A. V. Strickland, "the religion of Jesus was about the divinity of humankind. Jesus's ministry was all about teaching humankind how to discover, express, and become one with the divinity in us. He didn't call it the Christ. He called it the Father or the Son of God."[230]

In *The Power of Myth*, Joseph Campbell shed light on this matter:

According to the normal way of thinking about the Christian religion, we cannot identify with Jesus, we have to imitate Jesus. To say, "I and the Father are one," as Jesus said, is blasphemy for us. However, in the Thomas gospel that was dug up in Egypt some forty years ago, Jesus says, "He who drinks from my mouth will become as I am, and I shall be he." Now, that is exactly Buddhism. We are all manifestations of Buddha consciousness, or Christ consciousness, only we don't know it. The word "Buddha" means "the one who waked up." We are all to do that—to wake up to the Christ or Buddha consciousness within us. This is blasphemy in the normal way of Christian thinking.[231]

Torus

As I state in the appendix, for reasons beyond what any human mind may comprehend, the Absolute reflected itself—the Reflective Absolute. Philosophically, these are like two multifaceted jewels that refract and reflect in limitless combinations. From the Absolute and its reflection, Reflective Absolute, was "birthed the duality that was nondual"—a void that was not void. Divine Humanity refers to the absolute and the reflective absolute as the *great silence* (the sound of the Hebrew letter aleph is silence), not the big bang, and the duality that was nondual as the *dark ocean*—containing the eternal male and eternal female. The reflective absolute (divine mind and consciousness) now interpenetrates this voidless void (dark ocean), and creation occurs. At this moment a sacred geometric form called a torus was birthed. Reflective in essence, it is the reason consciousness is reflective in its basic structure. "The torus, or primary pattern, is an energy dynamic that looks like a doughnut – it's a continuous surface with a hole in it. The energy flows in through one end, circulates around the center and exits out the other side.

You can see it everywhere – in atoms, cells, seeds, flowers, trees, animals, humans, hurricanes, planets, suns, galaxies and even the cosmos as a whole."[232] In other words, the universe is a torus pattern. So is our heart. "The Heart's electromagnetic frequency arcs out from the Heart and back in the form of a torus field. The axis of this Heart torus extends from the pelvic floor to the top of the skull, and the whole field is holographic, meaning that information about it can be read from each and every point in the torus."[233]

One and the Many; Many and the One

> *Throughout this varied and eternal world*
> *Soul is the only element, the block,*
> *That for uncounted ages has remained,*
> *The moveless pillar of a mountain's weight*
> *Is active living spirit. Every grain*
> *Is sentient both in unity and part,*
> *And the minutest atom comprehends*
> *A world of loves and hatreds.*
> —PERCY SHELLEY, "QUEEN MAB"

As a religious belief, this premise of the "one and many" extends as far back as the ancient Egyptians and Greeks. The Egyptians' numbering sequence began with one, not zero. They felt that "zero represents a nothingness, an absence, and implies that something does not exist and for the Egyptians everything *is*—even Chaos, the negation, *is*."[234] In other words, "the great Unity, the number One is the totality of all existence; all things are One in essence, and love is the cohesive force that makes possible the recognition of all the parts."[235]

Greek theology recognized the unity of creation as well as its diversity in their myths of Apollo, the sun god. Apollo represented the principle of unity, and Dionysus, the fertility god, represented the principle of multiplicity. "Apollo is 'recollection,' the return movement of multiplicity toward divine unity, while Dionysus is 'manifestation,' the first movement of unity toward divine multiplicity. As one philosopher neatly summed up the matter, "When Dionysus had projected his reflection in the mirror, he followed it and was thus scattered over the universe. Apollo gathers him and brings him back to heaven, for he is the purifying God and truly the Saviour of Dionysus."[236]

In simplified terms, this ancient philosophy of unity and multiplicity or the "one and many" means that the One, God or the Divine, is in all things, and all things are in the Divine. This is the mystery of God as the all-originating first principle, which includes all multiplicity and the multiplicity that is included in the unity. In other words, spirit is within matter, and matter is within spirit; all mutually penetrate. Thus, reality is interpenetrating radical nonduality—oneness. There is no separation between the absolute and the relative, dark and light, spirit and matter, or mind and body.

Jesus knew this principle intimately. From his bathing experience of the Holy Spirit, the dove, descending into him, he knew firsthand the truth of spirit within matter and matter within spirit the same way that I do from my own experience in October of 1987. Both Jesus's and my descending-spirit experiences were a state of *unio mystica* (i.e., oneness or union with God). To shine light on this state of mystical union, the following words are the closest I can come to describing it:

> *Floating in that space between heaven and*
> *earth, I have a knowing of both.*
> *My soul's power suspends as a star in*
> *the luminous web of oneness.*
> *I am divine, and I am human; I am human, and I am divine—*
> *a child of God and a brother/sister to all creatures*
> *of the earth. A moment is an eternity as*
> *this knowledge engulfs my heart.*
> *Is it a dream? But isn't it all a dream?*
> *A scream, and I awaken.*
> —REV. DR. J. C. HUSFELT

Additionally, this knowing of the One in the many and the many in the One is recorded in the New Testament when Jesus says, "Believe me that I am in the Abba and the Abba in me, or else, believe for the sake of the works themselves" (John 14:11).[237] Jesus was referring not only to his message but also to having confidence in his message, his works, and his teachings, which he referred to as "faith."

In October of 1993 during the predawn hours, I experienced the divine "call" both as something heard and as something seen—in the form of a vision and a voice. This was additional knowledge of the One in the many and many in the One as well as revealing my intrinsic identity. It occurred on the Big Island of Hawaii early in the morning, when I was not sure if I was awake or still asleep. I saw the night sky before me with a star that was shining brighter than any other, and then a heavenly voice said, "This star is you; you are this star! The great purification is of the people! All are one."[238] This religious experience provided me with the awareness and knowledge of the essential oneness of the macrocosm and microcosm.

This star is you (my divineness); you are this star (my humanness and my intrinsic identity as the star)! But what star? The heavenly voice didn't give details. I needed to research to discover the identity of the star.[239] I know myself very well, including two of my past incarnations, so it was not very difficult for me to discover the name of the star. It was Venus as the morning star, which made perfect sense. There is no greater external sign of the Holy Spirit of God than the morning star, the star that symbolizes rebirth in Judaism. The sun and the moon, the two great eyes of God, represent the male and female dualities of the oneness of God, but the morning star—the planet Venus—as the most brilliant star in the heavens, signifies God's Spirit. This Holy Spirit, symbolized by the divine dove of Venus, brings balance to the dualities of life, resulting in a spiritual wholeness or a holiness of existence.

⚜

After Jesus's awakening, during his descending-spirit experience, he realized that all things had consciousness and that this consciousness permeated and interpenetrated all reality. To Jesus, God was not distant but was immanent in the here and now. The kingdom of God was not only within each person but also outside each person—a kingdom spread throughout the world. To Jesus the kingdom within was the One and the many, and the kingdom without was the many and the One. He knew that when we awaken our kingdom within, our divine spark within us, we pierce the veil of duality and awaken to truth and the paradise that is outside of us—lost Eden.

Prayer

Prayer is personal and not for the public display of one's unhealthy ego. It is the song, the language—communication with God or Alaha, the absolute and relative of existence. To God every word and every thought is a prayer that vibrates through the golden streams of time and creation. We must be aware of our words and thoughts, because each one does matter and may bring us and others joy or suffering. Every moment is sacred, and a life spent chattering in gossip, half-truths, and lies is a life squandered in dysfunctional darkness.

Prayer is the inner silence that will reveal the inner truth of our hearts. This stillness guides us along the crystal-studded pathway of our souls' destinies. Spend time alone out in nature and listen with the ears of the heart to the chorus of angelic knowledge, and you will know the oneness of heaven and earth.

A conscious prayer is like a seed that needs to be planted in good soil, watered, and nurtured. When the fruit of the seed is born, blessings and gratitude are given. On the other hand, many people pray as if they were lost in a desert, sowing their seeds on the top of a barren, sun-soaked soil. Our inner kingdom, darkened and infertile by fear, anger, guilt, and an unresolved past that lacks forgiveness, compassion, and love, can only provide us, as blinded ones, with a rock-strewn ground of unrealized joy and potentiality. Fear, uncertainty, doubt, resentment, anger, shame, and guilt only create barren soil.

Do not keep your seed lost in the desert. Awaken your indestructible seed of light so you may feel and know the awakening and growth of all the other seeds intertwined with this little mustard seed of eternal life.

⚜

The prayer known in English as the Lord's Prayer begins with the Aramaic word *avvon*. This prayer, which Jesus taught to his apprentices, was a teaching prayer and has gone through many translations since it was orally taught. It has not only been translated into different languages (Greek, Latin, Old English,

Modern English), but, originally, it was written in Aramaic—a language whose words had different and varying levels and shades of meaning. As a language, Aramaic conveys a sense of oneness where there is no differentiation between meaning and purpose.

The first line Jesus taught to his apprentices was *"Avvon d-bish-maiya"* (translated, "Thou art, from whom the breath of life comes..."). "The Spirit of God hath made me, and the breath of the Almighty hath given me life" (Job 33:4). I explain this fully in *Tequila and Chocolate: A Guide to a New Consciousness—the Awakening of Our Divinity and Humanity.*

Shema

"Shema Yisrael Adonai Eloheinu Adonai Echad—Hear[240] O Israel, YHWH our God, YHWH is One" (Deut. 6:4). This simple prayer, similar to one chanted by the ancient Hebrew priests, points us in only one direction, and that is one-ness—the many and the One of creation. God is both transcendent and immanent—in everything and outside of everything. "Indeed, Jesus himself stated that the *Shema* was the 'great commandment.'"[241]

Additionally, the six words stand for the six created directions and the six great elements. The sixth element is consciousness that interpenetrates the other five elements and would be mystically equivalent with *echad.*

Squaring of the Circle

There is great knowledge hidden within numbers. The number three is a divine number and heavenly (unseen universe), while four is a mundane number and earthly (seen universe). "Three is perfect and sacred; four is flawed and profane. Carpenters know this from experience. The triangle is the strongest geometric shape in construction because it will not deform under stress. The square, on the other hand, will collapse."[242] One of the oldest axioms of alchemy is known as "squaring of the circle." This axiom was "represented geometrically by a circle within which was a triangle, within which was a square, within which was a circle. From the unity of the circle arises trinity, and trinity gives birth to quaternity, which in the highest mystery returns to unity once again. The center and the perimeter meet and are the same."[243]

Therefore, the great circle (reflective absolute) gives rise to the triangle (divine trinity—unseen universe), which births the square (relative—earth and seen universe). And finally, we have the divine (small circle) interpenetrating and being contained in all parts of the square. When we awaken to the kingdom of God, we have squared the circle.

The Egyptians were the earliest known people to represent this concept physically—the square and the triangle. A few of the pyramids, such as the Great Pyramid of Giza, have a square base and triangular sides. Possibly even Solomon's temple was a step-pyramid. Once again, we observe the axiom "as above, so below."

Numbers are fascinating. I would encourage you to explore the magic of numbers. For instance, three (sacred) plus four (mundane) equals seven—the number of days in our week. Each day of our week is then the unity of the sacred and mundane. Even the names of our days are heavenly based: Sunday—sun; Monday—moon; Tuesday—Tiu (Tyr); Wednesday—Wotan (Óðinn); Thursday—Þórr; Friday—Frigg or Freyja; and Saturday—the planet Saturn. This truth reveals to us our need to have each day be a time of sacred reverence, not just Friday, Saturday, and Sunday. And the best place to spend this sacred time each day is in nature.

Be as Wise as a Serpent and as Pure as a Dove

Jesus taught his disciples to "be as wise as a serpent and as pure as a dove." At various times Jesus substituted the word peaceful (not harmless) for pure. In this statement he was referring to the archetypical concept of a feathered or fiery serpent—the interpenetration of the energies of heaven (fire) and earth (water). This concept was known to many ancient cultures, including the Egyptians. Jesus acquired this knowledge while in Egypt and from the handed-down oral teachings of Moses that were passed on to Jesus from John the Dipper that related to the story of Moses and the copper, bronze, or brazen serpent.

> "Make a seraph figure and mount it on a standard. And if anyone who is bitten looks at it, he shall recover." Moses made a copper serpent[244] and mounted it on a standard; and when anyone was bitten

by a serpent, he would look at the copper serpent and recover. (Torah Numbers 21.8–9, Jewish Publication Society [JPS] translation)

The standard is the "tau cross," and the seraph or Seraphim are an order of divine creatures or angels. "The root of Seraphim comes either from the Hebrew verb saraph ('to burn') or the Hebrew noun saraph (a fiery, flying serpent). Because the term appears several times with reference to the serpents encountered in the wilderness (Num. 21.8, Deut. 8.15; Isa. 14.29; 30.6), it has often been understood to refer to 'fiery serpents.' From this it has also often been proposed that the seraphim were serpentine in form and in some sense 'fiery' creatures or associated with fire."[245] Seraphim are the angelic beings that call out, "Holy, holy, holy" around the throne of God. And the prince of the Seraphim is the archangel Mikael (Michael).

The point of all of this is that the brazen serpent may be viewed as a fiery serpent ascending from the earth to the heavens. Accordingly, Jesus taught that the dove represented the divine spirit and the serpent embodied the wisdom of the earth. Taking this one step further, the dove may represent the element of fire (the fire of spirit), while the serpent may be identified as a water snake. This would indicate a feathered serpent and represents the marriage of opposites—the interpenetration of heavenly and earthly energies—fire and water, but even more mysterious is the blending of not fire and water but fire and ice!

Jesus was also speaking from his own firsthand spiritual experience—his descending-spirit experience while bathing in the Jordan.

Tau (Taw)—the Cross of Resurrection
"I am the Alpha (Al) and Omega (Taw)...the bright Morning Star."[246] These two statements have once again caused confusion and misinterpretation. In simple terms, "alpha and omega" means in ancient Hebrew, "the power (al) of new beginnings (taw)." Alpha is the first and omega is the last letter of the Greek alphabet, while aleph or al is the first and tau or taw is the last letter of the twenty-two letters of the Hebrew alphabet. Aleph also represents unity as well as power, and tau may also represent the perfection of creation.

The morning star is Venus in its morning phase and symbolizes rebirth. It is the star of hope and enlightenment. The sun and the moon, the two great eyes of God, represent the male and female dualities of the oneness of God, but the morning star—the planet Venus—as the most brilliant star in the heavens, signifies God's Spirit. This Holy Spirit, symbolized by the divine dove of Venus, brings balance to the dualities of life, resulting in a spiritual wholeness or a holiness of existence.

This balance resulting in a holiness of existence is to be found within the symbology of the Tau and the cross. Originally, the Tau was known as the Egyptian cross and "was used in the Bacchic and Eleusinian Mysteries. Symbol of the dual generative power, it was laid upon the breast of the initiate, after his 'new birth' was accomplished, and the Mystae[247] had returned from their baptism in the sea... The Tau was a magic talisman at the same time as a religious emblem."[248]

To the ancient Hebrews, the staff, column, and tree of life are all related to the Tau Cross. The Tau Cross shows us the human spirit bound to the cross of matter and is our crucifixion tree of suffering. We only suffer if we are locked within a dualistic, illusionary world of sensory gratification and materialism. Awakening from our egocentric sleep, our cross is no longer needed as one of crucifixion but is replaced and transformed from our tree of pure and impure into our tree of life and wisdom. Our tree of life now contains the wisdom of the radical nonduality of pure and impure or defilement and purity, just as the pure lotus grows within the "mud" of life. Since the "trees" are internal, the radical nonduality is of our body (heart) and mind and not external in any religion's dogma surrounding what is pure and impure, such as the religious segregation of men and women, doctrine against abortion or same-sex marriage, or dietary restrictions: "It is not the thing that enters the mouth that defiles a man, but the thing that proceeds from the mouth that defiles a man."[249]

One step further, if we look to the hidden knowledge of the tarot, we discover the twenty-second card—the World. It is related to the Hebrew letter tav with a numerical value of four hundred. This numerical value, "the number 4 with the two ciphers, symbolizes in number mysticism the whole material Creation, the entire universe with the Creator, with GOD."[250]

We may then realize Tau as the symbolic representation of the divine human where "I and the Father are one" (John 10:30).

The Beast Within

> *Jesus said: "Blessed is the lion which the man eats*
> *and the lion will become man; and cursed is the man*
> *whom the lion eats and the lion will become man."*
> —THE GOSPEL OF THOMAS

There is an ancient cross-cultural concept referred to as "the beast within." The beast is most commonly portrayed as either a lion or a wolf. It symbolizes the untamed nature of our primitive or hindbrain, where instincts such as survival, dominance, and mating are located. Metaphorically then, our beast is an inner quality that is intimately connected with our issues of safety, security, survival, and sex. All humans have a fierceness and ferociousness within them—the beast within.[251] Consciously, many people ignore this quality of self; many fear it, while others deny it totally. But our inner beast is neutral. It is not, by its nature, solely a positive (constructive) or a negative (destructive) quality. One way to think of our beast is as the sum total of our strength, willpower, and sexual potency. These are important qualities that we need in our lives in order to be fully human, fully healthy, and fully energetic.

However, these qualities and others may be turned negative or destructive through such things and emotions as denial, madness, anger, extreme anger or rage, substance abuse, revenge, envy, hate, jealousy, and fear.[252] Add to this list the issues of power, greed, and control over others, and it's easy to see the potential of unleashing the dysfunctional and destructive dark qualities of our beast.

Too often we forget that without the dark, there would be no light. Our lives are usually organized into a separation between the symbolic light and symbolic dark, with the light held up as our ultimate goal in spiritual and religious life.[253] The true secret that most never realize is that light and dark are equal components that interpenetrate as one reality. True spiritual and religious teachings are based on the acknowledgment of the interpenetrative aspect of dark and light within us and then the growth of our light or the divine aspect of our soul from the creative darkness of our humanity.

This is not the Jungian concept of the "shadow" but the actual and physical reality of dualistic concepts, such as light and dark, spirit and matter, that interpenetrate. The dualistic light and dark is the illusion, as our individual sense of reality (of separateness or duality) is an extension of the illusion of our basic core sense perceptions. Our eyes perceive separation between us and all things viewed. This constant reinforcement tricks us into thinking and believing that we are separate and an island unto ourselves.

The reality is that we are not separate at all but deeply interconnected. As we have discovered, Divine Humanity is based on the concept of nondifferentiating knowledge. This is the knowledge that fuses into nonduality all dichotomies such as subject and object. Its foundation is interpenetrating radical nonduality—oneness. There is no separation between the absolute and the relative, dark and light, spirit and matter, or mind and body. The most profound and essential nature of things is not distinct from the things recognizable by our senses.

Similarly, our symbolic light and dark are not separate but interpenetrate to define our wholeness as individuals. Additionally, the two sides of our inner darkness also interpenetrate. There is no separate shadow, just a darkness that is both creative and destructive at the same time.

The "shadow" is considered an archetype by Jungians[254] and connected with the unconscious, but Jung advanced no connection to physiological reality. With the concept of the dark, there is a connection to the body—testosterone. This hormone is our bodily source of physical strength, willpower, and sexual potency. Testosterone is the source of our beast within.

This important hormone is made in large amounts by the testicles. But testosterone is not limited solely to men. Women produce testosterone in their ovaries, even though it is only about one-tenth of what a male produces, just as a male produces a small amount of the female hormone estrogen. Additionally, both men and women produce a small amount of testosterone in their adrenal glands, which are the source of our fight-or-flight mechanism—the power of our beast. But "the modern, technological world gives us few positive outlets for this energy, and yet the pressures of our lives are constantly causing our bodies to send us hormonal messages to fight or flee."[255]

⚜

The beast within, ignored or turned negative, is the root cause of the seemingly ever-present abuse issues found within all levels and stratums of society. Abuse is not solely limited to physical actions. The untamed beast is literally ignorance running rampant. Ignorance, not to be equated to educational level or intelligence, is solely a materialistic dualistic view of life, which results in a spiritually unawakened consciousness. This ignorance then inflates and protects the unhealthy ego's sense of self-survival, resulting in arrogance and arrogant behavior. This arrogance, in turn, feeds the untamed beast. This is the very same arrogance that turns a blind eye to all forms of abuse, such as sexual abuse, especially if reporting or stopping the abuse would threaten the person's external power or position in the world.

The beast wants to constantly feed its source of power.[256] There is even a term for the most ravenous and power hungry—lionized. Particularly, the beast is the source of dysfunctional sexual behavior. These are not sexual issues that the church rules as dysfunctional, such as homosexuality, but the sexual dysfunctions that harm another individual, such as pedophilia, rape, and incest. It can also manifest in the manipulation of another through sex for power, pleasure, control, or influence.[257]

It is important to understand that the beast lies within each of us, male and female alike. As much as we may want to deny our beast within, doing so would be denying our own source of physical strength and potency. Our denial of the dark leaves our light in a vulnerable position in its so-called sole existence of truth. The dark is symbolic of our creative potentiality, a quality we would not want to destroy or inhibit. Additionally, denial may lead to a consciousness of passive victimization. Metaphorically, our "sword arm" is impotent and figuratively "cut off."

On the other hand, denying the beast within may allow it de facto permission to run wild in our spirits, in the process feeding and perpetrating a wasteland within us and outside us. The Roman Catholic Church is guilty of this denial. Look at how its denial has manifested in the world—vulnerable children abused. But to shift the blame, the church provides a substitute for the beast in the guise of the devil—the devil made me do it. In an interview the previous Pope Benedict "acknowledged some of the church's failings, like in the sexual-abuse crisis, which he called 'a volcano of filth' sent by the devil."[258]

⚜

We must "slay" our beast through the process of transmutation—in other words, tame and awaken our beast within. This will transform it into an inner quality of altruistic strength, divine willpower, and altruistic sexual potency—love as profane and sacred sexuality. These are the qualities that are based on love, not on fear, control, manipulation, or revenge. We still possess the "power of the beast," but it is tamed and will work for our benefit and the benefit of the earth and humanity. This is the strength and power to awaken our heart and inner spark while defending the downtrodden. No longer do we express excessive aggression nor have the impulse or need to abuse or destroy other people or other things.

⚜

As Jesus taught in the Gospel of Thomas, the lion symbolizes our beast within. If the lion, the beast within, stays unawakened (spiritually) and untamed (mentally and physically), our first chakra[259] actions and behaviors may be dysfunctional and possibly abusive. This is the unhealthy ego, seeing reality only from the "I" and seeing issues of security, basic needs, survival, profane sex, inappropriate sexual activity, and one's sense of "roots" and family and connection to the earth and nature as hostile. In Jesus's words, the lion has eaten the man, "the lion will become man," and the man is cursed. However, if we awaken the altruistic power of the lion, we have symbolically eaten the lion instead of the lion eating us. We are blessed, not cursed; "and the lion will become man." Being blessed is metaphorically the equivalent of achieving the healthy ego where reality is based on the "I" in the "we" and the "we" in the "I."

Metaphorically, our lion (power and fierceness), now tamed, has not eaten the lamb but has lain down with the lamb (compassion and gentleness). The lion and lamb are "one." With the focus of our lion power now on compassionately creating and not furiously destroying, we are able to journey into the unknown with gentle power and face our fears with compassion.

The Lion, the Maiden, and the Tarot

For eons humans have gazed at the night sky with feelings of awe and wonderment. For the earliest religious leaders and philosophers, the stars and the moon, as well as nature, were teachers and seen as a source of knowledge and wisdom. To these wise ones, the night sky was a starry script that could reveal the mysteries of life and death. With creative imagination, these wonderworkers assigned symbolic names for the various groupings of stars with the realization that "as below, so above; as above, so below." This was the knowledge of the oneness of heaven and earth—the one a reflection of the other.

In the night's angelic script, there were thirteen groupings of stars known today as constellations. Two of these were named Leo and Virgo—the lion in the night sky was followed by the maiden. These two constellations and their symbolic images are the gist of the eleventh tarot card—the Tamed Lion—Power. Modern tarot decks have a propensity to use the exoteric name for this card and call it Strength. Additionally, in some modern decks, it is tarot card eight, not eleven. But the esoteric number placement was eleven, and the card's name was Power.

And what is the greatest power? Love. Love conquers all, even the king of the beasts. The eleventh tarot card symbolizes the transmutation of the energy of the beast within—through love. This is the card of the mastery of one's self and one's own actions. It portrays a maiden with her hands on the open jaws of the lion, symbolizing that she has tamed the beast. It is only through the maiden's "loving acceptance of its bestial nature that the animal is not only tamed but is transformed as well...when human consciousness recognizes and accepts its untamed, primitive nature, it not only frees itself from the instinct's autonomous power but liberates and transforms the instinctual side as well."[260]

As the eleventh tarot card, the Lion and the Maiden are connected with the eleventh letter of the Greek alphabet—lambda, which symbolizes balance. In this case it means a balanced use of power. This is the ability to know when to let our lion roar, when to let it be silent, and when to "unleash" its power.

When we tame the beast within, we open the "book" of natural law as our behaviors become empathic and altruistic—prosocial behavior.[261] We become responsible for our actions and our behaviors. The key is once again the relationship of self and other—being responsible and caring means that we will not consciously hurt anyone else through our actions.

However, we do not metaphorically become a saint. We still have the basic primal survival, safety, and sexual wants and needs. Through the process of taming our beast, we are able to let go of some of our destructive behaviors but not all. When we don't let them go, we symbolically "press them down" or "bind them." (For this "binding knowledge" and further details of the beast within, please see my book on Divine Humanity's pathway, *Tequila and Chocolate: A Guide to a New Consciousness—the Awakening of Our Divinity and Humanity.*)

Awakening Our Kingdom

Awakening gradually occurs with our realization
of the oneness of subject and object.
—REV. DR. J. C. HUSFELT

Even though we are divine and human, our divine "spark" or "starlight" within us is not automatically awakened when we are born or, furthermore, awakened solely through outside influences. Certain New-Age authors and gurus preach that magically at the end of this age, all will be elevated to a higher plane of being, a higher consciousness—all will be enlightened through an increase in the vibrational frequency—no war, no need for power or material possessions. It might sound good and easy, but isn't this also the message of the church? Believe in us, have faith, pay us, and you, too, will spend an eternity in heaven.

In my opinion it doesn't make sense. Our divine spark is like a seed. A seed in nature does not automatically vibrate into a flower—it struggles to reach the light. It needs water, nurturance, and "feeding" to break through the earth and to develop into a beautiful flower, blooming perhaps for only a short period of time. Just like nature, awakening is not automatic. Awakening is not a quick fix; awakening is a way of being—a life journey of healing, love, and oneness. Awakening is a new consciousness, a new way of thinking, living, and being that requires self-responsibility and walking our talk. To awaken is to seek through direct personal experience the mysteries of heaven and earth—the mysteries of the kingdom of God.

Natural Law
The majority of present-day paradigms that rule humanity on earth are not natural-law[262] paradigms. They are based on a premise that human beings need rules and will not be motivated by altruism or exhibit behaviors that favor unconditional love, other human beings, or the greater well-being of humanity.

These present-day paradigms are based on a belief in fear; survival of the fittest (or is it the richest?); and the sinful, greedy, and selfish nature of people.

On the other hand, natural law is based on a belief in the inherent, natural, altruistic law of God that is found within the heart and mind of each person. It lies dormant until awakened. Once awakened, it will become each person's nature, and the world will be transformed through love, and Lost Eden will be revealed.

Thus, natural law is based on loving-kindness and doing what is best for the well-being of others and all things of the earth. It is not generated or codified by a society but is derived and flows from each and every person's natural, altruistic spirit.

Natural laws have their foundation in compassionate and loving actions between ourselves and others. In the Bible this appears as "love your neighbor as yourself." When we have a knowing within our hearts that we have starlight, a "spark of creation" within us, and a knowing that others do also, our ability to "love our neighbor" is heightened, as well as our capacity to forgive and have compassion for others. This is the kernel of magic we are capable of expressing through our own experience of the oneness of life and the heart knowledge of the humanness, joy, and suffering of life. When we open our hearts so thoroughly, we come to understand our own selves as well as others. This is true empathy and compassion.

As divine human beings, natural law is the source of our ability to express forgiveness, compassion, loving-kindness, and unconditional love to self and to others. This natural law lies dormant until awakened by each person. This is the true holy law of Moses; this is the law of our kingdom within and the basis for the teachings and the message of Jesus. Natural law and our divine spark may be awakened by what I call *participation mystique*.

Participation Mystique

Since the dawn of time, the purpose of life, religion, and spirituality was to be centered not in faith, belief, or a sacred book but in *participation mystique*. This is a knowing of the things of life and their inherent mysteries through the experience of the mundane as well as the spiritual. Jesus's emphasis was on a direct religious experience with the totality of body, mind, and spirit, not just the intellect. It was an immersion in the mysteries of nature and the seeking of knowledge and transformation through mystical participation.

Jesus was a "teacher of a way or path, specifically a way of transformation."[263] According to Jesus, what was needed was an inner transformation of the self at its deepest level. "Blessed are the pure in heart," he said, "for they shall see God."[264] His teachings emphasized love, which unites, over fear, which separates. Love and forgiveness begin with "self" (divine, intrinsic self) and then expand out to "others" (divine, intrinsic selves and things). This was, and still is, the *mystery of transformed consciousness*—the mystery of our kingdom within and the mystery of self and other. This was the message Jesus brought and taught to all who had the silence to hear.

Participation mystique may be as simple as sitting alone under a tree and listening to the sounds of nature and our own hearts or as complex as dawn bathing in a stream. *Participation mystique* will result in a *transformation of consciousness*. Albert Einstein, one of the greatest, if not the greatest, minds of the twentieth century, believed in seeking and experiencing the mysteries of life. He did not believe that it had been done for him; he needed to seek and experience the mysteries himself. Jewish by birth, he was not influenced by and had no loyalties to Judaism or Christianity. He felt that "the important thing is not to stop questioning. Curiosity has its own reason for existing. One cannot help but be in awe when he contemplates the mysteries of eternity, of life, of the marvelous structure of reality. It is enough if one tries merely to comprehend a little of this mystery every day. Never lose a holy curiosity."[265]

The Path and the Way of the Kingdom

> *The church is not the kingdom of God.*
> —REV. DR. J. C. HUSFELT

Jesus did not bring an easy path or a way of salvation. Jesus's original way focused on deeds of right action and sanctification practices within nature. His teachings emphasized doing the right thing based on natural law. Following one's heart was more important than following rules and laws, which in some cases were outdated and in most cases only served the elite. Jesus emphasized walking a narrow and difficult path of love and forgiveness—of self and of others. He taught a way of self-responsibility and the achievement of inner purity through spiritual work.

According to my undergraduate professor Dr. Phipps, "an early name for the Jesus's movement was 'Those of the Hodos,' meaning 'way' or 'road'...Jesus developed the notion found earlier in his scriptures, of two contrasting paths: 'Enter through the narrow gate; for the gate is wide and the road is easy that leads to destruction, and there are many who take it. For the gate is narrow and the path is rough that leads to life, and there are few who find it."[266]

With the majority of people's focus on the material side of life, the church and New-Age gurus provide wide-open gates and easy roads to follow. A path narrow as a sword's edge with the valley of the shadow of fear on one side and the valley of doubt on the other side is very difficult to follow. It is never the most popular way to go, nor does it attract the most followers: "Jesus associated the pursuit of the most popular way with false prophets. True prophets recognized that one's walk speaks more loudly than one's talk."[267] Even when miraculous signs are given, the majority will opt for the easy path.

Using common sense, why would Jesus bring a message that would bring him no popularity or riches as well as an accusation of sedition? A message and path of salvation would be considered the easy road, while a path of sanctification and deeds based on one's purified heart would require hard spiritual work. In other words, it is easy to talk salvation but difficult to walk sanctification.

His dedication to his message would have to indicate his commitment and unfaltering resolve. In his mind there was no separation between his work and his life. It was one and the same. He had a knowing about his destiny and dedicated his life to fulfilling it. His destiny, reflected in his life and work, was not focused on achieving external power. It was about bringing a message of a new way of consciousness and being. It was not about ego gratification or the accumulation of riches. This was one of the reasons for his indifference to money and why he saw the easy path of accumulating money, power, and wealth as destructive and a barrier to the kingdom.

Jesus saw the flaws in his people's religious laws, the Law of Moses, and realized that these were not the original teachings of Moses, teachings passed down to Jesus in all likelihood by John the Baptist and others. Jesus's teachings were primarily based on the original way of Moses, taught to him by John, the goddess tradition of King Solomon and the Egyptians, and his own studies in

Egypt. "The original religion of the Hebrews was, like that of all other ancient cultures, polytheistic—venerating both *gods and goddesses*. Only later did Yahweh emerge as the pre-eminent deity, and the priests effectively rewrote their history to erase—not very comprehensively—the earlier worship of the goddess."[268]

These teachings of the original way also viewed nature and the earth as divine. Many of these teachings could be traced all the way back to the Egyptian mystery-school tradition. "Morton Smith, in his *Jesus the Magician*, states unequivocally that Jesus's own beliefs and practices were those of Egypt—and, significantly, he based this assertion on material from certain Egyptian magical texts."[269] Additionally, it's important to note that Jesus's "contemporaries thought of him as being an adept of Egyptian magic, a view that is also expressed in the Jewish *Talmud*."[270]

In Jesus's eyes, the way of the Law of Moses did not even approach the importance of the original way or his own vision. Would this not partially explain Jesus's emphasis on nature as well as his many female disciples and his teachings of equality?

All of this got Jesus in trouble with the Sanhedrin, who considered him a heretic and a sorcerer. The priestly Sanhedrin were the keepers and the enforcers of the Law of Judaism. This patriarchal body ruled the law, which was totally focused on rules and regulations of secular and religious behavior. Their focus was strictly about a person's outward behavior, with no consideration at all to a person's inner consciousness or relationship of self to self and self to others.

It was no wonder the Sanhedrin had little patience for a rabble-rouser who preached against the law while emphasizing a new consciousness based on an egalitarian society and the importance of a person's inner kingdom and relationships with others.

I pose these questions: Was Jesus attempting to return Judaism back to its Egyptian roots and to the knowledge he had discovered in Egypt and knowledge about the teachings of Moses? Based on this knowledge, was he attempting to bring forth a vision of an egalitarian society that recognized the divine in all things—the reign of God, the divine that is within each of us, and the divine that is outside us in all things of the earth and the heavens?

The answer to these questions is yes. The kingdom of God is within us, and the kingdom of God is outside of us. This oneness of being awaits us when we awaken and return to Lost Eden. Have you ever sat alone in a mountain glade or on a deserted beach and heard, smelled, felt, and witnessed nature's inherent paradisiacal presence and intrinsic gifts? The kingdom only awaits our awakening.

Just as an apple tree grows from a tiny seed within the fertile darkest of the earth, our tiny, indestructible seed, our mustard seed of light, our divine spark, once awakened, will grow in its brilliance, bringing health, light, and life to our kingdom within us. With this light, we are now able to see with our heart and through the one eye of God the kingdom outside of us. As our light grows, our luminous body and mind brings us peace of mind and a sense of peacefulness with others. "May peace be upon you."

With our awakening comes the unveiling of the altruistic law of God—natural law. We now live a life where natural law and human-made law interpenetrate. Even if human-made law allows an action to be taken, if it harms others or the earth, we will not act on it. Our life is now dedicated and in service to the well-being of humanity and the earth.

We must keep in mind that for two thousand years, the philosophical and religious teaching of Jesus's kingdom of God has been misunderstood and misinterpreted (many times intentionally). The kingdom of God not only refers to our inner divineness and the divineness of nature and the earth; it also means a reign of equality and justice throughout the earth "where the only ruler is to be 'the Father which is in heaven,' and where 'all ye are brethren.'"[271]

This is in direct opposition to the inequality and injustice found on earth today, the great chasm between the haves and the have-nots, and the destruction of the earth and people through the greed of the political and capitalist elites. The foundation and the furtherance of this realm of wealth lies in the greed and lust many people have for material wealth and the earthly power that comes with this wealth.

In the *Gospel of Thomas*, even Jesus's apprentices were not quite sure about the kingdom: "'When will the Kingdom come?'...they receive the reply: 'It will not come by waiting for it. It will not be a matter of saying 'here it is' or 'there it is.' Rather, the Kingdom of the Father is spread out upon the earth, and men do not see it.' In terms of Gnosis, the Kingdom of Heaven is eternally present, yet it only becomes perceptible upon awakening, upon a transformation of consciousness."[272]

For two thousand years and even longer, Jesus's kingdom of the Father has not been acknowledged or become a reality on this earth. There has been no spiritual or religious unity, the underlying principle of Jesus's kingdom paradigm. Is it not true that in its purest form, religion does not separate people from each other or the earth? And is it not also true that institutional-hierarchal religion, such as Christianity, Judaism, and Islam, separates people and their relationship with nature and the earth? Contrary to the dogma of Christianity, Jesus's message was not one of separation but one of unity or oneness where all were equal, as all people, Jews and Gentiles, had the kingdom of God within them.

From the totality of Jesus's kingdom teachings comes an important idea and ideal for today's world. This is an antidote to the overuse of resources and the devastating effects of climate change. This is the concept and the need for awakened, sustainable communities. Within an awakened, sustainable community, the spiritual unity of people provides the glue to bond everyone together in peace, harmony, and oneness with a common focus on ecological harmony and sustainability.

This was another of Jesus's visions for humanity that never took root. "Jesus sought to transform his social world by creating an alternative community structured around compassion, with norms that moved in the direction of inclusiveness, acceptance, love, and peace. The alternative consciousness he taught as a sage generated a 'contrast society,' an 'alternative community with an alternative consciousness' grounded in the Spirit."[273] Let's make sure this time around that seeds are planted and that they take root, producing beautiful, peaceful gardens around the world.

The Key to the Kingdom
The Oneness of Self and Other

Today's cultural mantra is me, me, me! There is no consideration of others—human or the earth and its creatures. It's all about me—a shallow and highly self-oriented and self-focused worldview. Recognizing this worldview and the unhealthy egos of people who are totally focused on the I, the corporation marketing geniuses who are focused on maximizing their greed through the bottom line have subtly reinforced people's unhealthy egos through the names of their products—think iPhone, iPad, and iTunes.

To the majority of people, life is nothing more than an obsessive, materialistic philosophy of consuming. In our so-called democracy, it's hard to believe, but people seem to be more focused and concerned about the style than about the substance of a political candidate's debate, even a presidential one. Wealth and external status rule the day. "But what would happen if someone refused to define himself or herself by his or her economic status? What if someone came along and insisted that there's nothing ultimately valuable in material progress? What if someone were to treat the getting and spending of money, neither with contempt, nor with respect, but with indifference?"[274]

That someone was Jesus. The key to the kingdom was not to be found in external wealth and power. It was not to be uncovered in the rules and regulations of finite institutions. It was unearthed by discovering the oneness of self and others and following natural law. Accordingly, the secret to a peaceful and fulfilled life, one resulting in happiness and love, is to be found within our relationships to our own selves and to others—others including the world at large (animals, etc.). Love and forgiveness begin with self and then expand out to others. This was, and still is, the *mystery of transformed consciousness*—the mystery of our kingdom within and the mystery of self and other. When Jesus taught "love thy neighbor as thyself," he was referring to the metaphysical realization "that you and that other are one, that you are two aspects of the one life, and that your apparent separateness is but an effect of the way we experience forms under the conditions of space and time. Our true reality is in our identity and unity with all life."[275]

⚜

The kingdom within us and the kingdom outside us are based on the principle of interpenetrative radical nonduality—a oneness of being. This is not the concept of duality or nonduality. Duality states that reality is composed of two diametrically opposite forces, such as night and day. Nonduality believes that dualism is an illusory phenomena. There is no self and other in the concept of nonduality. It prescribes to an ultimate reality that is neither of the body or mind and may be termed *the one*. This state of being may not be achieved while on earth, only after death. Branches of this philosophy deem the earth and our physical body as corrupt and evil. People will refer to this as oneness—a state of being, possibly achievable only after physical death. This is not the oneness of Jesus or the kingdom of God.

The oneness of interpenetrative radical nonduality sees a reality where there is no separation between mind and body, dark and light, or spirit and matter. The most profound and essential nature of things is not distinct from the things recognizable by our senses. In other words, our sacred self and our profane self are nondual and interpenetrate; likewise, all other sentient beings' (things') sacred identities and profane identities are nondual and interpenetrate. This is true oneness.

Additionally, interpenetrative radical nonduality as a principle means that the kingdom of God is here and now. It is outside us and within us in our body and mind; even as imperfect and impure as they are, they are still perfect and pure. It makes sense then that we may be deluded and awakened at the same time. Furthermore, the seen and unseen universe, the absolute and the relative, interpenetrate and are nondual. In other words, the world of spirit and the physical world are in instantaneous union. This is the reason that Jesus said the kingdom was spread throughout the earth, but no one knows it or sees it. The reason: they were attempting to view the kingdom through minds that saw reality only as dualistic or nondualistic. The same is true today of the religious scholars, writers, seminary teachers, and preachers who have never experienced firsthand the realities that Jesus and I know.

Jesus taught his disciples the concept of interpenetrative radical nonduality as the foundation of the kingdom. Since this and other philosophical, spiritual concepts are difficult to understand and comprehend, Jesus utilized paradox and language with symbolic meaning. Furthermore, in this way he knew that his pearls of wisdom would be lost to the swine.[276] A person with one eye does not see or understand.

Symbolism is the preferred vehicle for esoteric knowledge. The lotus flower is a prime example. If I say that the kingdom of God is within us and outside us, which means that matter and spirit interpenetrate, and, furthermore, we are able to achieve enlightenment in this very same body, corruptible and deluded as it is, these are just written words. However, if we use the lotus to symbolize this concept, we will bypass the filters of our linear minds to understand and intuitively know, within our hearts, this knowledge. The lotus grows in the mud but opens its petals to the light of the sun. It remains undefiled even in the mud. This symbolizes the radical nonduality of delusion and awakening. It is still pure (awakened) while in defilement (deluded).

In chapter 22 of the Gospel of Thomas, we discover the following:

Jesus saw some infants[277] who were being suckled. He said to his disciples: These infants being suckled are like those who enter the kingdom. They said to him: If we then become children, shall we enter the kingdom? Jesus said to them: When you make the two one, and when you make the inside as the outside, and the outside as the inside, and the upper as the lower, and when you make the male and the female into a single one, so that the male is not male and the female not female, and when you make eyes in place of an eye, and a hand in place of a hand, and a foot in place of a foot, an image in place of an image, then shall you enter [the kingdom].[278]

This passage utilizes paradox and symbolic language in teaching about interpenetrative radical nonduality and oneness. Why would babies trigger this teaching? At birth we experience the oneness of self, not the exclusiveness of self (unhealthy ego) or the duality of self being separate from others. Our mother is not an object separate from us but a part of us, baby and mother. Breastfeeding is a vital part of this unity. An interesting question—how long does this last? I do not know and would not even attempt to conjecture the time period. However, at birth and for a time, short as it may be, each of us has experienced oneness with our mother and ourselves. Being one and not separate does open a window into our initial life experiences—the beginning of our earth walk and a knowing of oneness. It also reveals our innate but hidden connection to nature—the Great Mother.

Continuing on in the Gospel of Thomas, "when you make the two one, and when you make the inside as the outside, and the outside as the inside, and the upper as the lower, and when you make the male and the female into a single one, so that the male is not male and the female not female." This obviously alludes to interpenetrative radical nonduality—oneness. The next part, "when you make eyes in place of an eye," refers back to the suckling infants. When we have baby eyes (no separation) in the place of the one ego eye (total separation), we enter the kingdom. In our awakening we need to have baby eyes, which are nonjudgmental and tolerant, view the world with awe and excitement, and recognize the oneness of the light and the dark of existence. Baby Eyes is one pillar of the Three Pillars of Light of Divine Humanity.

Divine Humanity ("Humanity" represents not only the human race but all things of creation, all things of Mother Nature—terrestrial and celestial) is a living, spiritual philosophy and new consciousness. It is also a pure religion of the people, by the people, and for all the people. Divine Humanity is a religion of philosophy and a living, personal (not institutionalized) religion that "has less to do with religion and more to do with direct, open, ecstatic free experience of wonderment of creator through creation."[279]

As a world philosophy of awe and a religion of equality and simplicity, it conveys a love for all forms of life and acknowledges everything in creation as divine as well as honoring its own unique intrinsic expression. Therefore, not only is every human being a divine human with an intrinsic human expression and the light, holy spark, of God (the Great Mystery) within, but all trees are divine as well as being trees that in their intrinsic expression may provide food and shelter for us and for other creatures of the earth.

Divine Humanity is a personal religion and spiritual philosophy that is based on one's truth found within one's heart and mind. It is not based on faith, dogma, or doctrine. It is a green, ecological, and egalitarian philosophy and religion. Divine Humanity recognizes the divine in nature and the sacredness of all living things. Nature in partnership is one of the hallmarks of Divine Humanity. It acknowledges the equality and divinity of nature and the realization that humanity is not above nature, as a steward, or below nature, at the mercy of it, but is one with nature and in partnership with the earth in cocreating a paradisiacal state of life for all life—the kingdom of God.

Kingdom of God—Tree of Life and Knowledge

In Judaism one tree holds a special reverence as a tree of life. This tree is the almond tree.[280] Its fruit symbolizes concealed wisdom, and in Hebrew, almond means the awakened one, as the almond tree is known for early blooming bathed in white flowers. It symbolizes purity, perfection, and wakefulness and is referred to as the resurrection tree—the first tree to blossom. "Among the tribes of Israel, the almond was originally conceived as a Tree of Life. Moses' (and Aaron's) staff was of almond (Numbers 17:8) and was described as the 'rod of God' (Exodus 17:9)."[281]

Mystically, the almond symbolizes "the divine light that embraces us all equally. This is demonstrated in the other of the almond's ancient names, luz, which in Aramaic means 'light'. It is also the name of the mythical City of Almond of the Canaanites (who worshipped the goddess Astarte)."[282] The divine light of the almond is reflected in the menorah as the "tree of light." "The menorah within the holy place of the ancient tabernacle was a work of extraordinary beauty and consisted of three main parts: the base, the shaft and the branches. Out of the base a vertical shaft arose and from either side of the shaft there sprang three branches curving outward and upward.

"Each of the six branches and the center shaft ended in a cup made in the form of an open-almond flower. At the very top the opened petals of the flower held an oil lamp. The branches and the central shaft were skillfully decorated with that same open-almond-blossom design with three on each branch and four on the center shaft."[283] Within the symbolism of the menorah, divine light and the tree of life are combined as one. The tree of life is the tree of light.

But is all of this philosophical metaphor, or is there more to it? There is, and the key to understanding the tree of life and knowledge is to be discovered within the hidden meanings of the ancient word *luz*. Not only did *luz* stand for almond; it was also the Aramaic word for bone. Additionally, Luz was the name of the mythical blue city, the House of God that was the gateway to heaven.

First, let us explore Luz as it applies to the city of God. Luz, later named Beit El, was the ancient location of the biblical patriarch Jacob's vision of angels descending and ascending a ladder or stairway[284] that connected heaven and earth. After he had fallen asleep on the ground with a stone as his pillow, Jacob had his vision. It was during his dream that he got a glimpse of the celestial city of immortals where the "angel of death has no power." According to legend, the way into the city is hidden, and "you can only gain entry to the city through a secret cave that is concealed by an almond tree. By passing through a hole in the trunk of the almond tree, you gain the cave and, thus, the city."[285] It's slightly off topic but interesting to note that after Jacob awoke, he took the stone that was his pillow, stood it upright as a pillar, and sanctified it with oil.

Next, let's look at luz as the Aramaic word for bone. René Guénon, an author and intellectual in the field of metaphysics, referred to luz as the kernel of immortality. He goes on to state that "at the base of the vertebral column is the state of 'sleep' where the luz is to be found in the ordinary man."[286] Rabbi David A. Cooper, in his book *God Is a Verb*, when writing about resurrection, states that "the luz bone is sometimes referred to as the nut of the spinal column, a mysterious bone that rests at the base of the spine. The Midrash[287] says that it cannot be dissolved in water, burnt in fire, ground in a mill, or split with a hammer."[288]

Supposedly, the base of the spine is not the only location of the luz bone. The identity and location of the bone is so ambiguous that some feel that its location is not at the bottom (sacral and coccyx) but at the top of the spine (thirty-third vertebrae—the atlas, or first cervical vertebra). Just as there are many facets to a diamond, there are many sides to luz. Part of people's confusion is centered on the concept of resurrection. This is not bodily resurrection at the end of time but spiritual awakening and renewal.[289] And luz in all its facets gives us the clues and blueprints for our own resurrection of self from the unhealthy ego to the healthy ego and the awakening of our divine spark.

Divine Consciousness

What is consciousness? It seems the answer to this question is as slippery as an eel or as difficult to hold on to as a moonbeam. "Explaining the nature of consciousness is one of the most important and perplexing areas of philosophy, but the concept is notoriously ambiguous."[290] But I'm going to make it less so. Consciousness is the sixth element. This makes it no less ambiguous than fire. Fire is an element, and so is consciousness.

However, consciousness as the sixth element is, in reality, divine consciousness. Moses and Jesus both experienced the divine call as something heard and something seen—in the form of a vision and a voice. This was the voice of God or the divine consciousness. Both were awakened and became aware of the blended aspects of spirit and matter.

Divine consciousness does not exist alone. It interpenetrates the other five elements of earth, water, fire, air, and space. In other words, divine consciousness is within all things of the seen and unseen worlds. All things are conscious and aware. This means all—not only creatures but such things as trees and even the earth itself. We are all one, all conscious and aware.

Thus, divine consciousness is a consciousness of oneness. This is not the thought of oneness but the consciousness of it. In other words, our thoughts flow from our consciousness. And our thoughts determine our reality. As we think, we become.

We are born with a consciousness of oneness, but within an unknown period of time, it is overshadowed by a dualistic consciousness. This is the reason why the majority of people have a dualistic consciousness, which also means their thought patterns are dualistic—right and wrong, good and evil, win and lose, success and failure. Due to people's dualistic thought patterns, the ranks and coffers of the Christian and Islamic religions are filled with billions of people who need a sense of safety and security in their dualistic and fearful view of the world.

On the other hand, if we have awakened to radical nonduality where spirit and matter interpenetrate, our consciousness will be nondualistic, as will be the thoughts that flow from our consciousness. We will not seek our safety and security externally in an institution but within us as divine humans and other awakened divine humans—this is the essence of an awakened, sustainable community. This is the power we have to transform a desert into an oasis.

Our life quest is then to follow in the footsteps of the great ones who have gone before us. This journey of spirit is to reclaim our initial birth consciousness, a consciousness of oneness, which is referred to as awakening. As we awaken, we shift our consciousness and thought patterns from being dualistic to being a reality of radical nonduality.

⚜

A cautionary tale in recent history is the theories and writings of Jung. "His ontology seemed often to be dualistic, as well as persistently ambiguous, and was necessarily so because the science of his day could not envision a nondualistic conception of spirit and matter."[291] Jung's consciousness was dualistic, which led him to a wrong conclusion in his concept of a collective unconsciousness. There is not a collective unconsciousness, solely a human psychological inheritance, but a consciousness that is divine or relative and contained within all things of creation.

⚜

The message of Divine Humanity, Jesus, and the kingdom of God is oneness and divine consciousness. Could this have also been a teaching and belief of Moses that was passed down through the centuries until it eventually ended up with John the Baptist, who passed it on to Jesus? Or could Jesus have learned this knowledge during his time in Egypt?

What if Moses Had Brought the Concept of Oneness and Not Just a Theology of One God?

The following is my assertion and theory that Moses brought a message of the oneness of one God. The concept of oneness, radical nonduality, is foreign to many of the scholars, archeologists, philosophers, religious authorities, and historians who have put forth their own theories on Moses and monotheism. As a result, the meaning of the burning bush is lost to them. Their beliefs and assumptions surrounding monotheism are totally based on intellectual knowledge, as their hypotheses are not derived from experience or a knowing.

Moses knew oneness as he had experienced it, Jesus knew oneness as he had experienced it, and I know oneness as I have experienced it. My following theory is based on my intellectual knowledge as well as my experience and common sense of life and nature.

⚜

The three major Western religions are monotheistic due to the revolutionary efforts, trials, and tribulations of Moses, who led his people out of exile and supposedly established the first religion based on one God. His divine revelation to begin this quest was the burning bush.[292] This was a visionary and actual physical experience of interpenetrative radical nonduality, divine and matter as one—oneness.[293]

During Moses's time the majority of religious beliefs and practices in the lands of the ancient Near East were pagan, basically polytheistic. Some were tribal, but none were monotheistic, except for one.[294] In the fourteenth century BCE, a form of monotheism was developed and instituted by the Egyptian pharaoh Akhenaten, also known as Amenhotep IV, one of the first known religious revolutionaries. Supposedly, he did not have a divine revelation like Moses, but he did come to a realization of a single creator essence, the power[295] behind the sun—Aten or Aton. With his new paradigm, Akhenaten (also spelled Akhenaton) upset the proverbial applecart by rejecting the most powerful god, Amon-Ra, king of the gods; rejecting his priesthood at Thebes; and rejecting all the other regional gods. After Akhenaten had passed over, he became known as the heretic pharaoh. This was a discreditable title attached to his legacy mainly due to his religious reforms.

But Akhenaten was not the only heretic. In the eyes of the Egyptians, Moses was also a heretic and religious revolutionary—the cult leader of the Jews. In some scholastic corners, there is even consideration of the possibility that Moses was Akhenaten or Akhenaten was Moses's mentor—even the possibility they were childhood friends who were educated together and received their religious training in the great Egyptian mystery school of Annu (the Greek Heliopolis, the biblical On).

It is interesting to note that the symbol for Aton was the sun disk with rays coming off of it that ended in *hands*. The tenth letter of the Hebrew alphabet is yod. Its image is a *hand* with stretched fingers. The hand is the symbol of *power*. Yod is the seed, the primal vibration of the universe, and the smallest letter of the Hebrew alphabet. It stands as an important symbol for the Creator as well as creation itself, which is reflected in the first letter of the Hebrew alphabet—aleph. Yod may also be symbolized as the mustard seed within our hearts.

⚜

After Akhenaten passed over, his religion in Egypt died along with him. But what followed in the theology of Egypt is interesting to note. According to Erik Hornung, professor emeritus of Egyptology at the University of Basel: "After Akhenaten, and clearly as a result of the impression made by his monotheistic attempt, there was further thinking about the 'one,' as attested above all in hymns of the Ramesside Period...

"The Ramesside theologians saw or suspected the concealment of the 'one' behind the visible, polymorphic cosmos, and behind the divine world as well...This cosmic god is ever still the 'one' who existed before creation, though by taking action he transformed himself into the 'millions' in which he remains visible to the eye. This 'one'—and this distinguishes him from Akhenaten's god and from that of every monotheism—can therefore also be worshipped in the multiplicity of actual divine forms. Taken together, they constitute his body;[296] they cannot be separated from him, and they share in his essence."[297]

Furthermore, Professor Hornung writes that "with the 'one,' Egyptian thinking concerned itself above all with understanding creation, and in this respect we can speak with certain justification of an 'original monotheism,' for the divine was supposed to have been originally one and then differentiated himself only in the process of creation: 'the one who became millions,' as it is stated in a formulation popular after the time of Akhenaten. The Egyptians were always fascinated by the attempt to understand this derivation of multiplicity from an original unity, and they tended to describe this ultimately incomprehensible process by means of paradoxical statements regarding the unity...

"The solution to this paradox regarding the beginning of creation was that the original divine unity secreted something of his substance, whether as spittle, sweat, tears, semen, or even as the word that went forth from his mouth.[298] The first divine pair, and thus plurality, resulted from this original emanation. As early as the Coffin Texts, this process was described with a 'trinitarian' formula: 'when he was one, when he became three.' Multiplicity and the plurality of divine forms were thus derived from an original unity."[299]

⚜

It is plausible that the knowledge of the One and the many was a religious philosophy that was taught in the mystery schools of Egypt. But due to the priesthood's need for maintaining its power and wealth, it was never widely spread to the populace. It is conceivable that Moses would have been familiar with this principle of unity and multiplicity. And thus from this knowledge and from his divine experience of the burning bush, he would have brought a theology of the oneness of one God. Sadly, over the centuries this message was lost to the masses. But there was one who attempted to resurrect Moses's message through his concept of the kingdom within and without—Jesus.

However, today we are not left with a unifying message of oneness that would unite all people of the earth but only with a shell of Moses's message—patriarchal monotheism, a paradigm that only separates people.

⚜

Once we look to the past to evaluate sayings or events, we must understand that the past, especially one that extends back hundreds of years or even millennia, can never be empirically proven—only reconstructed. Even if the orally transmitted knowledge is close to the original sayings and teachings, what will stop a person from consciously changing it? The people or groups, such as the

Jewish scribes or the Christian Gospel writers, who commit to writing the oral teachings of prophets, such as Moses and Jesus, may still change, omit, and further dilute or adapt the stories, sayings, and teachings in a way that will serve their own ambitions.

The words recorded in the Torah were written by the Jewish scribes of approximately 600 BCE based on the handed-down oral knowledge of Moses's teachings and words from approximately 1200 BCE. After approximately six hundred years, common sense dictates that the words and teachings transcribed in the Torah may not have been the verbatim ones of Moses. Emphasis could have been put on certain things, while other aspects of the oral knowledge, and even written knowledge, could have been changed, minimized, or suppressed.

It is very evident that there were two primary areas of focus and emphasis for the scribes in their writing of the Torah—the traditionally known Laws of Moses, Israelites being the chosen people of God, and the establishment of a patriarchal religion. To the scribes Moses's divine experience of the burning bush was a divine statement of God speaking to the select one, Moses, which further established their mission of promoting their agenda of being special— the chosen people of God.

Was Moses's encounter with the burning bush true experience or metaphor? I would have to believe that the experience of the burning bush was real, as I have experienced oneness—interpenetrative radical nonduality. And it is recorded that Jesus experienced the interpenetration of spirit and matter when the dove descended upon him during bathing. But I question the exact religious teachings, practices, and words. This leads me to my assertion that Moses brought the concept of oneness, the One and many, and not solely a religion of one God.[300] I believe that his message was of oneness, which also indicates one God—the Absolute, the All. It seems that either by chance or on purpose, Moses's knowing and teachings of oneness got lost in the concept of one God.

If we delve further, we realize that a theology of one God based on knowledge of universal oneness is not dualistic in concept and cannot be classified as such or as solely patriarchal or matriarchal. Contrary to this theology of the oneness of one God, today's monotheism of the three main Western religions is *masculine* based and *dualistic* in dogma and doctrine.[301]

The Jewish scribes in their versions of the oral histories twisted Moses's oneness into a religion of a patriarchal God with the Jewish people as *his* chosen people. Fast forward to the originator of Christianity, Saul (Paul of Tarsus), and we have *not the one god of a chosen people* but *the actual flesh-and-blood Son of God. They one-upped Judaism*. They actually had the physical presence of God on earth. Each of the three Western religions ended up patriarchal and dualistic in context, far from the oneness of Moses or Jesus.

Finally, What Would Our Past Be Like if the Knowledge Had Been Spread That Moses Brought the Concept of Oneness and Not Just a Theology of One God?

The simple answer to this question—the world might be a very different place. The three major Western religions would have had a better chance of being based on gender equality and not the inequality of these male-dominated religions. This alone could have led to an equality and altruistic philosophy, thought, and action paradigm that would have permeated all levels of culture and society and not the prevailing male-dominated paradigm that has ruled the earth for thousands of years. In other words, there would be less inequality and a more altruistic spirit reigning throughout the earth.

It would not have solved all the problems over the millennia or the ones that we face today. There would have been greater periods of "peace on earth," but there still would have been wars. They probably would have been less frequent and not based on religious arrogance of being the one "true" religion, such as the church's war-based destruction of pagan and indigenous peoples.

Possibly, Francis Bacon's philosophy to conquer and exploit nature would not have been taken seriously, and we would not be facing the problems that we are facing today. We still would have social issues, and we would probably still have to deal with the environmental issues that we face today, but they would not be as extreme. All the problems that have faced humanity would not have been solved by Moses's message of oneness. But humanity would have been further ahead in its search for an enlightened society of equality, peace, happiness, and prosperity.

Additionally, we must not lose sight of the fact that if Moses had brought a message of oneness and a theology of one God, people would still have to be aware of it, understand it, and then do the work to awaken their consciousness to oneness. Jesus attempted to bring the same message, but we have seen what happened to his message of oneness. Instead of a message of the kingdom of God within and the kingdom of God outside, which is a way of teaching oneness, his message was turned into a lie where he was the fully divine and fully human one. This deemed the rest of society sinful humans, with their salvation only available through the church and through the grace of God.

Even if Moses and Jesus's message of oneness were spread worldwide, humans are still human with all their imperfections, fears, and unhealthy egos that constantly need a sense of safety and security and who see the world through a lens of us versus them.

No matter what, we must still awaken to this belief in oneness, which is in opposition to the accepted dualistic view of reality. And then we would have to live it. This has not happened. But if the message of Jesus had been heard, at the very least, humanity would have gotten a two-thousand-year head start on its transformation into a world that could be equated with the foretold Golden Age—a return to Lost Eden.

But all is not lost—hear the message now, awaken to oneness, and spread the good news of Divine Humanity.

CHAPTER 6

Mother Nature and Women

> *With forgiveness our seeds take root and produce the*
> *vines that through divine love bear flowers and fruit...*
> *with peace and harmony, we tend the flowers and*
> *pick the fruit, and with oneness we eat the fruit and*
> *share with all others as brothers and sisters.*
> —REV. DR. J. C. HUSFELT (1997)

Have you ever taken the time to go out into nature, away from human encroachment, and just sit on the earth and feel the beauty and love surrounding you, and if you let it, existing within you? You have no other reason than to just be part of nature—no smartphones or tablets, no hiking from point to point, but just you and the Great Mother, seeing, feeling, hearing, smelling, and even tasting the essence of the kingdom.

When was the last time you viewed the miracle of sunrise, the wonder of sunset, or the magical rise of the moon in its fullness, reminding us of the interpenetration of light within dark? Have you ever been in awe of the darkness of a new moon, knowing that all growth is born out of darkness? When are you going to awaken to the paradise spread before you—the kingdom of God?

When I talk about Mother Nature, I'm referring not only to the earth but to the whole of the seen and unseen universe. Mother Nature is wondrous, magical, and a miracle of creation. The universe as Mother Nature is a great concept to embrace. It expands our concern and consciousness for the well-being of all things out to the stars. This takes the religious, philosophical concept of the kingdom of God from just being earthbound out to the stars—the totality of the universe!

When Jesus would look up at the night sky, a bluish-black tapestry studded throughout with twinkling, silver pearls, he would be in awe of the beauty and vastness of God's kingdom. He would marvel at the deep, dark essence of a new moon and the fullness of light during a full moon. It was due to his descending-spirit experience that he had firsthand knowledge of this kingdom from his vision of the star of Venus and the voice from heaven. This conferred in Jesus's mind the philosophical, spiritual concept of "as above, so below; as below, so above"—the philosophy of macrocosm and microcosm. This is the premise that all occurrences in the microcosm (humanity and earth) are influenced by the macrocosm (the heavens), and it is Greek in origin, possibly dating back as far back as the fifth century BCE.

This philosophy, taken from *The Emerald Tablet of Hermes Trismegistus*, "underpinned the work of the great minds of the past, such as Plato, Aristotle, Pythagoras, and Ptolemy."[302] *The Emerald Tablet of Hermes Trismegistus* proposes that we are a reflection of the heavens. Thus, the manner in which the planets and stars are arranged in heaven when we are born is an imprint and reflection of who we are—a guide to our souls. This is the sacred science known as astrology. Astrology predates astronomy and may be traced back to at least 2300 BCE in Mesopotamia and Chaldea. This is not astrology as predictive but as a blueprint of our souls at birth as a guide in knowing ourselves.

According to Rabbi Joel C. Dobin, "the basic philosophical thrust of astrology derives from the conviction that the human being, God, and the universe are in some way a unity; that man and universe, if you will, both swim in the sea of space-time whose substance is God."[303] He goes on to state that "astrology was so much part of Jewish life and experience and so well respected in our tradition and law that the abandonment of astrology to follow the chimera of scientific linearality was one of the greatest religious tragedies that ever befell our people. For in so doing, we abandoned as well the mystical realities of our faith, our abilities to balance our lives and attain Unity, and we have created of our synagogues and temples arenas of contention for power and concern for financial sufficiency."[304]

Jesus's descending-spirit experience was not the only profound connection that he had with the stars. He was born under a major heavenly configuration with the conjunction of two major planets that figured significantly in

Judaism. These were the planets Jupiter and Venus—they were in close conjunction, and from the earth they looked like one bright star.

Jupiter was associated with the birth of kings and therefore called the king planet, and Venus was called *Meleket ha-Shamayim*, the queen of heaven, in Jeremiah 7:18 and was associated with fertility. In the Talmud *Zedek* refers to Jupiter, which also has the meaning of righteousness or justice. These two planets were known by astrologers as the Greater and the Lesser Good Fortunes of all the planets. Accordingly, the signs in heaven have presented to us the union of the king and queen, announcing the birth of the prince, the righteous one—Jesus.

Not only was Jesus born under the sacred marriage of the king and queen, but his descending-spirit vision was of the morning star (the dove of Venus). This is confirmed in the final verses of the New Testament in Revelations: "I am the root and the offspring of David, and the bright and Morning Star" (Rev. 22:16). Was Jesus virgin born? Yes. His mother was not a virgin, but Jesus was born under the sign of the virgin—the constellation Virgo. In other words, his sun was in Virgo, and he would be a son of the virgin—Virgo. Furthermore, he was born under a new moon—symbolic of the virgin. A new moon and Virgo: "Even today, astrologers recognize that the sign of Virgo is the one which has reference to a messianic world ruler to be born from a virgin."[305] We can see that the stars and the night sky were not only important to Jesus but were a reflection of who he was. In his heart and mind, Jesus loved the sky above him, whether night or day, and the beauty of nature and its creatures that was reflected by his love of the land and the sea—Galilee.

Mother Nature—Earth

> *The Holy Grail is not an item to possess. It is not an external thing. It is our awakened hearts and minds, and in a grand sense, it symbolizes what has been lost—humanity's, and our own, lost values. The primary one is the loss of the feminine—nature and the equality of men and women. This is the lost feminine principle. This world of ours only recognizes as authentic the light, not the dark; the material, not the spiritual; the male principle, not the feminine.*

> *This is then the quest—the quest to recover the feminine and nature. And to heal the wound—the separation, suppression, abuse, and control of the feminine. One of the greatest profiteers, activists, and advocates of this wound, the superior masculine paradigm, is the church.*[306]

Earth is a paradise of wonders all wrapped up in colors of blue and green. It is alive with a consciousness that responds to all the things that call it home. Jesus believed in a partnership with the earth and felt at one with it. He did not believe in being superior to nature, acting as its steward, but as being one with nature and in partnership with the earth in cocreating a paradisiacal state of life, for all life—this is the kingdom of God.

His connection to nature as a key to the kingdom was reflected in many of his teachings. "Like the sages of the Old Testament, Jesus often pointed to nature as a source of insight. 'Consider the lilies of the field; neither toil nor spin.' The observation could take the form of a question: 'Are grapes gathered from thorn bushes, or figs from thistles?' The appeal to the intelligence is clear: 'Of course not,' is the obvious answer. The similar saying, 'A good tree bears good fruit,' makes an equally commonsense observation. As with most of the proverbs of Jesus, it is the *application* of these lessons from nature that their particular power lies.

"Common to all these forms of traditional wisdom as used by Jesus was an *invitation to see differently*. He appealed to the imagination and intelligence, and not to the authority of a revealed tradition, as did the teachers of conventional wisdom. Indeed, Jesus used the forms of traditional wisdom to challenge conventional wisdom."[307]

Contrary to Jesus's belief and life, the entrenched mind-set of our culture is one of superiority to nature—being a steward. This mind-set reflects the patriarchal view of nature or the feminine as below them or inferior to them. Supposedly, men know what is best in managing nature or the feminine (women). By its definition, stewardship implies inequality, with the male side of duality being superior to the female, or Mother Nature, side. To put it in perspective, I am not a steward of my wife but her partner. Life is not about stewardship but about partnership. Stewardship is separation, while partnership is unity. My wife and I are not separate from each other but are together in unity as we journey through life.

This philosophy of patriarchal stewardship results in a separation mentality from the essential paradise God has provided, and so far still provides, to humanity: food, shelter, and beauty. Why then do so many go along with this separation paradigm? How blind can the majority be when "it is as true today as it was in those ancient times, dimly recalled by legend, that Nature can bestow upon human beings great wisdom and knowledge"?[308]

As a society and culture, our separation from nature underlies many of the problems and ills we face today, from climate change to the worldwide abuse and second-class citizenship of women. Being separate from nature, the keys to the kingdom remain hidden, buried beneath layers of church and institutional patriarchal rule.

But you can discover the keys to the kingdom. Discover nature as I did. As a child I remember lying in the grass while looking up at the immense sky; it was so majestic in its blue-tinged beauty. Then I fondly recall rolling over onto my stomach, smelling the earth and its life-force while gazing at the greenness of love the earth shares with all of her creatures.

I remember the magic of chasing lightning bugs in an attempt to capture their light for just a brief moment before letting them go on their way into the night. Even at a young age, I was ever seeking the light. I know I am not alone in these memories of happiness when our hearts, not our minds, beckoned us to be part of and connected to the earth. As children, from the depths of our hearts and souls, we recognized nature's wisdom as a gift to be shared by all. Many of us saw and lived in a garden paradise that provided the adventures and magic of life that only nature can provide.

My parents, on the other hand, had seemed to lose sight of this simple truth, nature's wisdom. Possibly, it was due to their excessive work habits in their effort to "provide for me." It was my great-uncle Albert who fostered and nourished in me the uncomplicated facts of life and the beauty and wisdom of the fruits and flowers of creation. He would let me help him while he tended his Concord grape vines and nurtured his pride and joy, the bright flowers with the sword-shaped leaves—gladioluses. Picking a grape and holding it between his thumb and forefinger, he once spoke these wise words to me: "Jimmy, this is the perfect color of purple; if you pick the grape when it is a lighter color, it will rob the vine of its gift. And if it is a deeper, bluish purple, you will have dishonored the vine by letting the grape stay on too long."

Life is simple and straightforward. We can discern others through the fruit of their vines. In today's world much fruit is rotten, evidenced by the lies of the church and the excessive consumption and accumulation of wealth that rots the fruit of the spirit.

But now is the moment of power. In seasons past, if your fruit has spoiled on the vine or stayed on too long, do not despair. Begin now to tend and nurture your vine, and your fruit will become sweet, loving, and compassionate.

⚜

There is a belief within some indigenous cultures that for every ill of humanity, there is the subsequent cure within nature. I also believe this. Not only have I seen the positive healing effects nature has provided for our students and others, but a simple example of the ill and the cure is the remedy for the sting of nettles. Wherever there are nettles, close by to them, you will find the natural antidote to their sting.

As a society we need to get our children away from the computer and TV screens, smartphones, Facebook, and iPods. All people, but especially children, need to spend as much time as possible in outdoor, self-directed play and in nature—not trying to conquer or exploit it or using it for recreational purposes that pollute and tear up the earth, but becoming one with nature. The simple act of hugging a tree will help increase a child's, as well as an adult's, well-being.

Every day as I gaze at the Pacific Northwest beauty before me, I feel a constant oneness with the tall cedars, our soaring eagle family, and the misty mornings—a joy to behold, a feeling to cherish, and the smell—fresh, alive, and mysterious—the gist of life. Why do people react so negatively to an overcast misty morn? Does it subconsciously vibrate their inner overcast and possibly darkened hearts? Tomorrow may bring a sun-filled view of the cedar trees—the darkness gone, the mist a memory. What about the darkened hearts of people? Does the sun ever metaphorically shine within them?

Separate from nature, many have walked through life as in a bubble—possibly seeing a flower and possibly even smelling its beauty but with hearts and minds separate from the truth of the flower and the experience of nature as their home, the kingdom of God. We lock ourselves away within the protective walls of human-made structures, slaves to institutions, and spend the majority of our waking hours commuting and working inside, separate from the rain, the sun, and, as the days darken, even the moon. And for what, I ask?

⚜

One last important fact, "it has now been confirmed by science that hugging trees can beneficially affect human health by altering vibrational frequency. In a recently published book by author Matthew Silverstone, *Blinded by Science*, evidence confirming trees and their healthful benefits includes their effect on mental illnesses, Attention Deficit Hyperactivity Disorder (ADHD), concentration levels, reaction times, depression, and the ability to alleviate headaches.

"According to countless studies cited within the book, children show extreme psychological and physiological effects in term of improved health and well-being when they interact with plants. It was recorded that children function better cognitively and emotionally in green environments and have more creative play in green areas.

"A large public health report studying the association between green spaces and mental health also noted that 'access to nature can significantly contribute to our mental capability and well-being.'

Human beings can only live outside of the laws of nature for so long before symptoms of disconnect be made manifest."[309]

Listen

Life doesn't occur inside the bubble anymore but inside a box! Science and organized religion separated us from nature, but now, technology has separated us from not only nature but each other. The illusion is connectivity, but the reality is isolation—we are boxes unto ourselves. When was the last time you had a conversation with someone heart to heart and eye to eye that lasted more than thirty minutes? When was the last time you sat and listened to the wind blowing through the trees while watching a bee settle its love on a flower? When was the last time you looked up at the cloud-filled sky's radiant white and blue?

There is great value in the world. Our world of everyday experience is the world of the divine. They are not separate. The cry of a crow is the sound of the divine. The daily chorus of beauty freely given to us by the winged ones reflects the heavenly music of the spheres. Our ordinary world provides us with an ongoing message of beauty, of spirit. But we need to listen—with quiet minds and hearts.

Nature is wondrous, a precious gem to embrace, and one not to be found within your smartphone or iPad. Your choice—wake up to the beauty of nature and each other, or stay asleep in a self-contained, secure illusion of life.

Sophia

Sophia is the goddess of wisdom. She is Mother Nature, the earth mother, sometimes depicted as the black goddess, the black soil of fertility. Additionally, she is closely connected with the serpent. "The serpent is Ophis; so too is Sophia (Wisdom), as in S-ophis, another name for Isis and the star Sirius. In most of the world's mythical, folkloric and religious traditions the snake/serpent is equated with wisdom, even in the Bible."[310]

As the goddess of creation, the aspect of creativeness, she is the eternal female—the feminine aspects of creation. If we look up into the dark of night, we will see her—the virgin goddess, Virgo, the "woman clothed with the sun." Sophia is the grail goddess. As the goddess of the grail, she beckons us to drink of its essence and awaken to Lost Eden—the lost paradise resulting from humanity's fall into dualism.

We may ask, from what well-source does wisdom such as this flow? Wisdom comes from our experience of knowledge. Wisdom does not come with age, like a fine wine. It comes through the experience of direct knowledge, our knowing. Knowledge may be discovered through books and oral teachings. But, ah, this is not wisdom. When we have a direct experience of knowledge, wisdom may be birthed within us. It is important to understand: wisdom is not to be discovered within books, ivy-covered institutions, or institutionalized theology. And it will not be discovered within human-made structures, such as a church. However, we may directly experience and discover wisdom within nature: the valleys and the mountains; the rivers and the oceans; the flight of an eagle; the croak of a frog; the sound of the rain; the crash of thunder; the path of the serpent; the sun, moon, and stars above. Mother Nature, or Sophia, is the teacher and the giver of wisdom. Before it is too late, humanity must seek truth and wisdom from nature, not nature's destruction for greed and power.

Just as Sophia is connected with the serpent, Jesus is also associated with the serpent and the light of wisdom or the Sophia light. We discover this in the Gospel of Thomas: "Whoever has ears to hear let him hear. There is light within a man of light and it illuminates the whole world. When it does not shine, there is darkness."[311]

The word for wisdom in Hebrew is *hokhma*, significantly featured within the Tanakh. Wisdom is the central topic in Proverbs, Psalms, Ecclesiastes, Book of Wisdom, and Song of Songs. Proverbs tells us about the value of wisdom. It is understandable that Jesus, being knowledgeable of these sacred writings, would teach various aspects of the Tanakh that matched his own philosophy and belief. One example would be the knowledge in Proverbs concerning wealth. We know Jesus's disdain for wealth. It is easy to see that he would be in sync with Proverbs: "Happy is the man who finds wisdom, the man who attains understanding. Her value in trade is better than silver, her yield, greater than gold. She is more precious than rubies."[312]

Do not confuse *hokhma* with the Jewish concept of *Shekinah*. *Shekinah* is the divine presence "that aspect of God that is close to and accessible to Creation. While it often simply means 'the presence of God,' it is more often treated as a personified hypostasis of the divine."[313] *Shekinah* is the feminine presence of the divine:

> She of celestial loveliness and purity, Divine in nature, whom they called the Spirit of God, the Dove, the Virgin Spirit, the Logos which is the Word of God, the earliest first Mother, whose name came to represent the essence of all that was beautiful and pure, and of most divine love. She was, in the Talmud, "The Spirit of God that hovered over the water like a dove, which spreads her wings over her young." She was the Shekinah, a mystic word often variously typified as a Lotus, a Rose, an Egg, and by symbols that were oval, as a Cup, a Boat or a Moon.[314]

In Exodus *Shekhina* is portrayed as a pillar of cloud and a pillar of fire: "The LORD went before them in a pillar of cloud by day, to guide them along the way, and in a pillar of fire by night, to give them light, that they might travel day and night."[315] I know this as truth, as three angels appeared to me and my wife as pillars of intense otherworld light—a light not of this earth.

✦

In all manners, Jesus looked to the earth and to the heavens for wisdom. He was a philosopher, a teacher and lover of wisdom—wisdom found within the sea, valleys, and mountains of his beloved Galilee. Nature fed his soul. It takes little imagination to realize that as a healer and lover of wisdom, intimately connected to the earth and the heavens—the otherworld—Jesus was without any doubt, and in all shapes and forms, a shaman.

Jesus as Shaman[316]

> *Jesus taught men and women to see the operation of God*
> *in the regular and normal—in the rising of the sun, the*
> *falling of the rain, the growth of the seed into the plant.*[317]

Predawn bathing in the Jordan River is about as shamanic as it comes. Ritualistic immersion in running water (stream or river) or the ocean is one of the oldest forms of symbolic death and rebirth, a foundational principle of shamanism, which is a cross-cultural form of religious practice and sensibility.[318] Shamans fulfill many roles, such as exorcist[319] and magician. "St. Austin asserted that it was generally believed that he (Jesus) had been initiated in Egypt, and that he wrote books concerning magic, which he delivered to John. There was a work called *Magia Jesu Christi*, which was attributed to Jesus himself. In the Clementine Recognitions the charge is brought against Jesus that he did not perform his miracles as a Jewish prophet, but as a magician, i.e., an initiate of the 'heathen' temples."[320]

One distinguished religious scholar, the late Dr. Morton Smith, believed that Jesus was a magician shaman,[321] as did another distinguished scholar, Bruce Chilton, who also identified Jesus as a Jewish shaman.[322] That Jesus was a shaman, or at the very least utilized shamanic methods, is acknowledged today by some shamans. According to one shaman from Mongolia, Zorigtbaatar Banzar, "Jesus used shamanic methods, but people didn't realize it…Buddha and Muhammad too."[323]

A recent discovery has unearthed further evidence. "An inscription on a bowl uncovered from the underwater ruins of Alexandria in Egypt reads 'DIA

CHRSTOU O GOISTAIS,' which archaeologists translate to mean either 'by Christ the magician' or 'the magician by Christ.' The bowl dates to between the late second century B.C. and the early first century...The archaeologists who discovered the bowl think that a magus could have practiced fortune telling rituals with the bowl and used the name Jesus to legitimize his supernatural powers."[324]

One of the key factors of a shaman's proficiency is the shaman's level of sensitivity, to be open and aware of the intertwining forces of heaven and earth and to have the ability to access both for knowledge and wisdom. Jesus displayed a high level of sensitivity, as proven by his descending-spirit experience and his ability to heal and perform other activities commonly associated with shamans, magicians, and mystics.

Shamans have a knowing about the mysteries of heaven, the earth, and the otherworld (world of spirit), whereas the institutionalized priest deals only with heaven, and then only secondhand. The most commonly known process of the shaman to reach the otherworld is through an altered state of consciousness brought about through various means, such as repetitive sound (drumming or chanting); movement; and extremes of temperature, such as bathing.

But Jesus was so sensitive and open to interpenetrative oneness that he could access the otherworld at any time, without relying on outside tools. In fact, the knowledge was always there in his consciousness. He viewed no separation from the kingdom within him and outside him. Jesus loved nature and could be labeled green for his beliefs and practices. This is one of the reasons that nature played such a prominent role in many of his teachings.

In Jesus's mind, the kingdom of God is not of human making by the church, temple, or mosque but is discovered only within the natural world of the earth and within us. The divine spark was in everything; not only was it within us, but it also interpenetrated all aspects of nature. This was the garden paradise of mythology, except Jesus knew the garden paradise was real—it was the kingdom of his teachings, a kingdom within and without. In other words, the vibrational love and light, the sun or starlight of God, is infinite and resides within each person and is outside each of us, where all things of earth and heaven are sacred and intrinsically unique.

"God makes his sun rise on the evil and the good, and sends rain on the just and unjust." With words such as these, Jesus invited his hearers to see in nature—looked at attentively from a certain perspective—a glimpse of the divine nature...he saw the earth "filled with the glory of God," permeated by the divine radiance...

Christians have sometimes been uneasy with the notion of God "permeating" creation, thinking it sounds like a more Eastern way of thinking. Yet it is intrinsic to the Jewish-Christian tradition to see God as both immanent (everywhere present) and transcendent.[325]

Of course, it is our choice if we listen to our hearts and then realize that our lives have the potential to be a paradise. This is a state of spirit, mind, and body where an atmosphere of love and peace extends outward to our families and to our physical surroundings. The kingdom is ever present, if only we have the eyes to see it and the hearts to feel it.

Common sense then dictates that a teacher who felt so connected and in partnership with the earth would use nature to demonstrate the truth of his or her knowledge and wisdom. Jesus exemplified this principle. He did not do his teaching in the temple but out in nature—by the seashore and the river, within caves and on hillsides.

⚜

Why is Christianity so utterly opposed to the indigenous practices of shamanism, magic, and paganism? Could it be that Jesus as pagan, shaman, and magician did not support the lie, whereas Jesus as God-man does? What about Judaism?

From its very beginning, Judaism was rooted in shamanistic magic, as witnessed by Moses's serpent power and his shamanistic ability to access the otherworld of spirit. It is reasonable to concur that "Moses was a shaman. He had been trained during his forty years as an Egyptian prince, and during his years as a warrior in Ethiopia, and as a son-in-law and apprentice to Jethro the Shaman of Midian."[326]

The earliest recorded shamanic rite of sanctification is to be found within Genesis, where the Hebrew patriarch Jacob awoke[327] early in the morning, took the stone that had been his pillow, set it upright as a pillar, and anointed it by pouring oil on top of it.[328]

In addition, it is known that rainmaking is basic to shamanism. No rain, no life, or as a Hawaiian friend has related, no rain, no rainbows. One of the ceremonial acts of rainmaking involves pouring water onto the ground or an altar. We discover this action recorded in the Oral Torah: "the Mishnah—that a golden flagon filled with water was carried to the Temple in Jerusalem where the priest poured water upon the altar."[329]

Jesus in Egypt

As was stated in the introduction, Jesus's crime "was that he tried to introduce pagan ideas and pagan gods into the Jewish lands." [330] Many of Jesus's pagan teachings and ideas were Egyptian in origin. These Jesus blended with the original teachings of Moses—the teachings that flowed from Moses's experience of radical nonduality: the burning bush. Of course, Jesus did not believe in interpenetrative reality—he knew it firsthand from his experience of the descending spirit symbolized by the dove.

The ancient Egyptians believed in this blended paradigm of reality. They "did not see a rift between the workings of the divine and mundane spheres. The sacred encompassed the secular in their worldview; the physical world—including natural phenomena and the plant and animal kingdoms—was seen as a reflection of the divine world, and everything in it possessed a divine nature."[331] Furthermore, "the gods manifested through the visible—human beings, trees, stars, wind and storm, even though these living things possessed an identity of their own as well. If we could express the essence of Egyptian philosophy over the thousands of years it existed, it would indisputably reflect this doctrine. A sacred text from the time of Rameses II describes this immanence of divinity in nature:

> The soul of Shu is the air, the soul of Neheh is the rain,
> The soul of Ra is the primeval ocean.
> The soul of Asar is the ram of Mendes,
> The soul of Sobekh is the crocodile.
> The soul of every god resides in serpents,
> The soul of Ra is found throughout the land.
> —The BOOK OF THE CELESTIAL COW, DYNASTY 19[332]

Common sense points to this Egyptian influence within Jesus's kingdom teachings. Even though religious scholars and historians label the period between Jesus's twelfth birthday and his thirtieth as the "lost years," they were not lost by any standard. Jesus spent part of these years in Egypt learning the knowledge of their mystery school[333] tradition—the same tradition Moses studied and mastered.

During Jesus's time, Judaism was not completely divorced from its pagan origins. Thus it follows that "the pagan, goddess-worshipping element of heretical Judaism could explain much about Jesus, his true motives and his mission."[334] This further explains the prominence of Mary Magdalene and other female followers as "virtually everything that Jesus said or did can be traced back to a mystery school—most likely that of Isis and/or Osiris."[335] Furthermore, this explains Mary Magdalene's authority as a priestess of Isis to be able to anoint Jesus. The sacred essential oil Mary used was spikenard, which she poured and rubbed over his head—an authoritative as well as a very sensual act.

Mystery School

Religious philosophy and truth evolve from the need to explore the mysteries of life. Many times throughout the twists and turns of our existence, we have wondered about the following universal questions: What is death, and what is the meaning of life? Who are we, and where are we going? Is there such a thing as reincarnation? Is life truly everlasting? What is God? These are just a few of the divine mysteries that are a part of the great mystery. These mysteries are to be sought after—and in the seeking you will experience, and in the experience you will understand, and in the understanding you will believe and know. This belief and knowing will be based on your own knowledge and wisdom—not what you may have read in a book, any book, including the Bible, or what someone else has told you, including all authority figures, religious as well as secular!

Historically, this search for the divine mysteries was the foundation for the formation of various mystery cults, schools, and religions. These systems of spiritual seeking had evolved over thousands of years from the shamans of hunting-and-gathering cultures. One of the core themes utilized by the mystery schools and religions was the transformational experience of symbolic death and rebirth—the oldest of these practices is submersion in living waters (stream, river, and ocean).

The ancient mystery schools "revealed through direct experience the perennial mystic teaching that life is a journey of spiritual awakening; a process by which humans may find their higher nature and become what the ancients called 'gods'. The pagan mystics taught that each individual is a spark of the one fire of life, as represented by the sun. The name of the Greek Sun God, Apollo, means 'not many', and the mystic path was seen as a journey with the aim of finding, within the multiplicity of things, the underlying oneness of God."[336]

In other words, to know the mysteries is to know life and happiness. It is the discovery of truth through experience. It is a transformational journey that allows at any and all moments a chance to experience the divine—the mystery—and thus embrace the essence of one's soul. A mystery allows a knowing that transcends the unhealthy ego and dualistic consciousness. Through direct personal experience, the brilliant light of knowledge and wisdom may be revealed.

For our souls to grow, we must discover the mystery of the kingdom of God ourselves—through our own direct experiences. We may read or be preached to about the ageless baptismal tradition of purifying in a stream and the power that can be gained from it. But until you and I actually step into the deep, dark waters, we will never experience the love and power of this mystery of the kingdom of God that awaits us. Spiritual lessons are very personal. They require humility, patience, and perseverance—plus intent, focus, and confidence. Through our direct experiences with the earth and nature, we learn about the sacred realms and the ways of the earth and the heavens. Through our personal experiences, we learn to see with an inner vision, a vision that lets us see the truth from our hearts—the all within all, the equality of all things, and their intrinsic identities and special and sacred worth.

Jesus's sense of the mysteries is revealed in the following pantheistic teaching: "I am the light which is on them all. I am the All, and the All has gone out from me and the All has come back to me. Cleave the wood: I am there; lift the stone and thou shalt find me there!"[337]

Women

> *The Magdalene could remind all the "Peters"*
> *that it was she who was the Beloved of Jesus*
> *and who held the keys to Heaven.*[338]

Philosophically and practically, it makes sense that "the Earth is female, reflecting the consonance between nature's fecundity and the fertility of women."[339] Millennia ago, the earth as divine Mother was acknowledged and honored as truth. This was a time when a human's consciousness was one of partnership with nature, not one of domination. This predominator mind recognized "our oneness with all of nature"[340] and "was far advanced beyond today's environmentally destructive ideology."[341] Both men and women worked together in equality and partnership for the well-being of society and the community.

As the wheel of time turned, things changed, and not for the better—for humanity or for the earth. The goddess traditions were gradually replaced with a paradigm of male domination in all areas of life. The serpent honored by the earth-based religions as a symbol of wisdom, prophecy, and death and rebirth was slowly transformed into an image of evilness by the Jewish scribes' editing of Moses's oral teachings and traditions and by the liars of Pauline Christianity. According to Riane Eisler's *The Chalice & the Blade*, "the vilification of the serpent and the association of women with evil were a means of discrediting the Goddess."[342]

Judaism is based on the supposed teachings and Laws of Moses. What then was Moses's original belief about nature and the serpent? As I have revealed, Moses experienced the oneness of reality during his firsthand experience of the bush that would not burn. Raised as a prince in Egypt and married to the daughter of a Midian[343] high priest, or shaman, Moses would have recognized his experience of the burning bush as proof of the divine (fire) within all things (nature—the bush), a concept that he had most likely been taught by his father-in-law or during his mystery-school training in Egypt. Knowing firsthand the divinity of the natural world in such an intimate way with the burning bush, Moses would have felt a kinship and partnership with the earth and thus with the serpent representing the wisdom of nature.

According to the Dartmouth Bible, "the most sacred symbol of Hebrew religion, the ark of the covenant, probably did *not* originally contain the Ten Commandments. In this ark, which to this day holds the central place in Jewish rites, there was a serpent made of bronze.

"This was the brazen serpent we are told of in 2 Kings 18, which as Joseph Campbell writes, was 'worshipped in the very temple of Jerusalem along with an image of his spouse, the mighty goddess, who was known there as the Asherah.'[344] As we also read in the Bible, it was not until circa 700 B.C.E., during the great religious persecutions of King Hezekiah, that this brazen serpent, said to have been made in the desert by Moses himself to prove Jehovah's power, was finally taken out of the Temple and destroyed."[345]

⚜

Women and religion would seem to be a natural mix, as is the blending of wine (fire) and water. But that has not been the case on earth for thousands of years."Even that enlightened being, Gautama the Buddha, when he was finally forced to allow women monks into his company, sadly declared that his real living message, which would have lasted 2500 years without women, would not survive longer than 500 after all.

"According to some Islamic theologians women can't enter Paradise and should not receive religious instruction. There are still many orthodox mosques which retain the signs, 'women, dogs and other impure animals are not permitted to enter.'

"The Jains of India, while they have many women among their monks, do not believe a woman can become enlightened, unless she takes a male body in her last reincarnation. Orthodox Hindus will not allow women in some of their temples and no woman is allowed if she has her period.

"But no religion, even today, is so tyrannical and unjust to women as the Christian church, Roman or Reformed. In its entire history there is not a single case in which women are accepted as equals to men."[346]

⚜

Therefore, it is a fact of history that the earth and women have lived under male domination for thousands of years and have suffered, emotionally, mentally, physically, and spiritually, the consequences of this domination. If you dominate women, you feel entitled to dominate the earth, as the earth, or nature, symbolizes the feminine. If the religious dualistic paradigms of the day put forth and endorse the belief that men are superior to woman and rule the earth and all its creatures, the gate of hell on earth flies open to social, economic, and ecological servitude, abuse, death, and destruction by justifying any patterns of behavior toward the dominated. One of the primary means of domination is control of wealth, bodies, reproductive health, and sexual activity.

The church, the mosque, and the temple have all relegated females and the earth to a lesser status in regard to the rules and authority of males— the mandate that is supposedly God-given. Under this mandate, the rape of the earth, overseen by the patriarchal, capitalist religious or industrial czars, is acceptable—all approved by their god of power and greed.[347] What subconscious message does this mandate give to males?

There are multitudes of examples of the male-dominated religions controlling, or is it dominating, women's bodies, reproductive health, and sexual activity. These range from the covering of the head or female body in Islam[348] to the condemnation of birth control as a sin by the Catholic Church. These examples even extend to the founding and subsequent history of Iceland. The Land of Fire and Ice was founded by the Norse in the ninth century after the courageous Norse pagan purists left Norway to escape from the Christian tide that was overwhelming other pagan cultures and religions. In their new homeland, their freedom of body, mind, and spirit only survived about two hundred years until their Althing, the oldest surviving parliamentary institution in the world, declared Christianity the religion of Iceland. As a concession to the Norse pagans, their beliefs and practices were allowed to go underground. The point of this is that before the church took over Iceland, men and women were equals in society. The primary crime was blood feud. After the church established its dysfunctional beliefs, women were regarded as inferior to men, and the most frequent crime—incest! Men now owned *all* women's bodies.

Expanding on this, one of the most devious methods of control that has ever been conceived is the Catholic Church's communion and its rite of confirmation. Communion involves eating the wafer, symbolic of the body of Jesus, and drinking the wine, which is the blood of Jesus. During confirmation, little girls, all dressed in white, are Jesus's brides, and then, confirming their bodies, minds, and spirits to the church, they each eat the body and drink the blood of their groom.

Symbolic or real, it still affects the consciousness and subconsciousness of the blind participants. You are still eating the body and drinking the blood and, in the case of confirmation, marrying young supposed virgins to a dead person hanging on a cross.

Females were not the only ones dominated by the church. Conquered indigenous cultures faced cultural and spiritual annihilation and forced domination of minds and bodies. One example of the church- and government-sanctioned domination of male bodies by other males was the practice of cutting off the long hair of captured Native American warriors. Their long hair, just like that of the Spartans and other warrior cultures, was a symbol of their spiritual and physical power—to cut it was a symbolic act of castration.

⚜

Sadly, first-century Jewish attitudes toward women were the same as they are today. Women were inferior to men. To the Jews of Jesus's time, women were secondhand creations—men were created first. "The synagogue prayer recited at each service included the words, 'Blessed art thou, O Lord, who hast not made me a woman.' In synagogues women typically were required to sit in a separate section and were not counted in the quorum of ten people needed to hold a prayer meeting. They did not teach the Torah, and as a general rule were not even to be taught the Torah."[349] The liar Paul (Saul) took this belief and ran with it. No wonder—he hated women. He proclaimed the inferiority of women and said that they must obey the will of men.

The editing of the Jewish scribes after the Babylonian captivity and the lies of Paul and the Roman Nicaea Council gave momentum to the belief in women's inferior status. For all of this to work, the ruling males needed to keep the populace ignorant and to subtly implant the notion that thinking for oneself goes against the dictates of God.

"According to the holy books, original sin, error, the desire for knowledge, all stem from the decision of one woman, Eve. Adam was an innocent fool, content to obey and submit. When the serpent speaks...He addresses the woman and starts a dialogue with her...Seducing serpent leads to seduced woman leads to woman the eternal temptress. It is an easy progression.

"Hatred of women is like a variation on the theme of hatred of intelligence. To which might be added hatred of everything women represent for men: desire, pleasure, life. Curiosity as well—many dictionaries confirm that inquisitive women are widely dismissed as 'daughters of Eve.' They generate desire; they also generate life. Original sin is perpetuated through women—that sin, which, as Saint Augustine assures us, is transmitted from the moment of conception, in the mother's womb, via the father's sperm. The sexualization of sin!"[350]

⚜

Contrary to the past beliefs of Judaism and the present ones of the church toward women as being inferior, women played an important role in Jesus's life and teachings, and he viewed women as equals. "As Jewish scholar Claude Montefiore notes, 'There can be little doubt that in Jesus's attitude toward women we have a highly original and significant feature of his life and teaching." [351] Additionally, "in the early first-century Church, and in accordance with Jesus's own rebellious policy of treating women with respect and having them among his chosen followers, leadership was conferred on women, and they were accepted into the roles of prophets, teachers and evangelists...

"Jesus's close association with women set him sharply apart from other Jewish teachers. The basic Jewish attitude to women at this time was that they were inferior to men because they were a secondhand creation—men had been created first...In fact so great was Jewish religious prejudice against women that it was perfectly legitimate for men praying in the synagogue to thank God that they had been born male not female."[352]

As another example, Jesus encouraged one woman, the sister of Martha, to learn from a rabbi, a male role, instead of serving food. He ranted about the injustice of the Jewish divorce laws that were exclusively a male prerogative and the Laws of Moses that deemed women impure during their moon time. Why, then, in the name of Jesus Christ, does the church deem women second-class citizens?

Sexual, racial, and economic inequality is rampant throughout society and culture, most evident within political institutions, capitalist institutions, and organized religions. Think about this for a moment: What if Jesus's true message, feelings, and oral teachings had survived intact with very little variation? What if equality were the religious and culture rule of the day instead of the inequality exemplified and supported by the one-sided patriarchal religions?

Consider how different the earth would be today if Jesus's message of equality had survived. Would we have various egalitarian types of cultures spread throughout the earth? Would Judaism or Islam be as they are today? Would the indigenous cultures of the world and their knowledge have survived intact without being destroyed? Would the Crusades have ever happened? Would there be a group of Islamic terrorist named ISIS? Would Marx and Lenin have had anything to write about? Would Hitler have come to power? Would capitalism even have appeared? Would we be on the verge of a worldwide biodiversity collapse, as we are today?

Think about a world of equality, not only of men and women but of races and cultures and economic classes. It is interesting what the truth, instead of a lie, might have done. But only Christianity's lie concerning Jesus and his message survived. Even with the long-term survival of the lie, it is hard for me to fathom that in the twenty-first century, people still abide by the dogma and doctrine that belittles and denigrates women. How ignorant and stupid to follow these patriarchal beliefs that surely limit and separate and are so destructive to nature, when we consider that the earth is viewed as the feminine. Religion is the underpinning of society and culture. If this is true, then we may surmise through common sense that any religion that is purely patriarchal or matriarchal will birth a culture and a society that is out of balance. These cultures will be founded on dualism and will result in separating beliefs that will never germinate true peace and harmony but only inequality and conflict.

Mary (the) Magdalene

Jesus honored women and found in them his most devoted followers, especially Mary (the) Magdalene. The Magdalene, his partner and wife, and other women helped spread his message of spiritual and secular equality. Mary was not only a partner in teaching others about the kingdom of God but was also a grounding factor and most probably a benefactor in his life. She "had a special knowledge of Jesus's teaching—an insight, or understanding, not necessarily shared by the other disciples."[353] This indicates a special relationship between Jesus and Mary, one of marriage, where you would share your inner knowledge with each other and have a knowing that your students would not be privy to. I know this is true, having discovered my modern-day John the Baptist in the form of Vince Stogan—an elder indigenous shaman. He and his wife taught and shared with Sherry and me the secret, inner teachings of their tradition, such as bathing, feeding the spirits, and healing. Many of these we have not shared with any of our apprentices. Only a wife teaching with her husband would know certain knowledge and inner teachings of the mysteries of the kingdom of God.

According to Malcolm Godwin's *The Holy Grail*, Mary's "insightful visions and actual 'knowing' far exceeds that of any the other disciples. Peter is especially galled by the fact that a mere woman should be in such an honored position. His particular hatred of her was seemingly transmitted down to all the other 'Paters,' who shared both his hatred and his mistrust of what, after all, was yet another one of the daughters of sinful Eve.

"We see the polarity within Christianity from the second century onwards between Mary Magdalene and Peter. All the countless manuscripts and hymns which extolled her role as favored disciple and bearer of his inner teachings were carefully excluded from the canon. In *Pistis Sophia* we learn the real cause of the problem when Mary tells Jesus of her fear of Peter. *'Peter maketh me hesitate,'* she says, *'I am afraid of him for he hates the female race.'* So here we have the twin, but polar, traditions within Christianity. On the one hand is the Church of Peter, the Rock—orthodox, male, dominant and aggressive. On the other hand there is the rival Church of Mary, of Love—Gnostic, heretical and worshipping a male/female deity. Of course the aggressive Church of Rome, dedicated to Power, triumphed over its gentler rival but it turned out to be a hollow victory. The Church's exclusion of the female principle crushed the heart out of Christianity and drove Mary's church underground where it remained until briefly bursting forth on the wave of a revived and radical spirituality. This new sense of a balanced religiousness was spearheaded by the Catharis' alternative Church of Love and secretly supported by the Templars, the cults of Mary Magdalene, the Black Virgin and the writers of the Grail romances."[354]

⚜

Jesus was married to the Magdalene; I know this as truth. Besides my knowing, it stands to reason that Jesus was married, as "marriage has always been central to the Jewish way of life,"[355] and "a man of over thirty not to have been married would have been virtually unique."[356] Most recently, "A historian of early Christianity at Harvard Divinity School has identified a scrap of papyrus that she says was written in Coptic in the fourth century and contains a phrase never seen in any piece of scripture: 'Jesus said to them, My wife...'"[357] Of course, the church has disavowed this as a fake. Supporting the premise that Jesus was married is my undergraduate professor Dr. William E. Phipps, who argued that Jesus's status as a Jewish male, a teacher, and a rabbi, would have virtually required that he be married.

Besides the Magdalene, there is also another Mary that figures prominently in Jesus's life. This is Mary of Bethany, the sister of Martha and Lazarus, who in reality is the Magdalene. According to Dr. Phipps, Mary of Bethany and Mary Magdalene are one and the same. Thus, Mary of Bethany who anointed Jesus was the Magdalene. And since in Jewish tradition only priests could perform anointing, it stands to reason that Mary was a female priest or priestess. The religious authorities would be shocked that Jesus felt and taught that to segregate spiritual and religious life into boxes where men can do this and women can only do something else is foreign to the kingdom of God, where all are human beings with the divine spark within and thus equal in the eyes and mind of God. A human being anoints; it doesn't matter if the person is male or female as long as he or she is awakened to the kingdom within. Rules and regulations that separate men and women are a direct affront to the kingdom and to God.

The Great Rip

From its beginning, Pauline Christianity ripped the spirit from the flesh. In all likelihood, this doctrine was created and propagated by sexually and bodily dysfunctional men. Sacred sexuality was taboo to these pillars of the church. The concept of a sacred marriage of love, equality, and the bliss of sex was a blasphemy in the view of the church fathers. Their doctrine proclaims that sex and sexual desires are wrong, except in the case of sexual intercourse for the creation of a child. Of course, even a worst sin is same-gender sex—except when it's convenient to look the other way when it is a male priest and a male child. Not even a slap on the wrist, just a transfer to an unsuspecting congregation.

Contrary to all of this, philosophically, spiritually, and practically, the body, our flesh, is our temple containing our spark starlight or, if you will, our holy grail. What this means is that our bodies are sacred vessels containing our personal soul—our holy of holies. The body is not to be denied or to be viewed as evil or corrupt. It is not separate from spirit but one with it. Our bodies are most precious, and each one is special and unique, just as each snowflake or leaf is unique and different.

⚜

This ripping of the spirit from the flesh included the separation of spirit from all matter. Up until the time of Pauline Christianity, cultures across this vast planet saw spirit as a part of nature or matter as a given truth. Thunder and lightning were not only a physical sound and visual experience of the sky's wonders, which foretold the birth of life-giving rains; they were also the voice of the Norse god Þórr and his hammer streaking across the sky. Thunder and lightning were both spirit and matter as one. Then there is the question of fire (spirit) and matter. If we say they are kept separate, "we boldly disregard the fact that certain stones strike off sparks and certain kinds of wood produce fire when rubbed. Primitive men arrange the facts in another pattern, saying that fire belongs to the nature or soul of tree and stone—the sparks are conceived and begotten by the fire drill; consequently there is an innate kinship between stones and trees on the one hand and the fire that comes down from the heavens on the other."[358] Philosophically, this is an alternative view of reality—one connected with nature, not separate from nature.

Christianity and the resulting cultural separation of spirit from matter have caused pain and suffering over the centuries and have finally resulted in today's worldwide ecological disasters and biodiversity deterioration. In addition, the Industrial Revolution and the capitalist paradigm gave speed and power to the church's doctrine of separation. These destructive twin paradigms have brought humanity to the edge of total death and destruction. Technology will not save us; the only thing that will is the destruction of the twin paradigms of organized religion and capitalism.

Seductive Temptresses—Women

Ah, Eve, the first temptress! The marching orders: separate them, keep them down, and cover them up—for thousands of years the patriarchal institution's slogan for women. During Jesus's time, "a respectable Jewish man (and especially a religious teacher) was not to talk much with women, apparently for two reasons. There was no benefit to be gained, for they were viewed as not very bright and as preoccupied with trivia. Moreover, women were considered to be seductive and sexually rapacious temptresses. Their voices, hair, and legs were felt to be especially enticing. Thus, in part because they were regarded as inferior and in part because of male perceptions (and fears) of their sexuality, women were systematically excluded from both the religious and public life of the social world."[359] Jesus was in direct opposition to these beliefs and practices. This type of nonsense only revealed the weakness of men's minds. In his eyes men and women were equal, and the male's inappropriate sexual thoughts were the problem of men, not what women were wearing or doing.

In the present day, the church views sex and sexual freedom as opening the gates of hell and letting loose the devil. The church's stance on sexual relationships and sexual freedom produces nothing more than guilt and shame in their followers. You can't enjoy sex and get into heaven. This leads many people to feel guilty about very natural sexual desires. If you yield to these urges of the body and mind, shame is added to the guilt. Sex for procreation only is sexual blackmail and the purest form of power and control over a woman's body. In Jesus's eyes sex was beautiful, not sinful.

Freedom in all aspects of life is most important. It is the cornerstone of life and an essential characteristic of the kingdom of God. It is freedom of the body, of the heart, and of the mind. Underlying all of this is the purity of sexual freedom—a concept the institutional religions forbid.

> Flesh, blood, libido, naturally associated with women, give Judaism, Christianity, and Islam welcome excuses for stressing the theme of the illicit and the impure. Thus they wage war against the desirable body, against the menstrual blood that briefly liberates women from the burden of motherhood, and against hedonist energy...
>
> And during menstruation she is at no risk of pregnancy, meaning that sexuality can be dissociated from fear and practiced for its own sake. The possibility of sex divorced from conception, and thus of sex alone, of pure sexuality—that is absolute evil.[360]

Sexual freedom does not imply sexual irresponsibility. In truth, it means that we have to be responsible for our actions and our behaviors. It is our choice based on our hearts and not on an institution's dogma and doctrine. The key is once again the relationship of self and other—being responsible and caring means we will not hurt or wrong anyone else through our actions. This takes away the stigma and the sin of same-sex relationships, as it is not about procreation or sexual preference but about a relationship of love between two divine human beings.

✤

A final disgusting note. The dysfunctional darkness of a patriarchal mindset leading to evil acts such as the rape and murder of a 23-year-old medical student in India was illustrated by the words of one of the rapists/murderers who blamed the victim for fighting back: "A decent girl won't roam around at nine o'clock at night," he says. "A girl is far more responsible for rape than a boy."[361]

Complementarianism—the Church's Theology of Inequality

Complementarianism is a dogmatic, doctrinally based term few outside of the clergy have probably heard of. It is "the belief that men and women have different roles in a marriage and religious leadership—husbands are spiritual leaders, and wives submit to them in love. To be 'complementary' is to complete or fill the lack in the other thing. It opposes egalitarianism, the theological belief that men and women are equal in all respects in marriage and in religious leadership positions. Traditional Catholic, evangelical, and LDS belief interprets the Bible to support a complementarian relational structure."[362]

As we can see, it opposes egalitarianism. This is further proof of their lie and need for patriarchal power, as egalitarianism was one of Jesus's basic beliefs. A November 20, 2014, *Time* article entitled "Vatican Strengthens Ties with Evangelicals and Mormons Against Gay Marriage" stated, "This week the Vatican hosted a three-day, international, interreligious colloquium called Humanum, 'The Complementarity of Man and Woman: An International Colloquium.' Its goal was to 'propose anew the beauty of the relationship between the man and the woman.' Speakers came from nearly two dozen countries and a variety of religious traditions, including Muslims, Jews, Sikhs and Taoists.'"[363]

Furthermore, the article goes on to state that the illusionary "Pope Francis did not spearhead the colloquium, as many casual observers might think. It was organized and led by German Cardinal Gerhard Müller, a strong conservative voice at the Pope's Synod on the Family last month. Müller is the prefect of the Congregation for the Doctrine of the Faith, the Vatican group that sponsored the event. Still, Pope Francis gave an opening address to attend-ees, in which he affirmed the Church's teaching that children have a right to a mother and a father."[364]

As a Jesuit and a PR Pope, Francis gives the illusion of equality, but the reality was demonstrated by the written statement of the colloquium: "On pa-per, the colloquium concluded with an affirmation of marriage. 'For on earth marriage binds us across the ages in the flesh, across families in the flesh, and across the fearful and wonderful divide of man and woman, in the flesh. This is not ours to alter,' it reads. 'It is ours, however, to encourage and celebrate... This we affirm.'"[365]

The Meaning of Pro-Life in America

Abortion was legal when America was founded.[366]

Pro-life as it is used today is, in reality, selective life. The male-dominated church and institutions are focused not on life—that is, all life—but on con-trolling women's bodies through fear, dogma, rules, and regulations. The illu-sion presented is the concern about life, but not all life, just the life of the fetus. For pro-lifers there is no choice for a woman to abort after becoming pregnant through rape, as it is "something God intended."[367] An example of pro-life be-ing selective life is that it is God sanctioned and OK to kill an abortion doctor or nurse, but aborting a fetus is murder.

Pro-life is totally focused on the fetus, not the welfare and life of the child after he or she is born—another form of hypocrisy. As I stated in the intro-duction, today, if you evoke the name of Jesus, then you better believe in and promote social justice and a culture and society of unity, freedom, equality, choice, and an egalitarian way of life. If you do not, then you are a hypocrite.

What was Jesus's view on this issue? Even though he was a religious revolu-tionary whose radical ideas threatened the male-dominated society, religious and secular, Jesus was still Jewish, and Jewish law states that life begins at birth. Additionally, there are no specific prohibitions of abortion in the Bible. Jesus taught that the kingdom of God is within us. It is then up to us to perfect our kingdom. This perfection does not come from an institution's rules and regula-tions, religious or secular, but from our own conscious choices in life. We can awaken to our kingdom or follow others as blind, fearful sheep. It is our choice to be compassionate and help others less fortunate or to be controlling and dominating, enforcing rules and regulations that many times only serve a select few, mainly the ruling elite—secular and religious.

Jesus, on the other hand, followed the natural law of God, not laws or rules that dominated others and forced circumstances on them that they did not choose or would choose. Finally, pro-life versus pro-choice is dualistic thinking. Jesus brought a message of radical nondualism—in Jesus's mind pro-life is pro-choice.

Pro-Life Is Pro-Choice

Being pro-life, and this means all life, even down to the smallest ant, does not mean that we are not pro-choice. In fact, the reality is that being pro-life makes us pro-choice. Believing that all things are alive, responsive, and intrinsically important and precious, we determine our actions and behaviors, words, and thoughts totally based on this most basic, but important, paradigm of life. This is a paradigm of life that encompasses choice and power.

Yes, power—empowerment. Self-power based on our belief in the divineness that is within us as well as within all other things of creation. This is *true* faith, not the hollow faith of the church. If we have the power within, we do not need religious or secular institutions telling us what to think and what choices to make—especially if it concerns our bodies.

For women, pro-life as pro-choice presents a different view of abortion, one based on common sense and love, not fear and guilt. We know that the question of when soulful human life begins is the source of the conflict between pro-choice and pro-life. It is also one of the greatest human spiritual and religious mysteries. And because it is a mystery, it cannot be proven one way or the other. On the other hand, even a mystery such as this may still have some light shed on it. However, the church would rather keep you ignorant and in the dark.

Christianity's dogma states that the soul enters at conception, while Judaism believes that ensoulment occurs at birth.

> Jewish law not only permits, but in some circumstances requires abortion. Where the mother's life is in jeopardy because of the unborn child, abortion is mandatory.

An unborn child has the status of "potential human life" until the majority of the body has emerged from the mother. Potential human life is valuable, and may not be terminated casually, but it does not have as much value as a life in existence. The Talmud makes no bones about this: it says quite bluntly that if the fetus threatens the life of the mother, you cut it up within her body and remove it limb by limb if necessary, because its life is not as valuable as hers. But once the greater part of the body has emerged, you cannot take its life to save the mother's, because you cannot choose between one human life and another.[368]

Since ensoulment is a spiritual and religious mystery, where can we turn to discover some truth? It seems that common sense, as well as biblical teachings, may provide us with the key to the contentious issue of when soulful human life begins. The key is breath.

Have you ever seen or felt a baby's first breath of life? Have you ever heard a baby's initial cry—the soul's cry of life? Have you ever looked into the eyes of a newborn baby and seen that spark of life? And have you ever viewed a person that has died—passed over—and recognized the absence or lack of breath and that spark? At the moment of our first breath, the divine spark, pure and untainted (no sin, no metaphoric dirt), entered us from the heavens.

⚜

Have you ever experienced near drowning? Have you ever choked on a piece of roast beef or a pretzel? As a child have you ever competed with a friend to see who could hold his or her breath the longest? And when you could finally breathe again, no matter what the circumstances, that initial gasp of air, that precious handhold of life, was the sweetest moment you could experience. I know this to be true, as I have choked on a piece of roast beef and a pretzel and was unable to breathe until my dear wife dislodged both. During and after graduate school, I was also a lifeguard and saved three people from drowning. I know and felt their terror when they could not breathe and that sweet moment when they took their first breath. I was at the birth of my daughter and held her as she took her first breath and screamed her announcement of arrival to the whole world.

I know by experience the fact and truth that breath is life. Inversely, the lack of breath is death. In all cultures breath was accorded a special place within their spiritual and philosophical traditions. In the Hebrew Tanaka, the word *ruach* is translated as "divine wind, breath, or spirit." "And the LORD God formed man of the dust of the ground, and breathed into his nostrils the breath of life; and man became a living soul."[369] In other words, it is a striking image of "an apparently lifeless body being slowly revived by artificial respiration. God himself breathes the breath of life into the first human being. For all his earthy substance, man has something divine about him."[370]

To native Hawaiians, "the living human being as a foetus is not considered a 'live' person until birth when the kino (corporeal body) breathes (hanu) the 'air' (ea) of the god(s), so that the material body quicken with the 'spirit' (ea) of the universe in the 'breath' (ha) of the human being as it ingests the atmosphere (ea) of 'god.' Abortion of the nonbreathing foetus is thus not considered deprivation of life inasmuch as 'life' (ea) is a condition of the 'spirit' (ea) and requires the ability to breathe (ha) in the god's breath. To be a full, living personality there must be corporeal life (ola), spiritual life ('uhane), the soul personality (kino wailua) and breath (ha)."[371]

And finally, the first line of the Lord's Prayer in Jesus's original tongue of Aramaic is "*Avvon d-bish-maiya*"—"thou art, from whom the breath of life comes."

⚜

Ironically, but still a glimmer of light within some who consider themselves Christians, the following is excerpted from the website TheChristianLeft.org in support of ensoulment at birth, not at conception:

According to the bible, a fetus is not a living person with a soul until after drawing its first breath.

After God formed man in Genesis 2:7, He "breathed into his nostrils the breath of life and it was then that the man became a living being." Although the man was fully formed by God in all respects, he was not a living being until after taking his first breath.

In Job 33:4, it states: "The spirit of God has made me, and the breath of the Almighty gives me life."

Again, to quote Ezekiel 37:5&6, "Thus says the Lord God to these bones: Behold, I will cause breath to enter you, and you shall live. And I will lay sinews upon you, and will cause flesh to come upon you, and cover you with skin, and put breath in you, and you shall live; and you shall know that I am the Lord."

According to the bible, destroying a living fetus does not equate to killing a living human being even though the fetus has the potential of becoming a human being. One cannot kill something that has not been born and taken a breath.

There is nothing in the bible to indicate that a fetus is considered to be anything other than living tissue and, according to scripture, it does not become a living being until after it has taken a breath.[372]

⚜

One last point, the fetus is a potential human being, not a separate, soulful life. Of course, it is alive and receiving the essence of the mother as well as the genetic or the earthly lineages of both the mother and father—a potential human being. But it is still not a soulful human being. The mother and the fetus are alive but are not two separate, soulful lives. Thus the loss of the potential baby, in my estimation, although I am not a woman, is one of the greatest losses outside of losing an actual child that a woman may experience during her lifetime, either through abortion miscarriage or stillbirth. I am not equating abortion with miscarriage and stillbirth. Abortion is a choice; miscarriage and stillbirth are the sufferings and struggles of life happening. And I believe that there is not enough help and support in our male-dominated society for women to heal from this loss (if they can actually ever totally heal). I know this as much as a male may know—my dear daughter has had an abortion, during which my wife, son, and I were there to support her, and a stillbirth, and then she gave birth to a beautiful little girl: our granddaughter LilyRose.

In my mind, the conscious choice to abort a fetus is the hardest and greatest choice a woman must face in life. But again, it is a choice. The woman is not killing or taking a human soulful life. She is losing a part of herself and a potential child. This loss is great, and it needs to be mourned and then healed—not only the loss itself but also any guilt or sadness. If there is anything lacking in legalized abortions, it is the absence of comprehensive emotional and spiritual healing after the abortion.

Two Lineages
There are two bloodlines. Every human being has not only an ancestral line of the earth but also an angelic lineage of the heavens. Our earthly bloodline flows from our parents' ancestral lines, while our heavenly evolution stems from our previous incarnations.

Each of us has two lineages. This is one of the reasons why there is emotional confusion surrounding the fetus and life. I have had people in their attempt to prove that the fetus is a living person state that their baby in the womb responded to various styles of music. Of course, there is an emotional attachment to the feelings of having life growing within you. Yes, it is alive, just as the heart of the mother is alive. Yet, it is not a soulful human being at this point in time. It is developing its earthly DNA lineage. It is a potential human being, as it has not as yet interpenetrated with its soulful heavenly lineage. This occurs at birth with the first breath of life, God's breath, and the descent of the heavenly DNA—the golden dew.[373]

To sum things up, the reality is that Divine Humanity (kingdom of God) recognizes the oneness of humanity and the equality of men and women and all things of nature.

Sound of Power—Word of Power

In Genesis the ancient Hebrew name for God is Elohiym (Powers). Powers is a euphemism for God and an appropriate functional name to help comprehend the indescribable. Following this train of thought, the above Sound of Power—Word of Power may be viewed as Sound of God—Word of God.

In humbleness we must view these and all other attempts at understanding the unknowable and the unseen through the prism of our humanness and our limitations in understanding the unknowable. But the spark or starlight of the unknowable is within each of us and within all other things. Utilizing a commonsense approach to commonplace things and happenings that occur to all humans, we are able to split the veil ever so slightly and allow a speck of light to shine on the mystery of the self-existent and eternal, the One, the Great Mystery—Powers.

Breath is life, and life is breath; from our first breath to our last one, we experience a journey of life in all of its shades of being. Our initial word of power was our birth cry announcing our immortal soul's entrance into a mortal body. Our initial cry is our mustard seed of power. But will it grow in stature until it turns into our voice in the world expressing the brilliance of our kingdom within? Or will it be stifled in silence—the fruit of our soul withering away on the vine of life? Is our life filled with words of power or powerless words and lies?

All of the mysteries of life are amazing as witnessed by the descent and entrance of the heavenly DNA—the golden dew—at birth, which results in our initial sound of power. Our birth cry is not the first sound that we make on earth. Our first sound is the sound of God's breath (our soul) entering our mortal body—silent as it may be. Then our soul's cry—I exist.[374]

Exploitation or Egalitarianism

The Industrial Revolution and capitalism were gifts to the church. During the sixteenth century, one of the architects of capitalism was John Calvin. Ironically enough, Calvin was not an economist but a theologian radical of Martin Luther's Protestant Reformation. Calvin insisted on the literal translation of the Bible and deemed work, and profit, a sign of God's grace. He himself didn't financially benefit, but what his reforms did was open Pandora's box and let loose the evils of capitalism. By repudiating the separation of sacred and secular duty, work became a way to glorify God. This allowed capitalism to flourish due to his message that hard work will be rewarded by wealth and by a guaranteed ticket into heaven.

John Calvin and Calvinism were no different than the Pharisees of Jesus's time who believed and taught that material and spiritual wealth were not separate issues but that one actually guaranteed the other. According to Duncan Holcomb in *The Gospel According to Us*, "The Pharisees, according to Jesus, taught that an oath offered on the Temple's gold was more binding than an oath on the Temple itself! Financial success they always interpreted as a clear indication of God's blessing."[375]

Following in the footsteps of the Pharisees, the founding fathers of Christianity capitalized on their elaborate lie purely for profit and power, even though Jesus was totally opposed to the inequalities that money provided and to the concept of profit. "Profit, in Jesus's provincial understanding, was a chimera unworthy of human effort; in his Galilean vision of fertility and exchange, commerce was a blight."[376]

This seems all in the past, but it is not. Today in America, the blight is called the Great American Dream. Illusion, illusion, illusion is the dream, and hidden behind its exploitive veil is the truth that it is a killer of our spirit, our connection to the earth, and the earth itself. Common sense deems that the exploitation of nature and the earth is solely for power, wealth, and greed—a brown philosophy.

The capitalist paradigm, profit at any cost, is based on inequality and greed. In other words, nothing matters except the bottom line. This leads not only to inequality but to the exploitation by the plutocrats of workers, women, and natural resources. The earth and its creatures are not only exploited but destroyed in the greed-fueled, never-ending quest for the excessive accumulation of wealth and power.

The question is, what type of world do you want? One based on exploitation and domination? Or one based on egalitarianism?

The Church and Capitalism: Complicit Partners in the Destruction of the Earth

Church doctrine denies the divineness of nature and the earth. This makes Christianity a brown, not green, religion, dogmatically promoting man's domination of the earth. The driving force of this domination and consequent destruction of the biosphere is the capitalist paradigm.

Climate change, such a benign word instead of the appropriate destruction of earth, is directly due to the inherent materialistic greed of capitalism. In her book *This Changes Everything: Capitalism vs. the Climate*, Naomi Klein has the courage to state what others do not want to hear. She reconnects environmental devastation and the warming planet back to capitalism itself. The following is a review of Klein's book by Rhyd Wildermuth:

> The last twenty-five years have seen what started out as a critique of all the logics of profit-taking, extraction, and private property

becoming untethered from their foundations instead become an attempt to treat symptoms caused by destructive human behaviors rather than the cause itself. Instead of demanding an end to economies based on greed, oil, and the destruction of people and land, environmentalism—at least as far as both the public consciousness and the major environmental NGOs portray—it is now about composting, recycling, and buying the right sort of shoe, car, or light bulb rather than about anything that might actually inconvenience the wealthy.

But why does addressing capitalism even matter? And why have the last two and a half decades seen a shift from cause-based solutions to a symptomatic approach?

According to Klein, the answer's simple. Connecting capitalism to climate change unveils an awful consequence.

> The only kind of contraction our current system can manage is a brutal crashing, in which the most vulnerable will suffer most of all.
>
> So we are left with a stark choice: allow climate disruption to change everything about our world, or change pretty much everything about our economy to avoid that fate. But we need to be very clear: because of our decades of collective denial, no gradual, incremental options are now available to us.
>
> ...By posing climate change as a battle between capitalism and the planet, I am not saying anything that we don't already know. The battle is already under way, but right now capitalism is winning hands down. It wins every time the need for economic growth is used as an excuse for putting off climate action yet again, or for breaking emission reduction commitments already made. (21–22)

Throughout her book, Klein dashes every single hope...that we might be able to stop the damage done without too radically changing the world. Not only are technologies like geoengineering untested, they are largely funded by billionaires, such as Bill Gates in particular, and come with further political problems. Artificially cooling the earth will cause droughts in some of the already poorest places, and flooding in others, which leads to the potential of a cooler United States and Europe, causing suffering elsewhere.

She builds a narrative of human technology...Men in the enlightenment, bloated with the certainty they could transcend natural limits, developed theories and technologies that would help them do just that. Francis Bacon, the founder of empiricism, spoke of conquering the earth as if by rape; James Watts, the inventor of the coal-fired steam engine, spoke of humanity's final liberation from nature. These fathers of modernity get particular attention. Klein continues:

> ...these are the tools and the logic that created the crisis geoengineering is attempting to solve—not just the coal-burning factories and colonial steam ships, but Bacon's twisted vision of the Earth as a prone woman and Watt's triumphalism at having found her "weak side." Given this, does it really make sense to behave as if, with big enough brains and powerful enough computers, humans can master and control the climate crisis just as humans have been imagining they could master the natural world since the dawn of industrialization–digging, damming, drilling, dyking? (266)

In page after brutal page, Klein unknots each connection between climate change and our economic activities. While Al Gore's film, *An Inconvenient Truth*, did much to raise awareness of the issues of human-caused climate change, it did little to address precisely how much of our human activities would need to change in order to stop the damage those activities have caused. The actual "inconvenience" of that truth is staggering, but only if one is heavily invested in keeping capitalism around. Klein continues:

> Climate change pits what the planet needs to maintain stability against what our economic model needs to sustain itself. But since that economic model is failing the vast majority of

the people on the planet on multiple fronts, that might not be such a bad thing." (155)[377]

Return of a Green Philosophy

Someone who has not found the vine cannot pick the fruit, and someone who has not "found" the earth cannot plant the vine!
—REV. DR. J. C. HUSFELT (1997)

Hardly a day goes by without the media presenting some grim new findings as to how the world´s ecological environment is on the brink of imploding and that if there isn´t a radical and immediate change in how we think and live our lives on this planet then Doomsday is a mere few decades down the road.

Two major contributing factors as to why we seem so complacent about these constant warnings are firstly how divorced an ever-growing urbanized world has become from the natural environment and secondly our increasing failure to nurture an inner spiritual self.

For centuries Christianity preached that Man was the supreme ruler and the earth´s resources were his for the taking. This Christian worldview encouraged Europe´s aggressive drive to dominate and exploit nature in a spirit of complete indifference. With the bible in one hand and a sword or gun in the other, indigenous peoples were conquered, empires built and the Western world rode the wave of the Industrial Revolution and so-called progress. Granted, industrialization brought many advances, but it all came at a terrible price, both to the environment and that existentialist sense of soullessness that so often haunts us in the first world.

Science and technology alone are not going to get us out of the present ecological mess; we need to reconnect spiritually with the larger whole of reality. Unfortunately mainstream institutionalized religions seem incapable of offering such a holistic perspective; however many ancient indigenous religions do and we should be looking to them for ideas and inspiration. As the Yale scholar John Grim states:

Indigenous peoples are ecologists and purveyors of an environmental wisdom absent in the technologically developed, industrialized "first world."[378]

⚜

The rich source of creation and the mysteries of life are encoded in the pulse of each moment of our lives. As I write this, I can feel the holy blood streaming throughout my body, bringing the breath of life to every part of my soul. Stop for a moment and allow yourself to feel each of your senses: Feel the air that brushes your skin—feel it as it enters your body and nourishes your blood. How does this air taste? Look around and focus your eyes on the colors surrounding you; open your ears to the music of the earth and nature that is available to you. Now, close your eyes, and with each breath experience a moment of sacredness, holiness, divinity, the gift of life. Life is precious and not to be wasted in a wasteland of our own doing. Each one of us, you and I, can transform our wasteland into a paradise on earth—a return to Lost Eden. We can achieve peace on earth and a oneness of humanity where we all share equally in all things and view each other as brother and sister. And we will discover that the world is truly an enchanted place where nature speaks to us and we can truly know our own intrinsic place in the symphony of life.

⚜

Jesus loved nature[379] and could be labeled "green" for his beliefs and practices. Jesus as Green Man recognized the divine in nature and the sacredness of all living things. Common sense dictates that a teacher who felt so connected and in partnership with the earth would use nature to demonstrate the truth of his knowledge and wisdom.

As is well known, nature and the earth are viewed in a dualistic way, as female or matriarchal. In disagreement with the patriarchal nature of Judaism, Jesus emphasized the balance between the opposites with the acceptance and acknowledgment of his female followers as equals. He also acknowledged the earth as the "mother," feminine, and the heavens as the "father," teaching the wisdom and the love that is intertwined within all things of creation.

He would in all ways feel the love and the power and see the wisdom of his "mother's gift" and would in all ways respect this gift and be in partnership with it. According to Chilton's Rabbi Jesus, Jesus saw the divine in nature.

> Part of the beauty of the concept of God's Kingdom was that it opened one's mind to see the divine hand in the natural world. A Galilean could stand under the stars, view the mountains, watch young animals gambol, and recollect the words of a well-known psalm that all the Lord's creations give thanks to him and attest his eternal Kingdom to all people (Psalm 145:10–13). Divine power was already present in nature, yet only just dawning in human affairs. Jesus came out of the Jewish tradition of seeing God's immanence everywhere, in forces as simple and powerful as a mustard seed and yeast. Later, as a rabbi, he took the leap of seeing the divine Kingdom in how one person relates to another. But even as a child, Jesus saw God's Kingdom not simply as a hoped-for future—he had a direct intuition of how his Abba, moment by moment, was reshaping the world and humanity.[380]

It is time and necessary for the return of Jesus's green philosophy—an egalitarian philosophy of humanity's partnership with the seen and unseen things of the earth and nature.

CHAPTER 7

Be Comforted I Know the Truth of Our Heavenly Partners

To lift your eyes to heaven
When all men's eyes are on the ground,
Is not easy.
To worship at the feet of the angels
When all men worship only fame and riches,
Is not easy.
But the most difficult of all
Is to think the thoughts of the angels,
To speak the words of the angels,
And to do as angels do.[381]

Firsthand personal religious experience has always
carried greater authenticity than the secondhand
offerings of collective religious authority.[382]

During Jesus's time, Jewish culture "took for granted the central claims of the primordial tradition:[383] there are minimally two worlds, and the other world can be known. At the heart of Jewish tradition, indeed constituting it, was Israel's story of the intersection between the world of Spirit and the world of ordinary experience. For this is what Israel's scriptures were. The Hebrew Bible is Israel's story of events which were seen as disclosures of Spirit, of people who experience as mediators of Spirit, of laws and prophetic utterances which were believed to have been given by the Spirit. This multi-layered picture of reality runs throughout the Bible."[384]

Jesus had experienced *firsthand* the otherworld or the world of spirit and knew its importance in his life as well as in his people's tradition. A principle most important to the Hebrews states, "Spirit is not seen as abstract and remote as a hypothetical first cause. Rather the world of Spirit is seen as alive and 'personal,' populated by a variety of beings: angels, archangels, cherubim, seraphim. At its center (or height or depth) is God often spoken of as personal: as father, mother, king, shepherd, lover. Non-anthropomorphic terms can be also used: fire, light, Spirit."[385]

The knowledge contained within this book has been accumulated from my experience of "listening, looking, and learning" from indigenous elders, healers, and shamans from all over the world. It also comes from my interactions with the young and old of other races and cultures and emanates deeply from my own soul and the wisdom contained therein.

This knowledge is what I refer to as the "first knowledge."[386] It is knowledge that is woven throughout and found in all the indigenous spiritual and religious traditions on this earth. This "first knowledge" has been referred to as primordial knowledge, or the *primordial tradition (perennial philosophy)*. As such, it portrays universal themes, principles, and truths. In other words, "the term Primordial Tradition is utilized to describe a system of spiritual thought and metaphysical truths that overarches all the other religions and esoteric traditions of humanity."[387] Furthermore, "the perennial philosophy proposes that reality, in the ultimate sense, is One, Whole, and undivided—the omnipresent source of all knowledge and power. We do not perceive this reality because the field of human cognition is restricted by the senses. But the perennial philosophy claims that these limitations can be transcended."[388]

⚜

Following this belief in the primordial tradition and Jewish tradition, I don't believe in angels—I know angels: "If you are blind and have never seen the sun rise it doesn't matter how many hypotheses you can array, you still don't *know*. Belief is simply the adoption of someone else's idea. Once you have seen the sun you don't *believe* in it, you *know* it."[389]

I have been in the presence of angels. Having been in their presence, I know angels in the same way that I know a sunrise, the buzz of a bee, or rain falling on my head. Traditionally, the North is the symbolic realm of heavenly beings, including the ancestral spirits. I know this is correct, as the archangel and the two assisting angels appeared in the North—not the East but the North, as traditionally recorded. It is important to keep in mind that all things of creation are unique and have a precise, intrinsic quality and identity.

The term angel is used within a certain philosophical tradition. Depending on the culture influenced by environment, oral tradition, and geographic location, the word could just as well be god or goddess to identify unseen energetic beings. An angel to one tradition could be a god or goddess to another. The important knowledge is that unseen beings of the heavens and earth are real. In addition to the visitation, I have experienced earthly unseen beings known as *huldufólk* (the hidden ones) in Iceland. I don't believe; I don't have faith—I know.

⚜

There are four commonly known archangels. Each archangel is real, and each one is its own unique heavenly being. They are Mikael (Michael), Raphael, Gabriel, and Uriel. Supposedly, besides these archangels, there are a multitude of other angelic beings within nine celestial orders. These nine orders are divided into three triads, with the highest order known as *seraphim* and the lowest as angels. The most interesting of the nine are the *seraphim*, winged serpents or feathered serpents.[390] "Popularly known as the 'fiery, flying serpents of lightning,' who 'roar like lions' when aroused, the *Seraphim* are more identified with the serpent or dragon than any other angelic order. Their name actually suggests a blend of the Hebrew term *raphe*, meaning 'healer,' 'Doctor' or 'surgeon' and *ser*, meaning 'higher being' or guardian angel.' The *Serpent* or dragon has long been a symbol for the healing arts, being sacred to Aesculapius."[391] In fact, the Jewish priests translated the word *seraphim* into Greek as *drakon*, from which we get our word for dragon.

Heavenly Guardians
Of all the spiritual mysteries, one that has consistently fascinated and perplexed people is the existence of heavenly beings. The question always posed is, are they

real or myth? What does your heart see? Myth or reality? I can answer absolutely: they are real. I use the term "being," although "energy" may be more appropriate. These beings take on various forms that are dependent on the culture and the underlying spiritual or religious tradition that claim them. It is a fascinating subject to explore, simple on the surface but very complex underneath.

Angels

Every blade of grass has its angel that
bends over it and whispers,
"Grow, grow."
TALMUD

Throughout time, humans have always identified with heavenly guardians—the higher light vibrations of creation. In some cultures and religious traditions, these guardians are viewed as messengers from above—angels. Angel comes from the Greek word *angelos*, which is the same as the Hebrew word for messenger—*mal'akh*.

Carvings of winged messengers date as far back as ancient Sumer in southern Mesopotamia—present-day Iraq. Traces of the Sumerian civilization appeared as early as the fifth millennium BCE. To the Sumerians these beings were called *Anu-naki*, meaning "of the heavens." There is even evidence from excavations that Sumerian homes had personal altars to their guardian spirits. The early Hawaiians believed in the *awaiku*—the equivalent of angels. Their home was known by two names: *Lani keha* (heavenly breath) and *Kahiki Na* (serene spiritual country of God in the East). The awaiku were not only messengers but also guardians of nature.

Angels have often been referred to as "morning stars." This is symbolic of the light emerging from the darkness, being suggestive of the role that angels may play in our lives. These celestial beings are always around us and above us, providing us with a link and ladder to the heavens. In the dark night of our souls, there is always the shining brilliance of our own angelic selves, our guardian angels working toward the destiny of our souls' light evolution. We are all children of light, sons and daughters of heaven and earth, and sons and daughters of God.

However, Pauline Christianity sees angels, shall we say, in a different light. Even though Christians roll out angels during the Christmas season, the foundation and inner doctrine of the Apostle Paul and Pauline Christianity was ambivalent and basically antiangel. "To the extent that Christianity is essentially Pauline, it has no need and little use for virtuous angels. What Paul and Christianity needed were fallen angels, and their chief, Satan, in particular."[392]

Furthermore, in 2 Corinthians 11:14, "the Apostle warns that 'Satan himself is transformed into an angel of light.' Every angel of light was under suspicion by Paul, who attributed all his rivals, Jewish Christian and Gnostic, to the heretical influence of Satan. This attribution, original with Paul, will never leave us, since it has become deeply embedded in every variety of Christianity."[393]

Contrary to the liar Paul's assertions, angels are awesome and essential and are most assuredly significant heavenly beings of creation who exist in a state of timelessness, not linear time. But since timelessness and linear time interpenetrate, angels may appear at any time and are as close as a breath of air. But for them to physically appear and step into the stream of linear time and our reality, a purification of the elements that compose linear time must occur. This is not supposition on my part but is based on my experience.

Early on Sunday afternoon, August 3, 1997, the day of the angelic visitation, we experienced an otherworldly storm. One moment, the sky was crystal clear, tinged only with a few clouds, and in the next moment, the sky darkened into an ominous, swirling, bluish-black tempest. There was a pause of sound and movement as if a giant were holding its breath. And then...thunder, lightning, and rain. Torrents of rain fell as thunder boomed, and lightning struck all around my wife and me and our twelve apprentices.

At the time, we didn't know what to make of such an unusual natural occurrence. Approximately eight hours later, with the appearance of the archangel and two assisting angels as three immense pillars of light, the reason for the storm became apparent. The volume and intensity of the thunder and rain and the strength and force of the lightning that struck all around us was a purification of the earth and its elements. A major sanctification had taken place.

At the visitation, as messengers of God and in answer to my prayer, the archangel and the two assisting angels announced who I had been in my previous incarnation through their presence and the other signs that were shown along with their appearance. "In biblical accounts, angels traditionally appeared in order to make an annunciation or a revelation of transcendent import. Usually an angel's message is one of concern not only to the individual who sees the vision, but to the collective group as well. Such visionary experiences mark dramatic turning points personally and culturally."[394] In the case of our twelve apprentices and my wife and me, the visitation was not a visionary experience—it was an actual physical-sensory extraordinary event.

Reincarnation[395]

Reincarnation is a philosophical paradigm that causes "shock and awe" in Christian and Muslim circles. It is a threat to the power of organized religion. Early on the Church of Rome saw the danger in people's belief in reincarnation. Consequently, "those early Church Fathers who taught or believed in reincarnation were declared heretics, excommunicated, and their books were burned. Other heretics faced horrible deaths, such as being burned alive. Why? Think about it. If you believe you will reincarnate in another body, you cannot be controlled by fear of an eternity in the fires of hell.

"The church existed to hold power over the people, to tell them what to believe rather than have them think for themselves. Control by fear is not possible if an individual knows who she/he is (astrology) and that he will reincarnate again and again. There is nothing to fear when we know Truth; therefore, Truth must be hidden from the people."[396]

⚜

One of the pillars of Christianity is the redeeming power of Jesus Christ. With faith you will spend an eternity in heaven. Another take on this is, at the Second Coming, with faith you will experience bodily resurrection in heaven. Of course, the alternative is an eternity with the devil in hell. This threatening sword held over people's minds and hearts keeps the faithful fearful and obedient—and, of course, the coffers full.

Within the church and the Christian mind, the concept of reincarnation is not to be found. But what if reincarnation were a divine truth? If there were physical proof of the truth of reincarnation, then the foundation of Christianity would crack and begin to crumble. I have that truth! This was Jesus's truth as well, as "many of the early Christians[397] believed in reincarnation. It was a widespread philosophy at that time and it would not have been unusual if Jesus had taught it. Many other mystics of the time did so, where it was an integral and natural extension of the belief in an immortal soul as the essence and real nature of (hu)man(s)."[398]

Additionally, let's compare my knowing of the truth of reincarnation to Christianity's dogma in a single lifetime with death resulting in the gift of heaven or the punishment of hell. This dogma subtly insinuates that we are not responsible for the future well-being of the land or the earth and its creatures or future generations, as we will not reincarnate back on earth in a future time. As we are observing in this twenty-first century, this belief has opened a Pandora's box of ecological destruction.

If we look back in time, we discover that "by the 7th century the Church had rewritten Catholic dogma to obliterate most of the original teachings of esoteric Christian groups such as the Essenes...Most importantly, they edited out all references to the universal doctrine of reincarnation, a central theme throughout Eastern religion as well as Druidic and early Christian life.

"This had a profound effect on all succeeding ages. Before, people believed that their ancestors were still alive in the Otherworld, and that, like themselves, they would be reborn into the group or tribe to which they belonged. In this way, warriors felt it an honour to die in order to protect their people. But there was a deeper responsibility; if you were to be reborn, then the land must be preserved not only for your children, but for yourself when you returned. Short-term exploitation would have been inconceivable. You and your children were, in a very real sense, the land.

"The replacement of this with a 'one-way trip' to heaven or hell forever changed people's attitude as it permeated into everyday life. Under this doctrine that this life was the only one you were ever going to experience, it eventually became acceptable to seize as much as was possible in the short time available. The development of this impulse in recent times may be held to be directly responsible for many of the critical dilemmas facing the world today...

"How far we have come from the ways of antiquity can be shown by our approach to the land in which we live. Today we think nothing of changing the essential features of the countryside in an effort to maximize the yield we may achieve from it or to make living more efficient, even if it blights the lives of those around and has unforeseen and unknowable consequences."[399]

My Direct Angelic Experience—the Visitation

> The mother sea and fountainhead of all religions lie in the
> mystical experiences of the individual. All theologies, all
> ecclesiasticisms are secondary growths, super-imposed.
> —William James

I've seen angels. This is the reason that I don't believe in angels; I know angels. Most importantly, I have not seen angels in my mind, in a cloud formation, in my dreams, or as some type of human figure. I've been in the presence of and witness to an archangel and the two assisting angels. To verify this, my wife, Sherry, and twelve of our apprentices were witnesses to the same sacred visitation. It occurred on the night of the new moon on August 3, 1997, in the woods of Maine. And it just happens that I was born on a new moon.

Numerically, the date is a ten. The number one symbolizes the Absolute, the One, the Divine, the Great Mystery, the Creator. The number ten symbolized the reflection of the Divine or the perfection of creation. "In the number 10 creation reaches perfection and fulfillment. The masculine-positive, creative principle of God has penetrated and fertilized space, the negative, maternal aspect, and has become one with it."[400] In the Jewish tradition, the tenth letter of the alphabet is yod. "Yod is the very first flame of the divine fire, of the spirit of God."[401] In the Jewish esoteric system of kabbala, "the tenth *sefirah*[402] is *Malkhuth*[403] and means kingdom."[404] And in the original tarot, the tenth card is the Wheel of Fortune. This is a card of choice where we will continue to maintain our dualistic consciousness or let go of it and begin the journey to awaken to a consciousness of radical non-duality where we shift our focus from materialism to one of spirit.

Winter 1997

The first indication of what was to come occurred in the winter of 1997. At that time, even in the wildest part of my imaginative mind, I had no idea or inclination of what the future might hold for our apprentices and us. In addition, this was the winter of the appearance of the comet Hale-Bopp in the Northern Hemisphere. It was only many years later that I would recognize its connection to the visitation.

It was early April, and I was conducting a weekend corporate community-building seminar in the foothills of Maine. There was still snow on the ground, but the temperature was tolerable. To say the least, our seminars were not your typical corporate fare. We would explore territory that was many times taboo within the corporate mind-set. We got away with it because we did get results and great feedback from the participants. One exercise pushing the envelope of acceptability was an experience demonstrating the power of the mind over the body.

On Saturday evening I asked for volunteers who would like to "go for it." After I explained the exercise, only a handful out of the twenty-some volunteered. In simple terms, through directed focused attention and intention, they would be able to spend some time barefoot in the snow without the benefit of coat or hat. Even though the sun had been shining throughout the day, once the sun dies, it gets cold. It was well below freezing as I took the few outside and explained the exercise in detail.

Standing barefoot in the snow, I slightly adapted the exercise, as the comet Hale-Bopp (the twins – two tails; the Hopi Blue Star)[405] was visibly streaming through the heavens like an icy-blue angel. This was a very special occasion and an extraordinary view, to say the least. The last time this comet visited the earth, the Great Pyramids were young, and Stonehenge was only a vision waiting to happen. The year of its last visit was around 2215 BCE, which would have been around the time of the life of the biblical patriarch Abraham! A few scholars date the event differently and feel that the last time Hale-Bopp appeared was some four thousand years ago during the time that Noah was building the ark.[406]

Down through the ages, according to mythology, comets such as Hale-Bopp have been considered celestial messengers and harbingers of prophecy. It was recorded that Hawaiian king Kamehameha, great warrior and unifier of the Hawaiian Islands, was born during the appearance of Halley's Comet. Since Hale-Bopp was a greater comet and seldom visited the earth, what then was the message this time around? I wondered...

As the comet was flying overhead, I had each person focus his or her eyes on the comet—a once-in-a-lifetime vision of heavenly magic. What a sight it was, a memory forever etched within our souls. At the conclusion of the exercise, everyone was simply amazed at not feeling the cold. While watching the mystical sight of the comet overhead, everyone's feet stayed warm and melted the snow. Little did I realize that the magic was just beginning.

The next morning was Sunday, the conclusion of the seminar. As I was ending the class, a strange and unexplainable thing happened. In front of everyone in the meeting room, a white feather mysteriously fell out of the air and dropped into the palm of my hand. Since it was early spring and still cold outside, all the windows in the room had been closed and locked for months. There was no rational explanation for the feather's appearance. It just manifested out of thin air.

Over the next several months, the mystery deepened. Two more feathers inexplicably appeared. Again they manifested out of thin air and in front of our students. During one of our weekend teaching sessions, two of our apprentices had independent visions of me riding on a white horse—even though it was known that I was not a horse person due to an incident that occurred in my childhood.

During the summer in Maryland, a carnival would set up for a few days every year in our small town. I was young, probably eight or nine years old, when my grandmother took me to the local carnival. This one summer night, they had pony rides. As I was waiting in line, I happened to move to a spot where I was now behind one of the ponies. Before I knew it, I was in intense pain and crying. The pony had kicked its hind legs, or leg, and hit me—in the groin! Ironically, my wife-to-be, Sherry, loved horses and rode often. And on our honeymoon, I agreed to go riding with her. Well, that experience lasted maybe two minutes before I got off. That was the first and last time I've been on a horse. But the smaller Icelandic horses do intrigue me. You never know... (in 2014 I overcame my fear and rode a Viking horse in Iceland).

Spring 1997

The last time that we had visited England was in 1982. Now it was fifteen years later, and for reasons known and unknown, we needed to return to the British Isles. Over the years we had focused on journeying to Japan, Hawaii, Mexico, and Peru. It seemed that I was being drawn back to England because of its connection with the Holy Grail and other legends and mysteries, such as the one surrounding Joseph of Arimathea.

The last time we were in England, we had not ventured to Cornwall and its many mystical sites. Since we were last here, my many visionary and otherworldly experiences of the past fifteen years had led me to research the legends and lore of this part of Britain. As in times past, I stumbled on information and knowledge that tugged at the inner recesses of my heart and mind.

Doing research, I knew Tintagel and St. Nectan's Glen were two sites we needed to visit. There was something more. Our first time visiting England, we had spent time in Glastonbury and on the Tor with its tower dedicated to the Celtic goddess Bride and the archangel Michael. We had also visited Avebury, a supposed serpent temple also connected with the archangel. Could it be that the archangel and his[407] connection to Cornwall were pulling me back to England? If so, it was not the only reason. There was another purpose to our return that only my wife and I knew.

I determined that we would bring a group here at the end of May, but first, we needed to check out the sacred sites and lodging in Cornwall. In mid-April we arrived in England and headed for Cornwall and the small town of Tintagel—the magical birthplace of King Arthur. In addition, this was the land of Merlin and the archangel Michael, the ancient patron saint of Cornwall and its hills and high places.

Michael, whom I call Mikael, is known as the dragon slayer. The archangel is also known as "the spirit of revelation, giving inspiration and visionary glimpses of divinity, the great initiator into the hidden mysteries. In the esoteric tradition, he is the one that transmutes lower, base energies into those of a more refined, spiritual type...This would seem to be the real meaning behind the glyph of the slain dragon—the archangel transfixes the raw dragon energy of the Earth with the Will (of which the sword is the traditional symbol), and transmutes it to a higher rate of vibration."[408]

Tintagel was everything we had expected and even more. It was situated on the cliffs overlooking the sea, and I immediately felt at home, feeling the breeze and the sun shining on my face and seeing the sparkling, blue ocean before me. Tintagel was more of a village than a town, with few options for lodging within the town itself, except for one inn that we fell in love with—the Wootons Country Hotel. The inn was situated right next to the cliffs and overlooked Tintagel Island and the mythological ruins of Arthur's castle. Located below the castle ruins was an ocean cave known as Merlin's Cave—the supposed part-time sanctuary of the legendary wizard. Since we conduct many experiences at dawn or after dusk, staying at the inn would allow us easier access to the cave than other lodgings outside of town.

Even if Merlin never set foot in this cave, it was still reputedly a place of power. Partially, this was due to the geomancy of the area—the meeting place of land and sea. But there was more to it than just this aspect. Tintagel Island's origins were volcanic, with an ample supply of quartz crystals deep within the interior of the island. It seemed that the odds of it being a place of power and an energetic vortex were great.

From a shamanic point of view, caves are considered repositories of power and the birthplaces of legendary people. Caves, since earliest times, have been places of enchantment, invocation, and initiation. Being in the "womb" of Mother Earth generates magical power as one experiences a symbolic death in the dark only to be reborn in the light as one emerges from the cave.

To enter Merlin's Cave required knowing the schedule of the ocean tides. During high tide the cave was partially underwater, which would cause an un-aware person to be trapped within the cave until the tide receded. In addition, it was a tourist and New-Age site. Planning a visit to do spiritual work required the proper timing of the tides, the ocean, and the people.

I believe it was late afternoon as we made our way down the partial stairs on the side of the cliffs and reached the beach that fronted Merlin's Cave. It was a ways away over the stony landscape, but we could still sense the power emanating from it. As with all places of power, care and respect were essential. We needed to do the proper prayers and ask the land, the sea, and the spirits of this area permission to enter the cave. We did this, as well as a simple purifica-tion of ourselves using what was naturally available to us.

As we silently entered, I noticed Sherry looking down at the floor of the cave as she walked. There was little light within the cave, giving it a further mystical feeling. Interestingly enough, there was light at the symbolic "end of the tunnel," which happened to be the opening to the sea at the other end of the cave. Time seemed to be frozen in a vortex of sounds—the ocean and the wind and every so often a subtle thump as if a dragon's heart were beating.

With a look of amazement etched on her face, Sherry asked, "Did you see what I just saw?"

"No," I replied, wondering what she was talking about.

"After we passed the entrance, I saw purple lights arranged in a serpen-tine form almost like a purple serpent moving across the floor of the cave. My first thought was, oh, they have lights in the floor of the cave to help visitors see. And then I realized this wasn't Disneyland, and with that thought, they disappeared..."

✦

The next day we awoke to an overcast sky but brightness within our souls after our experience in Merlin's Cave. We were going to explore the mystical valley that contained St. Nectan's Glen and its magical waterfall, rumored to be the place where King Arthur's twelve knights were purified and then took their vows to quest for the Holy Grail.

Twelve is a magical number—the number of constellations and months in a solar year. With the twelve knights symbolizing the twelve constellations, King Arthur as the sun god, and Queen Guinevere as the moon goddess, we have presented to us a heavenly cosmology mythologically reflected on the earth. Additionally, the Norse recognized twelve heavens, as related in the poem *Grímnismál* of the *Poetic Edda*.

Many myths have common threads. Arthur fought twelve battles as well as having his twelve knights. This may "recall a mystical system of initiation that was once universal. All the different cultures have memories of this, from Hercules and his twelve labours to Odysseus, Samson and the twelve-part Babylonian epic of Gilgamesh. For each, there are twelve trials of the spirit that mark the progress of the adventurer on his quest. In the Celtic world, this twelvefold system was translated into a central heroic figure surrounded by twelve followers. Charlemagne had his twelve peers, King Lot of Orkney ruled over twelve minor kings, King Conchobar of Ulster was supported by twelve of his best warriors, and King Arthur had his twelve knights."[409]

Arthur's "twelve battles have a zodiacal significance: the progress of the candidate on his pilgrimage through life reflects the passage of the Sun through the constellations on its annual cycle from birth to death, and rebirth. The actual nature of the trials or battles may vary in different cultures in accordance with the psychological makeup of their people, but they all seem to refer to the evolution of the individualized human consciousness."[410] Last but not least, we must not forget to mention the power of twelve in the Twelve Tribes of Israel.

✦

As with Tintagel, we were not disappointed with St. Nectan's Glen. The secretive glen itself had an otherworldly feeling and aura to it, and its waterfall and location only added to the land's mystical power. It was definitely a place of initiation into the mysteries of life and death. Here, "nature has contrived to create a most unusual waterfall. The river rushes out from a dark hole and cascades for some forty feet into a rocky basin (or kieve in Cornish) that has been sculpted by the timeless rushing of the waters. Here it forms a foaming cauldron of boiling water, which issues out through another remarkable hole in the rock outcrop, to hiss and splash into a pool below. A vertical rock face is covered with dripping dark-green weeds, and billows of spray spread a glistening dampness over everything. It is an intensely magical place."[411]

Standing on a rocky platform to the left of the waterfall and its pool, I turned to my wife and said, "This is awesome."

"I know," she replied.

We spent time doing inner work and energetic work, becoming one with the elements of this earth and the magic of the otherworld. This was so powerful a place that at any time, an elf or a faerie might appear, laugh at our humanness, and then disappear. This was definitely a place of vow-making, and it was here that we decided we would conduct a vow ceremony. Our students would vow to participate in a three-year quest for the Holy Grail. This quest would emphasize not only the experiential knowledge of the Grail but also the experiential knowledge connected with the archangel Michael and his places of power. This knowledge would include his roles as warrior, captain of the heavenly hosts, psychopomp, and dragon slayer.

Four weeks later, after a purification and initiatory ceremony, we were standing on the same rocky platform to the left of the waterfall, listening to each of our apprentices dedicate himself or herself to his or her own personal quest for the Holy Grail. My heart was happy as Sherry and I listened to each one state his or her vows as we began the first of three adventures questing for knowledge and power—questing for the Holy Grail.

Summer 1997

Our adventures in England had been an extraordinary experience. However, there was still something that kept gnawing at the edge of my mind—that there was a hidden reason for our need to return back to England after so long an absence. And it wasn't that we were both bored with Hawaii or Mexico.

During the summer we always conduct longer-term trainings out in nature. This summer it was scheduled to be four days, beginning on Friday, August 1, and ending on Monday, August 4. The theme of the training was initiation, fear, and death and rebirth, including the experiential experiences of a twenty-four-hour solitary quest, a stone-built ceremonial death spiral,[412] and bathing.

Since we mostly take novices into the outdoors, I always perform prayers for safety, love, and power before the trainings. This time I did a different prayer.

Based on what I knew within my heart and my vision, I prayed for a sign to be given of who I was in my last incarnation: "Let them see a sign knowing that I was [name stated]." I mentioned the name as people would recognize it today. I then let go of any expectations about the prayer. Little did I expect the sign—in reality, signs—that would be given.

The Sunday of the four-day training had dawned bright and very dry. Little rain had fallen that spring and summer. We had planned on constructing the death spiral early in the afternoon so we could conduct the ceremony late in the afternoon. In addition, during the evening, I wanted to work on the issue of *phobos*—the Greek word for fear and the origin for the word phobia. The exercise I had chosen was one I had conducted many times before. In my mind it was an excellent way to help a person release a fear that had haunted him or her.

It was a very simple exercise. Our apprentices had to identify a fear and then fashion an image of their fear out of natural materials. At night they would fight their fear with a wooden sword and burn the remains in a ceremonial fire. This was an excellent exercise of body, mind, and spirit, and besides, many of our apprentices were martial artists. The common assumption would be that they would take to this exercise like ducks to water. On the contrary, many were too structured in their bodily movements. This inhibited their creativity and spontaneous "immovable and no-mind" actions.[413]

However, we were concerned that we might not be able to conduct this exercise. Sherry and I faced a major hurdle in the dry condition of the land. It was basically drought conditions that summer, which generally prohibits an open fire. Without the fire, the experience would not work. But the heavens provided a solution to our dilemma. Early in the afternoon, an intense thunder-and-lightning storm developed within minutes. And "intense" does not do it justice.

One moment the sky was crystal clear, tinged only with a few clouds, and in the next moment, the sky darkened into an ominous, swirling, bluish-black tempest. There was a pause of sound and movement as if a giant were holding its breath. And then...thunder, lightning, and rain.

Torrents of rain fell as thunder boomed overhead and lightning struck all around us. Everyone ran to huddle underneath the cooking tarp, shaking and scared by the otherworldly intensity. People were terrified at the suddenness and force of the wind and the rain, the thunder and the lightning.

As the storm abated, the earth felt different—a purification of sorts. It was only later that I had a sudden realization that the pre-Christian Hawaiians would recognize this sudden downpour as a sign of the presence of the *Akua Lono*—the white god.[414]

Our apprentices were milling around, slightly disoriented by the storm. The good news—now we could have a fire. However, the storm changed the timing of building the death spiral. It would now occur later than we had planned.

For the remainder of the afternoon, we finished building the death spiral and prepared for the death-and-rebirth ceremony. When we were almost finished building the spiral, one of our apprentices took a picture of me within the center of the spiral. One of the universal symbols of the serpent is the spiral. Our spiral was a narrow path, the way of the serpent, to reach the center where our apprentices would experience the death of their old selves (shedding the skin and leaving the old self behind) and then the rebirth of their new selves.

As with all things, there is an opening, a middle, and an ending to the ceremony. Previously, I've opened many spirals, but this one was extremely different. I had a feeling that this was not just any ordinary spiral. When I was ready to open the spiral, I let go of any attachment or anticipation and cleared my mind as I prepared to enter it.

Sherry and I had chosen two apprentices as symbolic birth guardians. They would stand at the mouth of the birth canal of the spiral, which was also the entrance, and pull the new ones into existence. The others would stand on the outside of the outermost spiral, chanting a phrase linking heaven and earth, until it was their turn to enter and face their symbolic deaths. Each one who chose to enter the spiral would stand at the entrance, praying and contemplating his or her desire to enter the spiral. If the person still chose to enter, he or she would take the first step into the vortex with the left leg as a sign of intent and focused will to let go of his or her old self.

Before anyone entered, I needed to sanctify and open the spiral by walking to its center and then repeating my steps to leave it empowered and blessed. As I stood at the entrance to the death spiral, I could feel that this spiral was an extremely powerful one, possibly due to the thunderstorm. As I began to take my first step into the spiral, my last fully conscious thought was, "My spirit song's coming."[415]

And with that, my left foot stomped the ground inside the spiral, and as my right leg caught up with my left, my spirit song sprang from my lips, and I began walking the spiral with serpentine movements of my body. Sherry later related to me that the response from our apprentices was immediate—fear and wonder became etched on their faces. It was so intense that a few apprentices chose not to participate—one being a person that had been raised in a strong Catholic household and had been an altar boy.

⚜

After the death spiral, the apprentices fashioned images out of wood of one of their fears. The fear was to be minor, one that they could let go of in the night's exercise. Darkness came around nine o'clock when I lit the fire to begin the experiential exercise. Everyone sat on the ground in a semicircle with the fire in the center and the west direction open so that each apprentice could approach the fire from the west. Symbolically, this is the black direction of fear but also the direction of rebirth.

One after another, the apprentices approached the fire and laid the symbolic image of their fear before them. When they were ready, they fought their fear with the wooden sword and then tossed the remains into the fire. Whether it was tiredness or the effects of the death spiral, the apprentices only halfheartedly fought their fear.

When all were finished, I looked around the semicircle, and each apprentice's head was hanging low, staring into the fire. It was evident that they knew they had listlessly and with little heart fought their fear. A few were accomplished martial artists. How was I going to tell them that they blew it? They had squandered an awesome opportunity to release one of their fears. With these thoughts going through my mind, I decided to stand and talk more philosophically about releasing fear rather than giving them a searing commentary on—you blew it.

I stood and began a more nurturing synopsis of the exercise, only stating a few things before...before I felt my neck twitching and an icy-fire sensation around my head—I recognized the feeling. It is the one I always get when there are otherworldly energies around. But this time it was different, much more intense and strange. I turned my head to look behind me into the woods. Everyone else was still seated on the ground, staring into the fire. No one else was looking up.

This was the night of the new moon, and the only light in the clearing was cast by the small fire. The night before, while the apprentices were sitting alone in the woods on their vision quest, I had stood in this very same spot observing the dark woods. I was listening and making sure that everyone was all right. When I had turned off my flashlight, I couldn't see more than a few feet in front of me.

"What...no." These two short thoughts coursed through my mind as I turned my head back around to see if there was some other light source coming from my front other than the small fire. And when I observed nothing that could explain what I just saw, I turned my head back around again in disbelief—making sure I saw what I saw. This all took less than a minute.

"Please stand, and be quiet. We have visitors," I said as calmly as possible, all the while not knowing what I was seeing.

As Sherry stood up next to me, looking at the lights, I leaned over and whispered into her ear, "What are they?"

Without any hesitation she said, "Why, they're angels!"

And then I remembered my prayer for a sign of who I had been. It all made sense, but I never expected a sign like this.

"A shooting star," someone said as we all looked up as it blazed across the night sky.

"A white dove," an apprentice exclaimed as it flew over our heads.

"Look at the stones of the death spiral," another said.

The stones had increased at least fivefold in size; some were now the size of boulders. But the most unusual thing was the greenish, otherworldly glow that surrounded each.[416]

After this, no further words were spoken. Time seemed to be suspended as Sherry and I and our twelve apprentices witnessed in awe a massive pillar of light[417]—a living pillar of iridescent light a few feet off the ground, at least six feet wide and five or six times as tall. This light was in the north by the entrance to the death spiral. It was a light that was whitish and not of this world. Suspended higher up by it were two other pillars of light, not quite as bright or as large. The legends have always told that an archangel is always assisted by two helping angels. Many traditions believe that the north direction is symbolically the direction of heavenly beings, such as angels. After an unknown amount of time had passed...

"We need to leave and go to bed now," Sherry whispered to me. "There are only a few hours left until we have to get up and go bathing."

"You're right," I replied.

I then turned and said to the others quietly, "It's only a few hours until we put you in the stream and bathe each of you. We all need to get some sleep, so please return to your tents; be respectful as you leave, and give prayers, blessings, and a thank-you for this experience."

Sherry and I were the last to leave and return to the shelter where they were staying. Sherry slept soundly the few hours we had left, while I couldn't sleep. My mind was focused on the visitation and trying to figure out the identity of the archangel. The last little doubt of who I was had left my mind; I again gave blessings for the answer to my prayer for a sign of my past incarnation. Right before I was going to wake my wife up to go bathing, I thought, "Will they figure it out...who I was? And will they figure out about Sherry?"

Summer turned into fall. I had finally solved the mystery of the identity of the archangel. The archangel was Mikael, known to most as the archangel Michael. I had determined this through my research of the connection between myself and the archangel.

- ❖ Michael was denominated by the kabbalists and the Gnostics as "the Savior," the angel of the sun, and the angel of light.[418]
- ❖ The archangel Michael's day is Sunday, and the astrological sign is Leo.

❖ The visitation was on the night of the new moon, and I was born under a new moon, symbolic of the virgin. The full moon symbolizes the mother. Additionally, I was born under the sign Virgo—the virgin.

❖ He is the fiery manifestation in the burning bush (Exod. 2:5).[419] The angelic fire and light (spirit) interpenetrated with the bush (matter). This is the earliest known biblical reference to radical nondualistic interpenetration.

❖ Michael is the angel of sanctification and is recorded in the Talmud as the prince of water. I am one of the few Caucasians who carry the lineage of the sanctification practice of bathing.

❖ Michael is the warrior archangel, captain of the heavenly hosts and the guardian of the "mysteries." I've spent fifty years in the mystical and practical side of the martial arts.

❖ Michael is the guardian of labyrinths (death spirals included) and the organizer of earth energies.

❖ Michael has always been connected with both water and lightning. He oversees nature, rain, snow, thunder, lightning, wind, and clouds. He represents the ability to conquer or overcome any obstacle and the struggles of life. And according to various prophecies, great events are often heralded by unusual weather conditions. The storm before the visitation was extremely unusual. Seraphim are "known as the 'fiery, flying serpents of lightning' who 'roar like lions.'"[420] This is exactly how I would describe the intensity of the lightning and the sound of the storm. In addition, Michael is identifiable as one of the seraphim.

❖ Michael is known as the angelic psychopomp, the mediator between life and death, and the archangel of the shamans.

❖ Michael assists the messengers—"light-bringers" of the different ages of humanity—and is the messenger of the prophets.

❖ Michael is the archangel of the Holy Grail.

❖ Finally, "it is foretold in Daniel that when the world is once again in real trouble Michael will reappear. Some religious scholars claim that this century is the one in which he will reveal himself once again."[421]

⚜

It was late on an October afternoon of the same year when one of our apprentices contacted me.

"J. C., you'll never guess what I have," he said in an excited tone. "While you were finishing the late-afternoon building of the spiral, I took a picture of you in the center of it. When I got home, I just threw the camera into my truck. Last week I finally got around to getting the pictures developed. I knew something was up when the photo shop lady said, 'One of your pictures has caused quite a stir.'"

He paused and then said, "Guess what? I have a daylight photograph of the archangel and the two assisting angels. They were observing us building the spiral...and no one ever suspected!"

The picture is sacred and precious. Closer examination of the picture revealed a very faint image of what looks like the shape of a sword (sword of light) or an elongated, four-pointed star pointing to the heavens. This dim image is within the center of the reflected light. This is the picture on the front cover of this book.[422]

Summary

After seventeen years, of the twelve students who were present at this visitation, only one remains as our apprentice. The reason eleven apprentices left our circle is a reflection of the downside to this experience. It was, and still is, so far outside the normal dualistic consciousness of people that the truth is veiled from their minds. Even for those who were physically there and experienced the presence of the angels with all their senses, most still could not rationalize the event within their consciousness or their basic beliefs.

For the majority of people, it would have been an impossibility with no precedents for such an unbelievable event. There is no such physical manifestation or event ever recorded in the Hebrew Bible, the Christian Bible, or the Koran. Of course, there are accounts of angelic visitations or interactions, sometimes in visions and other times with angels appearing as men. But none had twelve witnesses, such as we did, or the appearance of other physical signs, such as a dove (which has symbolized the Holy Spirit as well as the bird of Venus); a falling star; and a multitude of ceremonial stones, which increased in size at least fivefold and glowed with a greenish aura. Preceding this visitation, we also witnessed an otherworldly thunder-and-lightning storm, which purified the land.

And very importantly, none of the accounts in the Bible were ever written down by the people who experienced them. All the accounts of angelic events in the Old Testament were written down by priestly scribes after having been orally passed down for centuries.

The following are a few of the recorded biblical angelic events:[423]

❖ Abraham, when he was willing to offer his only son as a sacrifice (Genesis 22:11–12, 15–18)
❖ Jacob, after his famous dream of a stairway to heaven (Genesis 28:12; 31:11; 32:1–2)
❖ Joshua, before the battle of Jericho (Joshua 5:13–15)

Furthermore, from my experience, knowledge, and knowing, I would have to state that of all the stories recorded in the holy books, the first one that holds more truth in revealing an angelic or divine encounter is that of Moses and the burning bush. Three factors point to this truth.

❖ The image within the bush was one of fire and light. It was not in human form.
❖ The angelic fire and light (spirit) interpenetrated with the bush (matter). This is the earliest known biblical reference to radical nondualistic interpenetration (the basic belief of Divine Humanity). For Moses this was not a dream or vision but a physical-sensory firsthand experience.
❖ I have personally experienced firsthand radical nondualistic interpenetration with my descending-spirit experience.

Another revealing truth was Jesus's descending-spirit experience while bathing in the Jordan. The descent of the dove into Jesus, symbolic of the Holy Spirit, was a visual reference to radical nondualism—spirit interpenetrating matter or the body of Jesus through his head. This was his awakening and the formal beginning of his quest to bring his message of the divine in all things to all people of the world. In reality, extraordinary spiritual and religious experiences are difficult to metaphorically "swallow" for the average person.

The Effect of the Visitation on Spiritual, Philosophical, or Religious Knowledge

The visitation was a sensory, materialistic, firsthand experience witnessed by twelve apprentices and my wife and me. In other words, we experienced something that few, if any, humans can only believe in and not know. The majority of humanity's spiritual, philosophical, or religious belief is based on secondhand knowledge, either written or oral, from others who have also based their belief on secondhand, thirdhand, and further-removed oral or written knowledge.

This miraculous happening opened the gateway to knowing certain truths concerning spiritual, philosophical, or religious beliefs. I will attempt to lay them out as best as I can. One further note: I believe that the visitation provides Occam's razor validation for some aspects of physicist David Bohm's theories.

Knowledge: The Interconnection and Interpenetration of Consciousness throughout the Seen and Unseen Universe

❖ David Bohm theorized a new reality of the universe. This reality he named the Implicate Order—the hidden aspect of the universe. "The theory of the Implicate Order contains an ultra-holistic cosmic view; it connects everything with everything else. In principle, any individual element could reveal 'detailed information about every other element in the universe.' The central underlying theme of Bohm's theory is the 'unbroken wholeness of the totality of existence as an undivided flowing movement without borders.'"[424] In other words, "within the Implicate Order everything is connected; and, in theory, any individual element could reveal information about every other element in the universe."[425]

❖ Bohm named the known or visible universe or manifest world the "explicate order." In the Implicate Order, "everything is enfolded into everything. This is in contrast to the explicate order where things are unfolded."[426]

❖ The visitation would provide proof of Bohm's theory, as the physical appearance of the angels (immense pillars of light) was due to my prayer. For the angels to respond while in the Implicate Order, they would have to have received the information from me in the explicate order.[427]

❖ After the intense, unusual storm, they were present in the afternoon but hidden[428] while they were still in a layer of the Implicate Order. It was only in the evening that they became visible to us in the explicate order. In Bohm's terms—until they unfolded.

Knowledge: Reincarnation

❖ Based on what I knew within my heart and my vision as the morning star, I prayed for a sign to be given of who I was in my last incarnation: "Let them see a sign knowing that I was [name stated]." I mentioned the name as people would recognize it today.

❖ The angels, as well as other signs, responding to my prayer indicate that I was alive before in a different body, place, and time. I am no different from anyone else. If I have had a past life (lives), everyone else has had a past life. This is proof, as far as we can take it, considering we are attempting to prove the unprovable mysteries of life and creation, that our lives on earth are not a one-shot deal with a result of heaven, hell, or oblivion waiting for us.

❖ But it is an ongoing death-and-rebirth evolution of our souls—our golden DNA or divine spark or starlight.

Knowledge (the Most Obvious)

❖ Sentient beings, which humanity has named angels, physically exist even though they are usually hidden from sight while they remain in Bohm's Implicate Order. This leads to a conclusion that other sentient beings exist, such as faeries and, in Iceland, the hidden ones. But once again they are in the Implicate Order and hidden from our senses and sight.

Knowledge

❖ With the visitation came silence, or what one apprentice referred to as the cone of silence. There were no summer sounds of nature—just silence. I am still attempting to figure this one out and reach a conclusion. On the other hand, silence is a key element in spiritual growth.

Knowledge: Sacred Power of Stones

❖ The stones of the death spiral had increased at least fivefold in size; some were now the size of boulders. But the most unusual thing was the greenish, otherworldly glow that surrounded each. Green is the middle of the light spectrum and esoterically is usually connected with the heart, the heart chakra's color being green. You may come to your own conclusions on this.

❖ The Japanese anthem is correct! Proof of being in the presence of the heavenly or divine power of the three pillars of light is reflected in the growth of the stones from ones that you could hold in one or two hands to boulders. Indigenous cultures believe in the spiritual power of stones. The Japanese believe that sacred power is often manifested within a sealed vessel that may grow. The vessels that contain this sacred power are known as *utsubo*. The stone is an utsubo vessel. It contains a sacred force that may grow under the right circumstances. Even the Japanese national anthem contains these words addressed to the emperor: "May your reign last for thousands of years until pebbles have become moss-covered rocks."

The Exorcist Who Came to the Sacred Mountain to Find Me
One Concluding Point

It can indeed be said that the one sure and inerrant key
to the Bibles is the simple concept of fire plunging into
water, the fire being spiritual mind-power and water being
the constituent element of physical bodies,--as well as
the symbol of matter. Soul (spirit) as fire, plunged down
into body, as water, and therein had its baptism. (The
blending of fire and water—radical nondualism)[429]

The following is excerpted from *Tequila and Chocolate: A Guide to a New Consciousness—the Awakening of Our Divinity and Humanity*:

As time was approaching midnight, we were approaching a bridge over a small stream that pointed the way from one world to the next—one of prophetic sanctuary. This wooden bridge separated the rest of the cemetery from the realm and mausoleum of the Great One. (A warning to heed: never cross a bridge such as this without prayers and permission asked...This bridge was a gateway separating sacred space, and permission to enter must be granted.)

After crossing the bridge, we beheld the Lantern Hall in front of us ablaze with hundreds of yellow-tinged specks of light. It was in front of this hall that the exorcist stopped and offered incense before he led us around the back to Kūkai's "meditative residence." And it was here that the exorcism took place.

I believe there were approximately seven others, plus Keikō-san (our Japanese guide), the exorcist, and myself. He positioned us, except for Keikō-san, in a straight line horizontally facing Kōbō-Daishi's mausoleum and told us, through Keiko-san's translation, to sit still and relax. I was last in the line with Keikō-san angled in front and to the side, facing me.

He began working on each person, leaving me for last. He chanted; toned; and, every so often, screamed a spirit shout. Out of the corner of my eyes, I could see him working rapidly, with mudra, up and down each person's spine. The sounds coming out of the exorcist were eerily of another world and another time. Feeling as if I was in a dream, I closed my eyes. And in no time at all, I could feel the exorcist's presence and was unafraid.

The next part is hard, to say the least, to describe in words. I had a strong sensation of being disconnected, yet connected at the same time. I was I, but not I. I was the I in the we and the we in the I and felt like a top swirling in an every widening circle. And power, not the illusionary power of external humanness, but the power of the bodhisattvas, the archangels, to put a name on it—power not of this earth, and I, not wanting to let go or return...But then...

A woman's scream penetrated through the night and ripped through the very fabric of time...

I was back...Who am I? What am I? As my eyes slowly opened, the portals to my soul gazed upon the surreal scene before me. Keikō-san's face, beautiful as the dew glistening on a lily, was now frozen into a mask of terror. It had been her scream that had brought me back; on the other hand, had I ever left? This part of the cemetery contained a few stone lanterns. The shadows, cast by what little light there was, only heightened the mystical sense of wonder for me as I felt incredibly powerful.

The visually shaken Keikō-san was stammering over her words to the exorcist. From a place of stillness, I silently watched the gestures and body language of the exorcist and Keikō-san, not knowing or, in fact, caring about the meaning of the words being exchanged. A moment ago, or was it an eternity ago, I was in a space of power. But, no, I was the power. What does it all mean?

Keikō-san turned to face me and asked, "Are you all right? How do you feel?"

"I feel awesome and powerful. I can see so clearly, as if it is daylight...but mystified," I replied. "Was I transforming into one of the guardians who serve the Great One—the Daishi?"

"Well, yes...but no. You may look at it as a merging or interpenetration of energies. Energies that few humans could accept, much less survive. It is the first quickening of your bodhicitta—your divinity. The others who were here will deny what happened, out of fear and envy. We sent them back to the temple," said Keikō-san.

She then explained to me that the descending-spirit exorcism was a way to discover a spiritually sensitive person. This is a spiritually evolved person able to tap into other realities. "He believes that you are the most sensitive person he has ever worked with or met. This is why he came to Kōyasan—to find you. He had a dream of you," she explained.

"But I had to stop him because I could see that your face was so red like fire; you were not yourself."

❖

This abbreviated story briefly portrays my otherworldly experience—an experience that thrust me through a tear in the fabric of dualistic reality. Even the setting for the happening, courtesy of a descending-spirit exorcism, was mythically mystical. Commonly, exorcism is known as a spirit being taken off or out of a person who is supposedly possessed. A descending-spirit exorcism is where spirit merges or blends, interpenetrates, with a person. As recorded in the Bible, this was an experience of Jesus with the descent of spirit in the form of a dove.

As I looked back on my experience, the exorcism was the initial quickening (means "to bring to life") of my awakening mind and a knowing of radical nondualistic interpenetrating reality. It was a sacred midnight happening I will never forget. The setting was a cemetery on a sacred mountain in Japan, and the time was October of 1987. The exorcism was performed by a Japanese esoteric, or shamanic, priest. It occurred in front of Kōbō Daishi's mausoleum on the sacred mountain Kōyasan. Kōbō Daishi was the founder of Shingon Esoteric Buddhism. He is believed to be in eternal meditation in his mausoleum, awaiting the arrival of the next Buddha—Miroku Bosatsu.

❖

"I always remember your sensitive, strong, sacred spirit. It was a great experience for me, too." Keikō-san, October, 1987

❖

Knowledge

❖ I have experienced and have a knowing of reality, which is interpenetrative radical nonduality. In other words, reality is the blending and oneness of the absolute and relative: spirit or divine and matter. We are in the divine, and the divine is within us. We are in the kingdom, and the kingdom is within us.

CHAPTER 8

The Kingdom of God— Divine Humanity

Go to the mountains, sit by a tree, and listen with heart and mind; walk in the valleys with the winds caressing your soul, and listen with heart and mind; lie by a river with its soothing lullaby, and listen with heart and mind; skip a stone in childlike innocence across the mirror surface of ocean or lake, and listen with heart and mind; feel the fire of the sun on your face, and listen with heart and mind; let the moonlight blanket you with its beauty, and listen with heart and mind; stand and gaze at the night sky with its star-studded tapestry, and listen with heart and mind to the sound of angels; and let the rain cleanse you of pain and suffering, and listen with heart and mind. Realize the voice of God.
—REV. DR. J. C. HUSFELT

We must keep in mind that for two thousand years, Jesus's kingdom of God has been misunderstood and misinterpreted (many times intentionally). The kingdom of God not only refers to our inner divineness and the divineness of nature and the earth; it also means a reign of equality and justice throughout the earth "where the only ruler is to be 'the Father which is in heaven,' and where 'all ye are brethren.'"[430]

The ruler of the kingdom of God is not the church or the Catholic pope. The church is not interested in the kingdom of God, just its materialistic kingdom.

> There is almost no evidence of an understanding of the Kingdom of God, which Jesus made so prominent, or an interest in it by the Christian Church. In a general way it was considered to be synonymous with the Church, visible and invisible. Paul showed but slight knowledge or interest in it. The great councils, in formulating the creeds tell us nothing about it. Modern catechisms only say that baptized believers become members of it...And Jesus's faith in the supremacy of Love, while held in theory, is often forgotten in the Christian's larger interest in theistic dogmas, competitive economics and private profit, nationalism and war.[431]

The Path and the Way

The pathway of the kingdom of God—Divine Humanity—is a partnership paradigm. It is not one of domination, whether that is male domination, as it is today, or female domination. The kingdom is of the father and mother interwoven together as a reality of oneness. The kingdom is love, balance, and harmony. Jesus emphasized this balance between the opposites with the acceptance and acknowledgment of his female followers as equals. Furthermore, he acknowledged the earth as mother and the heavens as father, teaching that their love and wisdom is intertwined within all things of creation and is spread out upon the earth and extends out to the farthest star.

In all ways Jesus would feel the love and the power of the kingdom outside of him. He understood the wisdom to be found within his mother's gift and would respect this gift and be in partnership with it. According to Bruce Chilton's *Rabbi Jesus*, Jesus saw the divine in nature.

> Part of the beauty of the concept of God's Kingdom was that it opened one's mind to see the divine hand in the natural world. A Galilean could stand under the stars, view the mountains, watch young animals gambol, and recollect the words of a well-known psalm that all

the Lord's creations give thanks to him and attest his eternal Kingdom to all people (Psalm 145:10–13). Divine power was already present in nature, yet only just dawning in human affairs. Jesus came out of the Jewish tradition of seeing God's immanence everywhere, in forces as simple and powerful as a mustard seed and yeast. Later, as a rabbi, he took the leap of seeing the divine Kingdom in how one person relates to another. But even as a child, Jesus saw God's Kingdom not simply as a hoped-for future—he had a direct intuition of how his Abba, moment by moment, was reshaping the world and humanity.[432]

Sadly, over the past two thousand years, the kingdom has morphed into one of heavenly patriarchal exclusivity only accessible through the rotten gates of the church. The patriarchal elites and the church dominate the earth. There is no acknowledgment of the divine within nature or the wisdom that is to be found there. In their minds the earth and its creatures are inferior and solely here for their exploitation.

The Four Winds

The kingdom's pathway is anchored in the transformational ability to let go or detach from the emotional, mental, and physical enemies, such as stupidity, ignorance, arrogance, guilt, anger, and fear. Add to these the mental illusion of ego and the spiritual separation of self. To awaken is to realize our divineness and our relationship, our partnership, with all other things of heaven and earth. This realization must occur within the heart and flow out from there to a new consciousness of being. This is a consciousness that first and foremost recognizes the unity or oneness of self and the oneness of others.

It is a consciousness that lets us know within the core of our souls the nondualistic interpenetration of all things, which our culture and society deems separate and opposite. The pathway is not a work of mental exercise. It is a guide in merging the mind and body (heart) into a oneness of being.

It is awakening to the knowing of the interpenetration of light and dark. We may achieve divinehood in this life—in this body and mind, even as corruptible as they both are. The kingdom's pathway is an exercise in the relationship of self and other. It explores the inner mysteries of self, the lesser and greater mysteries of life. This results in a greater understanding of ourselves and others and our struggle to achieve the happiness, hopes, and dreams we all seek.

In acknowledgment of the reign or kingdom of God outside of us on the earth of our birth, the kingdom's pathway of four gates and four paths honors and is structured around the four directions, or, if you will, the four winds of the earth, as well as the four basic elements and the four seasons delineated by the two equinoxes and the two solstices. The pathway is fully explained in *Tequila and Chocolate*.

Our pathway also recognizes the fifth direction—the center of the mandala, the center of the circle, where the interpenetration of heaven and earth occurs. The center is metaphorically a reflection of our hearts, the core of our souls (our divineness), and our minds (our humanness)—the interpenetration of heaven and earth, or a divine human being.

The Key to the Kingdom

The secret to a peaceful and fulfilled life, one resulting in happiness and love, is to be found within our relationships to our own selves and to others—others including the world at large, animals, and so forth. Love and forgiveness begin with self and then expand out to others. This is the *mystery of transformed consciousness*—the mystery of our kingdom within, the mystery of self and other.

"Turn the Other Cheek"

What power and enlightenment are to be found in those four simple words! Simple as these words may be, to live and experience them is a different story. They truly sum up the relationship of self to other—an atomized version of living an awakened life.

As it is with oral teachings that are spread, and many times changed, after the teacher has passed over, the meaning of turn the other cheek has been misunderstood and misrepresented with a Pandora's box of various interpretations. Many others, as well as religious authorities, have attempted to explain the meaning of this statement, which was one of Jesus's prime teachings. Turn the other cheek is an aspect of personal power—no meekness here. Here is the meaning of turn the other cheek, which is literally a volcanic explanation of self and other:

❖ A slap on one cheek is a symbolic wounding done by another person. Before turning the other cheek, we must release this wounding (i.e., through forgiveness). Ideally, this occurs immediately, but realistically it may take days, weeks, months, or even years.

❖ Next, we must talk our truth to the one that wounded (if possible) and then release any fear—such as the fear that it will happen again. When this is complete, we symbolically turn the other cheek.

I once got into an argument with a man about the meaning of this phrase. He insisted that its meaning was totally one of pacification. No matter what was occurring, you would let it happen, thereby symbolically turning the other cheek. I pressed him on this, and he finally admitted that even if his children were being abducted, he would let it happen rather than fight for them!

Now, of course, this is an extreme rendering of the pacification meaning. But still, this meaning rings true to many people and allows them to justify various causes and behaviors.

The Process of Turning the Other Cheek

Detachment is not separation from life but full immersion in life and all that life has in store for us. If we are attached to something, we automatically limit ourselves to the totalities of life. We constantly carry the fear of loss. We imprison ourselves in our own minds, and we seldom experience peace, joy, or the paradise that is our kingdom.

Turning the other cheek will help us release the past and detach from any fear that the same person or situation will harm or wound us again. The practice of turning the other cheek is as follows:

❖ Pick a small wounding with a person that recently happened and that you are still holding on to. Drop a stone based on this wounding.[433]

❖ After the stone is dropped and the wounding released, talk truth to the person. This dialogue may open up the reasons for the wounding. Keep talking, and let the person know that you were hurt through his or her words or actions. Establish or reestablish harmony with the person. (If the person is no longer alive or in your presence, you still need to talk your words of power to release the fear that the wounding will be repeated.)

❖ Release any fear that the person will wound you again by symbolically turning your other cheek.

Turning the other cheek will strengthen our minds and establish an inner peace and harmony within our kingdom. This type of detachment is of the past weeks, months, and years. However, to awaken and to have a strong mind, the idea is to be able to detach at the end of the day through a daily releasing ritual. This is a detachment to all the things that caused a disturbance within our minds through forgiveness. In this way we will be less stressed, be healthier, and sleep soundly.

"Love your enemy!"
Connected with turn the other cheek is the teaching to love your enemy. Again, this teaching has been misunderstood over the centuries. Neither teaching has anything to do with a state of passiveness or submissiveness. In fact, just the opposite—they are states of action. Both are acts of courage and fearlessness and are totally connected with a warrior attitude.

The foundation of this teaching is fear, which is the opposite emotion of love. Fear is separation, while love is unity.

To love your enemy is to have no fear of your enemy. With the absence of fear comes compassion. When you feel within your heart and mind the suffering of others, you begin to understand them more. People who were the unknown to you become the known, and so you grow less separate from them. This results in less fear and more love.

With more love and less fear, your enemy may become nonexistent and, quite possibly, even become your friend. (An enemy is not necessarily a human being.)

Kindness
Kindness is the caressing, angelic spirit of life. It's the light we bring to another's darkness through caring acts of compassion and love. A simple thank-you

from our hearts is a basic kindness. A word spoken in kindness to anyone, especially a stranger, may lift the person out of the depths of despair and in the totality of his or her being may ultimately save a life. Opening the light of our souls to all the ones that cross our paths may be the catalyst that helps them pass through the barriers of fear and anxiety, thus loosening the kindness that has been locked away within their hearts. Being kind and generous communicates a caring and respectful spirit to others and to ourselves—this is love.

By bringing joy to others through our kindness and our peacefulness, the world brightens, and our souls rejoice in the love that we have shown to others. To be kind is to be strong and to be forgiving. Our spirits, gentle as a breeze, and our hearts, glowing with kindness, provide us with the strength of the bamboo as it sways ever so softly, touched by the winds of life. Consistent kindness helps liberate one's self from the ongoing stresses of life and brings the divinity that is within us to the outside world. Kindness sets us free and lightens our hearts, while greed and materialism imprison us and harden our souls. To distribute kindness is to do the work of the heart that brings peace to our minds and joy to the world.

Let all who we come in contact with see the kindness of our hearts through our radiant faces and eyes. This expression of love will uplift others more than we will ever know.

Sometimes the greatest kindness is not what we think it would be. Words from our hearts may be kind words, but occasionally, they may be tough to hear, because they are the words that need to be said that no one has had the courage to say. They may sting, but a great kindness is done when we present to others a light to their darkness.

Heart of the sun
Gaze within,
And you will see.

What is there?
Flower or weed,
Broken or whole.
Do not despair.
It is all right.

Mend if need be.
Reseed and know
Your divine heart.
—REV. DR. J. C. HUSFELT

Quest for the Kingdom of God—the Holy Grail

*Anyone who puts a hand to the plow and then
looks back is not fit for the Kingdom of God.*[434]

The quest for the kingdom of God takes courage, total focus, and commitment. It is about becoming by growing spirit, not growing money! Because the church provides people's salvation, those people are subconsciously given permission to focus their lives on money and not on spirit. And the siren's song of wealth, and the power that goes along with it, provides further motivation. Wake up to these lies.

⚜

Our quest for the kingdom of God may be seen through the prism of the mythology of the Holy Grail. This timeless object and its myth bring us a collective imagery of universal truths. As a talisman of great power, the Grail is elusive in its shape-shifting identity—sometimes being referred to as a cup or chalice; a magical cauldron; or even a sacred well, such as the Norse-Germanic *Well of Urd*, or *Mimir's Well*. Sometimes it is symbolized as a vase, a magical stone or jewel, or even as the Golden Fleece of Greek mythology. More intriguing than any of the previous identities is the one as a bird's nest! It symbolizes both the cup and the heart. The winged one's eggs within symbolize the unawakened spark within our hearts. When we birth our eggs of spirit, we awaken and accept our heavenly wings, allowing us to soar with the eagles and the angels as we now understand the language of birds—a green language.[435]

Even though the Grail is enigmatic in its identity, it is essential to understand that the Holy Grail is not an item to possess. It is not an external thing. It is our awakened hearts and minds, and in a grand sense, it symbolizes what has been lost—humanity's, and our own, lost values. The primary one is the loss of the feminine—nature and the equality of men and women. This is the lost feminine principle. This world of ours only recognizes as authentic the light, not the dark; the material, not the spiritual; the male principle, not the feminine. This is then the quest—to recover the feminine and nature. This will heal the wound—the separation, suppression, abuse, and control of the feminine.

❖

Magical cauldrons and mixing bowls have played a primary role in many cultures' myths and legends. They all predate the Grail legends. These cultures were rich with legendary searches for magical cauldrons and bowls that can inspire, provide knowledge and wisdom, and furnish insight into the secrets of the otherworld and the mysteries of life, death, and rebirth. Wondrous cauldrons were "a recurrent motif in Celtic myth. Some overflow with plenty, others restore the dead to life, while still others contain a special brew of wisdom...Similar mystery bowls or cups feature in Greek and eastern myths as holy vessels of spiritual insight. Ultimately, the early Celtic cauldrons find expression in the Arthurian Grail, which overflows with spiritual sustenance and leads the hero from death to immortality."[436]

Common sense reveals that the miraculous cauldron or vat may be representative of the feminine and symbolic of the life-giving womb. It implies plenty, the powers of resuscitation, transformation, and fertility. Many times it is depicted as boiling (fire and water) or as a mixing bowl where things are blended and transformed. The mixing bowl concept is very important, and in my opinion, underutilized and undeveloped by authorities in the field of Grail scholarship. The Greek krater, in Latin crater, was a mixing bowl where wine and water were blended together. "The word grail is believed to be related to Crater...The **grail**, the Holy Chalice, the Cauldron, according to medieval legend is the platter used by Jesus at the Last Supper, and contained the blood of Jesus Christ turned into wine, from Old French *graal*, *grael*, from Medieval Latin *gradalis*, ultimately from Latin **crater**."[437]

❖

The Grail is our divine mind and heart. It is our heart as the cup of our sacred blood known as *san grail* or "sanctified grail." It is our skull, our chalice divine containing within it our sacred light—our pineal gland. This is the mystery of blood and spirit, both of which may be symbolized by the color red. Our red blood is the source of all that is life-giving. The religious and spiritual use of blood in the form of red paint or pigment or red ochre dates back far into the mists of time—250,000 years ago![438] It is thought that "Neolithic cave painters ascribed magic powers to the color red. The word 'magic' (*Zauber* in German) translates to *taufr* in Old Norse and is related to the Anglo-Saxon *teafor* meaning 'red ochre'. It can be stipulated that they painted animals in red ochre or iron oxide to conjure their fertility."[439]

It is interesting to note that in certain cultures, "the ritual used in manufacturing the pigment was to mimic the grinding motion of the celestial sky as it appeared to revolve around the pole star. Grain was also turned into a fine flour by milling in rotary and saddle querns, but red ochre seems to have been used to symbolize blood and immortality in specific birth and death rituals.

"There can be little doubt that the barley grains and hazelnuts, ground in the rotary stone mills, symbolized the female principle as food giver and as creatrix. The concave stone gave nutrition and wisdom, while the pestle or grinding stone represented the male principle, symbolizing will or force.

"To the earliest tribes of the Atlantic the food grinding ritual was the transformation of the soul, while the red ochre symbolized travail and sacrifice before and after the transformation. In this simple rite we see the beginning of sacrifice and vestiges of the quest for transcendence common to almost every religion in the world."[440]

My wife and I can attest to the magical use of red paint for various ritualistic and ceremonial practices. This knowledge was part of one of the spiritual or religious lineages that was passed on to us to carry and keep alive.

One final note: the Holy Grail and the return to paradise are metaphysical but also real, concepts that cannot be separated. In other words, at long last with our awakening and humanity's awakening, we discover the Grail and return back to Lost Eden. Our earthly Eden may be pictured as a return to an egalitarian model of social interaction. Finally, after thousands and thousands of years, we bury once and forever the domination model that has forcibly ruled the earth while decimating cultures and nature.

Jesus and the Grail

There are many threads that weave through and compose the tapestry of the legendary Grail. One of these threads is directly connected with Jesus. It is "an apocryphal tradition based, not upon the teachings of the Apostles, but rather on the mysteries surrounding a little known and very minor character within the gospels called Joseph of Arimathea. In the legend it is he and his family line who carry the true message given to the disciples at the Last Supper by Christ...

"While the Holy Grail is essentially a Christian sacred image, it has never been accepted into the orthodox church. It would seem, in retrospect, that there were simply too many disturbingly heretical threads woven into the texture of the legend. One such thread is a lineage which carries the transmission of Christ's inner teaching outside that of the accepted Apostles. We know from the Church itself that the deepest communion of Christ's teaching occurred at the table of the Last Supper. The Grail tradition sees this as the first of three great tables, the others being the Round Table and the Table of the Grail. It was here the true seeker could be in direct contact with God. So even though Joseph of Arimathea was not actually present at the Last Supper he was still chosen by Christ to be the first Guardian of the Grail."[441] You may wonder why Mary was not chosen as the guardian. As coteacher with Jesus, she was not the guardian but the carrier and holder of the hidden knowledge and wisdom of the Grail.

The message and teachings of this hidden knowledge was of oneness—radical nonduality, the divine in everything, and everything in the divine—only if we have the silence to know it and the eye to see it. "With the Grail quest, the duty of everyone was the search for the divine...The idea of the knowledge of God being in everything and every person had been an inspiration in the Arthurian romances, particularly in *Parzival*. In one sense, the trails of the Knights of the Round Table on their way to the Castle of the Fisher King were the outward description of the inner turmoils of self-discovery. Finally to see the Grail was a vision of the unity of oneself with the universe. The object seen was in the shape of what one's knowledge made one able to perceive. The goal was union with the ultimate Creator."[442]

As we can see, the church would not be happy to have this knowledge of the oneness of the kingdom of God spread throughout the world. This has always been the case since the early days of the Grail legends. These legends focused on right deeds and the perfection to be found within us—something the church does not teach or preach. "The Church of Rome would never quite swallow the quest for the Grail. For this search derived from the worst of heresies, which was preached in the Near East and in Britain before the time of King Arthur.

"The great offence to the Bishop of Rome was the idea of a direct approach to God without the intercession of the Church. In the early fifth century, two Celtic monks, Pelagius and Coelestius, were banished from the Holy City for preaching that through their deeds, human beings could perfect themselves. There was no original sin, as Saint Augustine was arguing. Therefore a priest, who might absolve sins, was unnecessary. The believer could reach heaven by his acts alone on a sinful earth. 'Everything good, and everything evil,' Pelagius wrote, 'for which we are either praised or blamed, is not born with us, but done by us.' This doctrine was condemned by the Council of Ephesus and was to breed the first crusade of Europeans against Europeans, when the *perfecti* of the Cathars would be destroyed by Simon de Montfort and the Inquisitors."[443],[444]

The Eternal Question

Whom does the Grail serve? It serves us as we serve it! Our awakening to the kingdom of God only comes from our dedication and focus and the practice of right thinking, right speaking, and right actions and deeds. Our sun (heart) must give light to our moon (mind). It has been said that when "the sun turned away from the moon and enlightened it no longer, there would be no day without maledictions and sufferings."[445] This is the current condition of our culture and society. The next question is, "Who is so wise among you as to turn darkness into light?"[446] We are—don't despair; when we quest and awaken to the divine within and without (oneness), the darkness of our moon will be enlightened by the sun of our love and compassion.

The Law of the Kingdom

> *I will put my law within them, and I*
> *will write it on their hearts.*[447]

This is God's natural, altruistic law—the law of the kingdom. This natural law is based on a belief in the inherent, natural, altruistic law of God that is found within each person. This natural law flows from the divinity within each individual but lies dormant until awakened by each person. This is the true holy law of Moses, the basis for the teachings and the message of Jesus and a foundational belief of Divine Humanity.

This natural law discovered within each of us may be awakened by what I call *participation mystique*. This is a knowing of life and its inherent mysteries through the experience of the mundane as well as the spiritual.

Does natural law make null and void human-made laws? Not at all; human-made laws are as necessary as natural law. Just as the divine interpenetrates the human or the absolute interpenetrates the relative, natural law interpenetrates human law.

Natural law is an essential segment of an enlightened society and is based on doing what is best for the well-being of others and all things of the earth. It is not generated by a society but is derived and flows from each person's natural, if awakened, altruistic spirit.

Human-made laws, on the other hand, are society based and are focused on the probations of societal life in an attempt to control behavior. Many times they are a necessary part of life. But they are not necessarily based on what is most beneficial for the well-being of life—the environment, the whole of humanity, and the earth and its creatures.

There are international laws against torture. However, torture is still conducted through the manipulation of these laws. While there are laws against child abuse (thou shalt not), there are no laws that state that parents must be in their children's lives (adult children included) in a supportive way (thou shalt). There is nothing in legal code stating that a divorce must not be so destructive and revenge filled that any children involved will be drastically affected in a harmful way.

While human laws are drawn up to protect the environment, they are not necessarily what are best for the environment. They do, however, tend to serve capitalist thugs, whether they are corporate elites or their paid-off political flunkies. Capitalist law is the law of the bottom line—profit by any means possible. In the capitalist world of market-based medicine, cures for diseases go unresearched and unrealized if there is no profit or not enough profit to be made. Natural law is the antithesis of this entire paradigm.

Human laws, secular and religious, are based on the concept of the beast within and need enforcement for secular laws and a good dose of fear and guilt if they are religious laws, because both are the don'ts of life. There is no compassion connected with human secular law, as it is based on blind justice, or religious law, as it is supposedly based on the word of God. On the other hand, natural laws are the dos of life and thus require no enforcement.[448] Natural laws have their foundation in compassionate action (love your neighbor as yourself). Thus, natural law is the law of our hearts—divine, universal love.

Both human secular law and natural law are inadequate as stand-alone systems. For an enlightened society and a Golden Age to flourish, we need the integration of both.

Natural Law

Jesus said to them, "Is it not written in your law, 'I have said, "You are gods"'?"[449] Jesus is alluding to the divinity within each person. This was his firsthand knowledge from his descending-spirit experience of the interpenetration of spirit and matter or radical nonduality. Jesus goes on to state, "If I am not doing the works of my Father, then do not believe me; but if I do them, even though you do not believe me, believe the works, that you may know and understand that the Father is in me and I am in the Father."[450] Here, works refer to his spiritual deeds and abilities, his belief in and practice of natural law, and his knowing that the divine is within him and outside him in the kingdom paradise that no one can see. The laws of the temple only preserve the power of the priests while keeping people from recognizing and entering or awakening to the kingdom within and without. He knew that the law was a barrier to the direct experience of the kingdom.

As I have said before, it seems that in two thousand years, nothing has really changed. A former oil executive, Justin Welby, was expected to be the next archbishop of Canterbury. In this position he would be the leader of the world's seventy-seven million Anglican Christians.[451] Holding one of the most illustrious positions in Christendom, he is far removed from believing in the kingdom within or the following of natural law, just as were the scribes and the Pharisees. Here is a view into his consciousness: "*I don't believe in good human beings,*" Welby said in an interview with the *Guardian* newspaper. "But I believe you can have structures that make it easier to make the right choice or the wrong choice."[452] Of course, the structure is the church. Once again the total focus is on the outside structure of the cup: "Now then, you Pharisees clean the outside of the cup and dish, but inside you are full of greed and wickedness."[453]

If Jesus was teaching the original way of Moses, what was Moses's take on natural law? The Pharisees said that they followed the Laws of Moses, but were these laws the only laws? We know that Moses also experienced radical nonduality when he came face-to-face with the burning bush. Anyone who has experienced radical nonduality as I have would not see life as one-sided. Yes, he brought the outward laws that the priests want to shout from the mountaintop, but he also fed his people manna—the inner altruistic law of God. Any awakened community, large or small, needs some rules and regulations, but such a hive of awakened souls also needs natural law and its honey of compassionate action (work).

Moses

The angel of the Lord appeared to him in a blazing fire from the midst of a bush; and he looked, and behold, the bush was burning with fire, yet the bush was not consumed.[454]

This was a bush that defied the logic of physics. This was Moses's experience of interpenetrative radical nonduality, or oneness, on Mount Horeb.
—REV. DR. J. C. HUSFELT

This is the earliest recorded religious verification and proof of the divine spark within and nondualistic interpenetration reality, both being the foundational beliefs of the wisdom, religion, and philosophy of Divine Humanity.
—REV. DR. J. C. HUSFELT

Moses's visionary experience of the burning bush revealed to him the knowledge of interpenetrative radical nonduality—oneness. This alone was universally earth-shattering. But equally important and momentous was what he heard—along with his vision was the voice of God. And God said to Moses,

"Ehyeh-Asher-Ehyeh."[455] The exact meaning of these three Hebrew words is uncertain, so the phrase may be variously translated as "I am that I am," "I am who I am," and "I will be what I will be." In Hebrew the middle word "Asher" in its use as a relative pronoun may mean "that," "who," "which," or "where." Each of them could work, but I feel the most appropriate would be "that." Considering that Moses heard "Ehyeh-Asher-Ehyeh" during his vision of the burning bush, I feel that "I am that I am" is the more fitting of the three. However, we are still not complete. "I am" indicates that "I exist." In my mind as well as others, this is the proper translation: "I exist that I exist."[456]

However you may translate "Ehyeh-Asher-Ehyeh," the meaning of this auditory experience has been explained as revealing the name of God. Yet, besides the name of God, there is further hidden knowledge within this divine axiom— "Ehyeh-Asher-Ehyeh." This is the knowledge of oneness—a unity of being.

Both the vision and the voice imprinted within Moses's consciousness the same knowledge. This is a knowing and understanding of oneness or radical nonduality, which is the divine, the "I am" within all things; in other words, "I exist" in all things—"I am that (bush) I am" or "I exist (in) that (bush) I exist."

Further along in Exodus (6:2), God once again speaks to Moses but with a different identity: "I am the LORD." This time the name is "Lord" instead of "I am that I am." It is important to note that Lord in Hebrew is Adonai and is a euphemism for God or Yod Heh Vav Heh (יהוה)—also designated with the tetragrammaton YHWH. This time God repeated to Moses not "Ehyeh-Asher-Ehyeh" but I am "Yod Heh Vav Heh." The meaning of YHWH is a never-ending theological maze of opinion. The result is that the meaning may range from the One that ever manifests to simply the Creator.

⚜

One of the keys to the kingdom and to compassion and loving-kindness is the relationship of self to self and self to others. Within our conscious there is a way to blur the separation between subject (self) and object (others). It is a focus on repeating either silently or out loud the axiom "I am that I am" and substituting the object after "'I am that": "I am that [state object][457] I am!" This requires consistent practice, just as in any exercise regime where it is more efficient and effective to walk for thirty minutes six or seven days a week, every week, than one hour only two times a week every so often.

It would be best to focus on the "I am" a few times a day, every day. At some point your separation between subject and object will become less and less. *This is the secret of the kingdom—to recognize the dualities in life while at the same time maintaining an underlying consciousness of the radical nonduality of life.* Spirit and matter are one; the secret is to know the balance of this unity to its time and season.

> There is a time[458] for everything, and a season
> for every activity under heaven:
>
> A time to be born and a time to die,
> A time to plant and a time to uproot,
> A time to kill and a time to heal,
> A time to tear down and a time to build,
> A time to weep and a time to laugh,
> A time to mourn and a time to dance,
> A time to scatter stones and a time to gather them,
> A time to embrace and a time to refrain,
> A time to search and a time to give up,
> A time to keep and a time to throw away,
> A time to tear and a time to mend,
> A time to be silent and a time to speak,
> A time to love and a time to hate,
> A time for war and a time for peace. (Eccl. 3:1–8)

⚜

> *Believe me that I am in the* Abba *and the* Abba *in me, or else, believe for the sake of the works themselves.... I am in my Father, that you are in me, and that I am in you.*
> —JOHN 14:11, 20

The next stage in awakening is to acknowledge the divine in all things. "I exist—I breathe." According to Jeff A. Benner, "The name hwhy (Yahweh) comes from the Hebrew root hyh (hayah). This root and the words derived from it can have a wide variation in meaning and application. The original concrete meaning is 'breath' and has the extended meaning 'exist', as one who exists, breathes."[459] He goes on to state that "the spirit in Hebrew thought is the breath. Just as the breath of man cannot be seen but is essential for life to exist, Yahweh also cannot be seen but it is his breath in man that gives him life."[460]

The ancient Hebrews were not alone in this philosophy. To the Hawaiians the magic of breath is known as *Ha*—breathe out, exhale. The loving essence of the Hawaiian Islands is contained within the concept of the aloha spirit. *Alo* means "in the presence of" or "to be with," and *Ha* is "the breath of life." Breath for the Hawaiians symbolizes life as well as the essence of life—the divine. Ha is the secret key within aloha. It is the breath that we all share. It is the life-force and consciousness that connects us all. It carries our words, words that may create or destroy throughout the world. To the wise ones of old, words were no less powerful than deeds. One way to experience the presence of the magic of life is to inhale through the nose and softly say "Ha" as you exhale through the mouth. This will help your body and mind relax and be in the present moment.

To the Greeks, "psuché was the breath, the soul, the vital breath, breath of life. Psyxḗ (from psyxō, 'to breathe, blow' which is the root of the English words 'psyche,' 'psychology') corresponds exactly to the OT phágō ('soul'). The soul is the direct aftermath of God breathing (blowing) His gift of life into a person, making them an ensouled being."[461]

These cultures were not the only ones with this knowledge; it was wide-spread across this earth, from the Celts and Egyptians to the ancient Japanese. To bring this knowledge of the divine alive within ourselves, our next step is to practice honoring and acknowledging the divine in ourselves and in all others. Once again we need to achieve a focused awareness, repeating either silently or out loud the axiom "I exist that I exist" with the addition of (in) and (thing): "I exist (in) that (thing)[462] I exist!" Some Buddhist put it this way: recognize the Buddha essence in ourselves and in others. "In the Thomas gospel that was dug up in Egypt some forty years ago, Jesus says, 'He who drinks from my mouth will become as I am, and I shall be he.' Now, that is exactly Buddhism. We are all mani-festations of Buddha consciousness, or Christ consciousness, only we don't know it. The word 'Buddha' means 'the one who waked up.' We are all to do that—to wake up to the Christ or Buddha consciousness within us. This is blasphemy in the normal way of Christian thinking."[463]

And finally, we discover a familiar axiom within "the Indian concept of the cosmic union of ātman and brahman, which is expressed by the phrase *tat tvam asi* (thou art that)."[464]

⚜

There are many great gifts to receive from the practice and consciousness of these exercises. One gift may be a peacefulness of body, mind, and spirit during certain times of stress and during various moments of our lives. Other gifts may be a sense of loving-kindness, compassion, and a consciousness where we harm nothing *intentionally* through words or deeds. The key word here is *intentionally*. We are divine humans, but in our humanness we make mistakes and may *unintentionally* harm others through words and deeds. This is not justification but a reality of our humanness. Forgiveness is needed. We must ask forgiveness of the ones we have harmed. We must learn from our mistakes so that we do not repeat behaviors over and over again—behaviors that bring pain and suffering to others and to ourselves.

CHAPTER 9

Divine Humanity—A Revolutionary Worldview

Be humble for you are made of earth. Be
noble for you are made of stars.
—Serbian Proverb

The Five Pillars (foundational beliefs and principles) of Divine
Humanity are the belief in the divine spark within, original
divinity, interpenetrating radical nonduality (oneness), the
consciousness of all things in and of creation, and natural law.
—Rev. Dr. J. C. Husfelt

Divine Humanity (humanity represents not only the human race but all things of creation) is a living, spiritual philosophy, wisdom, religion, and new consciousness. It is also a pure religion of the people, by the people, and for all the people. Divine Humanity is a religion of philosophy and a living, personal (not institutionalized) religion. As a world philosophy of awe and a religion of equality and simplicity, it conveys a love for all forms of life and acknowledges everything in creation as divine as well as honoring its own unique intrinsic expression. Therefore, not only is every human being a divine human with an intrinsic human expression and the light, holy spark, of God (the Great Mystery) within, but all trees have the divine spark within them and in their intrinsic expression may provide food and shelter for us and for other creatures of the earth.

Divine Humanity is based on the concept of nondifferentiating knowledge. This is the knowledge that fuses into nonduality all dichotomies, such as subject and object. In other words, Divine Humanity is not based on dualism. Its foundation is interpenetrating radical nonduality—oneness. There is no separation between the absolute and the relative, dark and light, spirit and matter, or mind and body. The most profound and essential nature of things is not distinct from the things recognizable by our senses. In other words, our sacred selves and our profane selves are nondual and interpenetrate; likewise, all other sentient beings' (things') sacred identities and profane identities are nondual and interpenetrate. This is true oneness.

There is no separation; no dualism—just two aspects of a single reality. We may be enlightened and deluded, even defiled and pure at the same time. An example of this is discovered within the biblical myth of Samson—the honey (pure) within the carcass of the lion, or beast (defiled). Jesus knew this truth. The following from *The Nag Hammadi Library*, "The Thunder, Perfect Mind," speaks to this knowledge:

> *I am knowledge and ignorance.*
> *I am shame and boldness.*
> *I am shameless; I am ashamed.*
> *I am strength and I am fear.*
> *I am war and peace.*
> *Give heed to me.*[465]

The morale and ethics of Divine Humanity are built on the relationships between people and all other things (self and other). There is no good or evil in its own right, but actions may lead to good or bad, or evil, consequences. There is no original sin, only original divinity. Every individual is responsible for his or her actions and has to bear the consequences.

Briefly, Divine Humanity, an ecological and egalitarian philosophical religion, is based on a partnership of nature (a green religion), equality, and a partnership of self and other.

A Pure Religion

Social and economic problems are very important issues that must be addressed by any religion that is pure and true. In addition, I believe the present and the past social and economic ills sprang directly from the dogma and doctrine of institutionalized religion.[466]

A religion that represents all people needs to embody social and economic concerns that focus on equality for all. This religion would need to acknowledge the equality and intrinsic value of all things on this earth based on the divine consciousness of love.

A Spiritual Philosophy

Divine Humanity is a spiritual philosophy that attempts to understand and explain the mysteries of life and creation. It is based on first knowledge or first principles. It is not solely based on earth knowledge, like the earth-based philosophies and religions, nor is it solely based on the heavens, like institutionalized religion.

Divine Humanity is based on both the earth and the heavens and is experiential and transformational in content. It is a stellar religion. Divine Humanity is a spiritual philosophy, and it may also be a personal religion that is based on one's truth found within one's heart and mind. It is not based on faith, dogma, or doctrine.

New Consciousness

Life is not about sin or guilt. Life is about awakening—awakening to a new consciousness that the divine is in all things, that all things have consciousness, and that we are divine human beings born in love and perfection. Our awakening gradually occurs with our realization of the oneness of subject and object.

The Divine Spark

Divine Humanity believes that each and every person has an immortal spark within him or her—an indestructible seed of divine light, starlight, the divine immanence. This indestructible seed of divine light may be likened to a mustard seed within our hearts. This divine seed of immortality or spark, which sometimes may be referred to as the divine golden dew, constitutes the soul—an eternal spark in its essence, since it is a fragment of God, and immortal.[467]

This is our sacred self. This inner, indestructible seed of light, that settles over and interpenetrates our DNA as divine golden dew, needs to be awakened, to grow in its brilliance, and to be brought to the surface until its radiance spreads to all others and to the world.[468] This is our luminous body that grows within and shines without. In so doing, our relationship to ourselves and to all other things of the world is transformed from being based on fear to being based on love.

In All Things
Divine Humanity believes that the divine light of creation, this immortal spark, is within all things of creation—all sentient beings (all existences such as flowers, dogs, trees, fish, worms, and stars) throughout the universe. This is sacred identity.

Humanity—Unique Intrinsic Identity
Every human being is unique with an intrinsic worth and identity. This is our profane self. In addition, every flower, tree, and animal (all sentient things of creation) is unique with its own intrinsic worth and identity. This is profane identity.

A Diverse Humanity
Humans are divine as well as intrinsically unique in all facets—some may choose to fish, and some may choose to build bombs. Still, our divinity is within us, even as it remains hidden. This is diametrically the opposite of Christianity, where each individual is intrinsically sinful.

Does Everyone Have a Divine Spark?
Yes, but unawakened. Even though we are born with this divine light of creation within us, our divine sparks stay hidden until awakened. This is the work

we must do. We must awaken our sparks and then grow these indestructible seeds of light.[469]

Interpenetrating Radical Nonduality—Our Oneness

Our sacred selves and our profane selves are nondual and interpenetrate; similarly, all other sentient beings' sacred identities and profane identities are nondual and interpenetrate. This is true oneness. In addition, Divine Humanity believes that all things of creation have an interconnected consciousness. This consciousness interpenetrates all things in and of creation.

Divine Humanity believes that the relative world of our everyday experience and the absolute world of the divine are inseparable aspects of a single reality. The relative and absolute are nondual.

Oneness means that the body and mind are nondual. Because of the fusion of body and mind, the attainment of awakening is not effected in the mind alone, but is also equally realized in the body. Spirit and matter are not separate from each other but interpenetrate:

> Christ taught that the kingdom of God is within us. What does this mean? The kahunas[470] teach the same thing! Within us are both Spirit and Matter. We must know them both. All the powers of the kahunas, to heal, to control nature, to bless, and to curse, are based on this one secret...
>
> What does it mean to combine the Spiritual and the Material? What does it mean, "Know thyself?" Some people are only materialistic. They become weak when they lose health and wealth. Others try to be only spiritual. They become weak when they are impractical. Both types of people have no real foundation. Life is the combination of spirituality with sensible materialism.[471]

⚜

Our individual sense of reality (of separateness or duality) is just an extension illusion of our basic core sense perceptions. Our eyes perceive separation between us and all things viewed. This constant reinforcement tricks us into thinking and believing we are separate and islands unto ourselves. Reinforced by messages from childhood, we build stronger and thicker walls around our islands to protect us (the unhealthy ego). This core belief leads to behaviors and actions based on fear and protective neurosis of the unhealthy ego. Constant vigilance is needed to overcome and release our dualistic thinking, dualistic believing, and behaviors that are attached to this false paradigm of dualism.

Keeping in mind that all things have consciousness, a behavior to adopt is to talk either silently or out loud to things other than humans, such as trees, flowers, and animals. During this communication imagine that each of you have a divine spark within, and understand that any feelings of love, sadness, or even hate will be felt not only by you but also by it.

⚜

Other spiritual, religious, and philosophical systems of belief similar to Divine Humanity (kingdom of God) include pantheism, with the addition of the related concepts of panentheism, pandeism, and panpsychism. In fact, putting all four concepts together paints for us a pretty close picture of Divine Humanity without spelling out the key elements of natural law and radical nonduality.[472]

Oneness Equals Mental Tranquility

When the two hemispheres of our brains are united in an interpenetration of the logical and the intuitive, we experience reality not as separate from us but as a part of us and us as a part of it. This breaks down the barrier between our ordinary minds and our enlightened minds. The mirror of our minds will then reflect things in their true, original state.

There still may be dust on our mirrors, but we will see clearer than the ones that remain stuck in a dualistic reality. When we realize that reality is not based on an either-or paradigm of duality, we will finally discover a great peace within ourselves. There is great solace in knowing that we may be both enlightened as well as deluded. We do not have to be one or the other. We do not have to win or lose. This shift alone will transform us from self-centered beings into divine human beings that are participating in a journey of life and experience along with all other humans and all other creatures of the earth.

Our minds become purer and calmer when we view and sense reality as united, not as a separate thing that may threaten our egotistic sense of safety and security. When we can see ourselves in all other things, not only another human being, but animals, moths, trees, and so forth, we achieve a state of being that is peaceful, benevolent, and compassionate. This is something not just achievable in meditation, but more importantly, in every waking second of our lives.

⚜

Oneness means that the world of physical phenomena is nondual with the divine. One of the best ways to realize this philosophy is by working with the elements. Divine Humanity prescribes to not four or five, but six elements. The six are earth, water, fire, air, space, and consciousness. Divine Humanity believes that all things of creation have consciousness, which interpenetrates the other five elements. These five elements are physical as well as metaphysical (e.g., water equals water, emotions equal water; fire equals fire, spirit equals fire; air equals air, mind equals air; and earth equals earth, body equals earth).

There is a carved inscription on the Porta Alchemica (Alchemy Gate or Magic Portal) at the Villa Palombara in Rome that reads, "He who knows how to burn with water and wash with fire makes out of the earth heaven and out of the heaven precious earth." In cryptic terms this is a teaching of oneness—the interpenetration of heaven and earth. Most researchers will identify this statement as a theorem of alchemy during the Middle Ages. I would date it much further back in time, possibly as far back as thousands of years ago.

In the New Testament, we find the words, "Baptize with the Holy Spirit and with Fire (Matthew 3:12)." We once again discover the veiled reference to oneness. But what does all of this mean? How can we wash with fire and burn with water? What is it to be baptized with spirit and with fire? Again, Christian religious leaders, whether they be ministers, priests, or bishops, answer these questions in theological terms, future-orientated events, or faith issues. But how else could they answer these questions? If you have never seen or eaten an apple, how could you actually describe its form and color and taste?

If you have never put your hands in fire where they were not burnt and never submerged yourself in a cold, running stream where you felt the icy fire rushing through you, how would you even come close to understanding the hidden meanings of these veiled teachings? You wouldn't; all you could do is rely on faith and discursive linear thinking. Socrates put written words, supposedly God inspired or not, into proper perspective when he "compared written doctrines to pictures of animals which resemble life, but which when you question them can give you no reply."[473]

There is no separation between the divine realm (the otherworld) and the material realm (the earth); they both interpenetrate. The awareness of this interpenetration of the two realms is most evident near flowing waters, such as mountain streams and rivers. It is here where the illusionary veil of separation may be dropped to reveal the oneness of life through the process of bathing. The first time that we step into the stream to submerge, die, and be reborn may be an apocalyptic experience that literally has the potential to be a volcanic implosion of our souls—an unveiling and purification of our hearts and minds.

But for the majority of the time, our conscious focus and awareness are only on the material realm, even though we exist in the divine realm as well. This is one of the reasons why Divine Humanity does not believe in sequestering ourselves away in so-called religious cages—such as a monastery or the Vatican. This is an artificial and illusionary state done more for power and control than personal transformation. It also provides a physical and visual form of legitimacy for the church's religious badge—authority. Add in the dresses and collars of Catholic priests, and you have achieved a statement of separation from the masses and identified yourself as the mouthpiece of God.

Our power is to be found by fully participating in the totality of life by weeding our fields and sowing and harvesting the precious flowers and jewels of our earthly garden paradise. When we realize and keep foremost in our minds that all things have a consciousness, not just humans, and that the elements that compose life are metaphysical as well as physical, we gradually break down the illusion of separateness between ourselves and our garden paradise. This results in loving-kindness, peacefulness, benevolentness, and compassion for all other things. The moth is you, and you are the moth; the cat is you, and you are the cat; the tree is you, and you are the tree. "I am that..."

This transformation of consciousness results in joy, happiness, and tranquility of the mind. We are no longer frightened children hiding, protecting, and hoarding on our own personal islands of fear against all things that are seemingly different and separate from us. Our islands of fear dissolve, and we realize that the garden has always been there for us, where all things are one with each other.

However, we have to be careful not to let five things interfere with this transformation of consciousness and the tranquility of our minds. These are desire, anger, ignorance, doubt, and false views. Desire is the attachment to materialistic and pleasant things. Anger causes wrath and vengeance. Ignorance, as well as pride and arrogance, can cause us to feel we are superior to others and all other things. Doubt keeps us from distinguishing between delusion and enlightenment and cause and effect. And false views allow us to believe in the doctrine and dogma of dualistic paradigms, such as the church.

Six Great Elements

Divine Humanity prescribes to six great elements that interpenetrate and are in eternal union. Six is the first number of perfection. The world was created in six days. "Order involves numbers, and among numbers by the laws of nature, the most suitable to productivity is 6, for if we start with 1, it is the first perfect number, being equal to the product of its factors (i.e. 1 x 2 x 3) as well as made up of the sums of them (i.e. 1 + 2 + 3)."[474]

The first five elements are earth, water, fire, air or wind, and space. These five elements are physical as well as metaphysical (e.g., water equals ocean, and emotion equals water). The sixth great element, which interpenetrates the other five, is consciousness. This belief opens up worlds of opportunity, knowledge, and the wisdom that form is inseparable from mind and the mind is inseparable from form—a nonduality or oneness. And we realize that we are never alone or out of touch. Everything has a consciousness that is all connected in a web of life extending out and back to the farthest star in the most distant galaxy.

LED—A Practical Example of Radical Nonduality

The Nobel committee said that light-emitting diodes, or LED's, would be the lighting source of the 21st century...[475]

And so they will...

Light-emitting diodes are unique in producing white light. This is due to the fact that the electric current (negative and positive) itself is the light, unlike incandescent bulbs, which use electricity to produce a glowing filament that emits light, or fluorescent lights, which use a glowing gas to produce light.

The birth of light-emitting diodes only came after the creation of blue diodes. Up until that time, the only diodes available were red and green, and without a blue diode, white light cannot be created. When red, green, and blue[476] diodes are combined and "an electric field is applied, negative and positive charges meet in the middle layer and combine to produce photons of light."[477] In other words, with the blending or interpenetration of negative and positive or, if you will, symbolic spirit and matter, light is produced. The magic of LEDs reflects the magic of radical nonduality. When we awaken to a consciousness of radical nonduality, we awaken our dormant sparks; our divine light awakens and begins the process of evolving into a body of light.

Three Pillars of Light of Divine Humanity

- ❖ Baby Eyes—eyes that are nonjudgmental and tolerant, that view the world with awe and excitement, and that recognize the oneness of the light and the dark of existence.
- ❖ True Talk—silence is golden—listening more often than talking, and when talking, speaking truth from the heart. It is to hear, understand, and perceive.
- ❖ Flower Heart—always expressing love from the heart and letting others, as well as ourselves, view the beauty and the divine perfection that is the true essence of our hearts. Smell is a powerful sense. With a Flower Heart, our fragrance is pure, sweet, and soothing to ourselves and others. The Flower Heart is also the Lily or Lotus Heart.

Consciousness

Consciousness is probably something that most people have never pondered. Ironically and simply put, this would be thinking about thinking and the source of those thoughts. But it might be the most important thing for us to consider. It may open a vista of realization on the whys of human behavior.

Divine Humanity proposes eight different states of consciousness.[478] The first five are our senses: visual consciousness discerns form, hearing consciousness discerns sounds, taste conscious discerns taste, smell consciousness discerns smells, and touch consciousness discerns tactile sensations.

Next we have mind and thought consciousness—conscious mind. This is the realm of the unhealthy ego (solely focused on the I), which constantly seeks external power, safety, security, and inappropriate sex. Our minds and thought consciousness are our decision makers, and the ongoing, prevalent decision that we make is where we focus our attention. Many times the focus of our attention will be based on our concept of power. This is the reason why millionaires and billionaires keep accumulating money instead of buying an island, kicking back, and contemplating the meaning of life. They see their power externally in status and wealth. It does not matter if their internal spirit is a stagnant swamp of an unresolved past that harmed others and harmed the greater well-being through their actions, such as those of tobacco, oil, and pharmaceutical executives and investment bankers, to name just a few of the many capitalist elites.

When we awaken our divine starlight, our unhealthy egos are transformed into healthy egos, with the I in the we and the we in the I—a consciousness of radical nonduality. Even though our unhealthy egos have been transformed, reality is not either-or. Even with healthy egos, we will sometimes exhibit traits and behaviors of unhealthy egos—we are humans, not gods or goddesses.

Storehouse consciousness—subconscious—is next. This is the realm of first attention. Just as it implies, this consciousness stores the seeds, and possibly stones, of every moment and experience of our lives and forms our beliefs, assumptions, attitudes, habits, and behaviors. It is our memory bank.

It is through our conscious minds that we are able to transform our storehouse consciousness and its first attention into a second attention. This enables a shift in consciousness of our beliefs, assumptions, and attitudes, which will then change habits and behaviors. To achieve this shift in consciousness, we need to begin shifting our first attention into a second attention, which will then begin a transformation of our conscious minds (thought and mind consciousness—dualistic consciousness) into a heart-mind consciousness (radical nonduality consciousness).

Finally, we have the supraconsciousness—soul consciousness. This may be looked at as our guardian angels or our higher selves. It is the divine-spark consciousness that is eternal. Mesoamerican indigenous shamanic cultures refer to this type of consciousness as the tonal of a person. Tonal is the birth guardian or the metaphoric animal twin of the person. The Norse referred to this concept as the *hamr* of a person. This is our birth guardian, not separate but a part of us.

In conclusion, do not look at these various states of consciousness as proceeding from sense consciousness to supraconsciousness, but understand that they all interpenetrate. Additionally, our sense consciousness is essential to the overall health of our bodies, minds, and spirits and the awakening of our divine starlight. You may see the Pandora effect of the unbridled technological advance based solely on capitalist gain without concern for the totality of people's bodies, minds, and spirits. The bottom line: humanity's sensory consciousness is deadening, affecting people's sense of reality, common sense, and connection to the earth and nature.

The Ninth Consciousness

If there were not a ninth conscious, each of us would be separate from, and not a part of, the web of life—islands isolated unto ourselves. Just as the sixth great element, divine consciousness, interpenetrates the other five elements of space, air, fire, water, and earth (physically and metaphysically), it also interpenetrates our individual eight states of consciousness. Our ninth means that the observer and the observed, self and other, are not separate but are connected in a oneness of being. We are not our brothers' or sisters' keepers, but we are our brothers or sisters.[479] We are truly one with the divine.

Heart-Mind Consciousness

Our heart-mind consciousness is our awakening and awakened minds. It is still corruptible and deluded but awakening to the reality of interpenetrating radical nonduality. It is a shift from viewing life totally from the I position to one where the I and the we interpenetrate—the I in the we, and the we in the I.

Our consciousness flows from our hearts through our minds—the sun of our hearts gives light to the moon of our minds. We no longer recognize people by race and gender but as human beings with a divine spark within. Judgments and discernments are not made on a label of color or sex but on the basis of the person's actions to us and to others.

True compassion is centered in the heart, not in the mind. Compassion is not an intellectual exercise but a feeling within our hearts and our bodies of the suffering of others. It is from our hearts that we may truly acknowledge our own suffering and our loved ones' suffering through the challenges and obstacles that life invariably throws at us.

For the sun of our hearts to shine brightly on all who cross our path, we must not carry the burdens of the past into the present. We must learn the lesson of detachment.

Detachment

Life and growth are absolutely amazing. As babies our souls relearn how to be human and continue relearning and learning all the different ways of being a human as we grow into adulthood and beyond. Initially, this is our first attention learned through attachment. We attach to the sensory input to learn how to speak, walk, and do the many other necessary motor skills. This is basically imprinted in our subconscious minds—our storehouse consciousness. This means we do not have to relearn all the motor skills. They become automatic actions and reactions. This teaches us how to attach and, the bad-boy offshoot, judge, which is based on our past experiences and not the present happenings.

If life were such that on a daily basis, we treated each other as we would like to be treated (e.g., compassion; kind, caring and supportive words; and unconditional love), we would lovingly see and interact with each other based on the present moment. But such is not life. We wound others through our words and sometimes through our actions, and others wound us. If these wounds are not released, we will attach to the past and make judgments in the moment that are based on the past and the fear of the repetition of words and actions. We imprison ourselves, and we seldom experience the paradise of a joyful life.

Lotus Heart—the Holy Grail of Oneness

The lotus is the perfect flower to symbolically represent the interpenetration of the divine and matter—the pure and the impure. The purity and beauty of the lotus grows and thrives in muddy environments but remains undefiled as it opens its petals to the first light of dawn. Our heart is our lotus (purity), which remains pure as it contains our divine spark or starlight, even though it is encased with the body of our humanness (impurity). Philosophically, we are pure within our impurity, which makes us pure.

Our lotus heart is our divine womb—our personal holy grail of oneness. Our personal lotus heart not only receives but also gives. Physically, it receives the blood that has coursed through our bodies and then gives it back to our bodies in a wondrous and magical process of life. This magical transformation depends on the spirit wings of our lotus heart—our lungs circulating the spirit of the heavens through our earthly body.

Spiritually, our lotus heart is the vessel—the grail, which received our divine spark—our starlight. After we have awakened this immortal spark, its starlight gradually brightens until it is brought to the surface and nourished until its radiance suffuses our loved ones, friends, community, and earth. In so doing, our relationship to ourselves and to all other things of the world is transformed from being based less on fear to being based more on love.

With our awakened heart, the separation between heart and mind disappears—the mind is the heart, and the heart is the mind. Our mind symbolically transforms into a perfect full moon reflecting the light of our lotus heart, our starlight or inner sun, which is the microcosm of the macrocosmic Sun—God—the Sun behind the sun.

But our holy grail remains unawakened and undiscovered if the mythical question is never asked. It somehow seems that we have been led to believe, and not question, the prevailing secular and religious codes of behavior. Such acceptance has caused great suffering to humanity and the earth—a wasteland that waits to be transformed by the foretold messiah and his heroes of spirit.

The legends of the Holy Grail reveal in various ways the destructiveness and commonality of blindly accepting and not questioning. "The key to the hero's subsequent failure when tested at the Grail Castle is the instruction that a true knight should avoid being too talkative. The young fool takes these rules at face value so when he is confronted with a situation which requires his true and natural response he falls back on someone else's authority, on a programmed reaction which is totally inappropriate to the situation."[480]

Does this sound familiar? From early in life, we are conditioned to accept authority and not to question it or its rules. This becomes an obstacle to our awakening and spiritual development. And we never get around to asking one of the primary questions of life—who am I, and what ails me? "What ails us all is that we cannot accept ourselves exactly as we are. We just cannot seem to accept ourselves as being perfectly natural, just as the whole of existence is natural. If only we can act spontaneously, without being programmed into someone else's belief system, we can ask the real question of ourselves. Then, miraculously, for one moment the vessel of the Grail is empty—and in the next it is filled with the wonder and glory of all and everything."[481]

⚜

The kingdom of God is spread before us, and no one knows it. In her book *The Sovereign Adventure—The Grail of Mankind*, Anna Murdoch writes about "Arthur sleeping 'bespelled' in Richmond Castle, where many in vain tried to find him. One man only, Potter Thompson, wandering one night among the ruins, stumbles into the hall where the king sits with his knights, his horn and his sword beside him. But Potter Thompson, who is not a true knight, runs away in terror. Behind him he hears a voice calling:

> *'Potter Thompson, Potter Thompson,*
> *Hadst thou blown the horn,*
> *Thou had's been the greatest man*
> *That ever was born.'*

"The blowing of the horn, the clarion call that wakes from sleep, is a feature of all sacred scriptures, and in innumerable sagas down to folklore and fairy-tale. All higher teachings in the East and West have described man as sleepwalking. Forever the voice of the angel has called him to wake up from sleep, that of every teacher to free himself from illusion, from the ceaseless turning of the wheel. Sometimes the task of blowing the horn falls to the hero."[482] I am blowing the horn to wake you up.

Wake up, embrace Jesus's message, and discover the path and way to love, peace, and compassion and a return to Lost Eden in *Tequila and Chocolate: A Guide to a New Consciousness—the Awakening of Our Divinity and Humanity*.

APPENDIX

Universality of Divine Humanity

Throughout the past centuries, there have been few Western alternatives to the institutionalized religions of Christianity, Judaism, and Islam. At various times there have been revivals of past religious traditions, such as Druidism during the Celtic Revival of the nineteenth and twentieth centuries. Over the past forty or so years, we have witnessed the establishment of neoshamanism, neo-Druidism, modern heathenry, and modern paganism. These were birthed as alternatives to the three major Western religions as well as from people's opposition to the destruction of nature and the biosystem.

What is lacking in these alternatives is a universal, foundational spiritual or religious philosophy that would underlie practices such as modern heathenry and modern paganism. Divine Humanity provides this philosophy There is no dogma, doctrine, or rules of practice connected with Divine Humanity. In other words, individuals and groups may conduct rituals and ceremonies in a manner they see and feel is effective and matches their own belief systems. This includes the honoring of one's chosen gods, goddesses, nature spirits, and so forth.

Divine Humanity is not institutionalized or hierarchal. It believes in original divinity, not original sin. It is a green, ecological, and egalitarian philosophy and religion and is all-inclusive. You do not have to pass a hierarchal "gatekeeper" to join, such as in the Christian church through baptism. There are no fees or donations required. All that is needed is the acceptance of Divine Humanity as your religion or philosophy and the willingness to awaken your spark or starlight within—with the additional acceptance of being in partnership with nature and walking gently on the earth with an open, loving, compassionate, and forgiving heart. These are asked of you with the realization that we are human as well as divine. We will make mistakes, get angry, and carry fear. Many times forgiveness of ourselves and others is needed. But life is a journey of becoming, not a destination of finality.

Divine Humanity's Philosophical Approach to Cosmology and Ontology Marrying Religion and Science

Science and religion at one time were combined as one study under the name of Sacred Science. This study I continue to conduct. Please understand that with the following, I am attempting to describe an indescribable process of divine creation.
—Rev. Dr. J. C. Husfelt

Divine Humanity acknowledges that the Creator, the Unknown and the Uncreated, cannot be identified or imagined by the human mind and cannot be put into human terms, just in absolute terms, as it is the greatest mystery of all mysteries. The Absolute—the All—which Divine Humanity refers to as God, is beyond form and conception, the unmanifest. It is outside of time and space; in a sense it is timelessness.

For reasons beyond what any human mind may comprehend, the Absolute reflected itself—the Reflective Absolute. Philosophically, these are like two multifaceted jewels that refract and reflect in limitless combinations. From the Absolute and its reflection, Reflective Absolute, was "birthed the duality that was nondual"—a void that was not void. Divine Humanity refers to the absolute and the reflective absolute as the *great silence* (the sound of the Hebrew letter aleph is silence), not the big bang, and the duality that was nondual as the *dark ocean*—containing the eternal male and eternal female.[483]

The reflective absolute (divine mind and consciousness) now interpenetrates this voidless void (*dark ocean*), and creation occurs. The *great silence* (divine mind and consciousness) has interpenetrated the *dark ocean*, and the divine is now in triple aspect (divine mind and consciousness, divine spark in the "dark," divine spark in the "light").[484] In other words, from the union of oneness and duality (which is its reflection), we have a trinity.

From this the reflective absolute and the *dark ocean* (in triple aspect) birth the *great sea*—the relative universe (seen and unseen). The *great sea* has wave action or vibration. Within this the absolute is nondual to the relative, spirit is nondual to matter, and divine is nondual to humanity (all things, seen and unseen, of creation—*Mother Nature*). The divine is in all things (*kingdom of God within*), and all things are in the divine (*kingdom of God without*). In other words, spirit is within matter, and matter is within spirit, and all mutually penetrate. Thus, reality is interpenetrating radical nonduality—oneness. There is no separation between the absolute and the relative, dark and light, spirit and matter, or mind and body. Consciousness permeates and interpenetrates all reality. God is both immanent and transcendent. This may be likened to the realization through religious intuition of the essential oneness of the macrocosm and microcosm. Furthermore, the macrocosm, the universe (*Mother Nature*), and oneself are essentially one. We are within the universe (*Mother Nature*), and the universe (*Mother Nature*) is within us.[485]

Dr. Husfelt's Original Concepts and Principles

- ❖ Creation occurred when the Absolute reflected itself. We are not made in the image but are a reflection of God, as are all other things of creation.
- ❖ Oneness is radical nonduality, not merely nonduality. Radical nonduality is the interpenetration of the absolute and relative, spirit and matter.
- ❖ The burning bush is the first written acknowledgment of radical nonduality.
- ❖ We are born in original divinity, not original sin.
- ❖ Our soul, which enters us at birth, is metaphorically "golden dew." This settles over, blends with our earthly DNA, and provides us with a heavenly DNA as well as an earthly DNA. We are creatures of heaven and earth.

❖ The beast within, referring to the darkness (functional and dysfunctional) within us, interpenetrates with the light within us. This concept is fully explained in *Tequila and Chocolate: A Guide to a New Consciousness—the Awakening of our Divinity and Humanity.*

The Return to Lost Eden

Awakened Sustainable Communities

Within an awakened, sustainable community, the spiritual unity of people would provide the glue to bond everyone together and all such communities as one. This follows the principle of Divine Humanity, where the divine spark is within all people. This equates to the equality of all—egalitarianism, one of the core beliefs of Divine Humanity. In addition, each individual is honored and recognized for his or her intrinsic value to others and the community. This is not socialism or the submergence of the individual for the benefit of the group or community. This is intrinsic egalitarianism, where equality and individual intrinsic ability interpenetrate. Deeds are honored over words unfulfilled.

Throughout history, "the vision of human unity, with its concomitant emphasis on a caring and committed response to collective need, is, in itself, one of the most inspiring products of the human heart and spirit. But like all Neptunian[486] products it contains a fundamental resistance to being translated into everyday terms. The degree of compromise necessary to anchor this vision in workable ways, while respecting the personal boundaries of individuals at every level of society, forms the rock upon which politicians and political parties have foundered throughout history."[487]

In short, social paradigms of the past have been principally dualistic in nature and nonegalitarian. This is one of the prime reasons for their failure, whether we talk about Marxism, communism, or socialism. These paradigms and others have all been based on dualistic principles, not principles and practices of egalitarianism and radical nonduality—oneness.

All three of the major Western religions are based on inequality. They are dualistic and male dominated, with women considered second-class citizens.

Inequality is not limited to organized religion but is to be found socially and economically throughout the width and breadth of our planet—the end result of the capitalist paradigm.

One of the key factors of awakened, sustainable communities is not only the equality and compassion of each person in the community, but also the honoring and acknowledgment of the intrinsic humanness of each person. In other words, the old labels of dualistic paradigms are nonexistent, as is any form of sexism. For example, the best intrinsically valued person within the community for, say, a blacksmith is the person with that intrinsic skill and ability, no matter what education, race, or sex. There are no hierarchies or class structures, only divine, intrinsic human beings.

Warning

"When machines and computers, profits and property rights are considered more important than people, the giant triplets of racism, materialism and militarism are incapable of being conquered.

"The choice is ours. And though we might prefer it otherwise, we must choose at this crucial moment of human history." [488]

"Data-driven insights, experts say, will fuel a shift in decision-making. Decisions of all kinds, they say, will increasingly be made on the basis of data and analysis rather than experience and intuition—more science and less gut feel."[489]

I do have a warning. Scientific and technological advances combined with the capitalist mind-set without subsequent spiritual awakening and transparency may lead to loss of freedom, catastrophe, and disaster facing the human race sometime in the future; whether that is the distant or near future is up for debate.[490] To these challenges are added climate change, extreme weather, and lack of drinkable water.

Rev. Dr. J. C. Husfelt

Rev. Dr. JC Husfelt, author of I Am a Sun of God and So Are You, The Return of the Feathered Serpent and Return of a Green Philosophy, is a philosopher, shaman, and mystic as well as a poet, martial artist, visionary, and exemplary prophet.

Since 1964 Husfelt has undertaken a literal and metaphorical journey through the mystical and practical aspects of the martial arts, mystery, myth, and spiritual lore of indigenous cultures throughout the world. He and his wife have traveled across the Americas to the icy plateaus and volcanoes of Iceland, through the windswept barrens of the British Isles and the Orkneys, and across Norway, Europe, the Mediterranean, Asia, and the Polynesian Islands.

Husfelt's teachings grew from his firsthand experience with multiple cultures and their spirituality. For more information, please e-mail him at spirit@divine humanity.com or visit any of his websites:

www.divinehumanity.com
www.revolutioninreligion.com
www.spartanwarriorphilosophers.com

NOTES

1. John 8:32 (New International Version).

2. In October of 1993, my wife, Sherry, and I conducted a spiritual journey to the Big Island of Hawaii. To begin the journey, we conducted a spiritual, or religious, ceremony called a burning or feeding the spirits of the ancestors. We performed the ceremony the day before my vision at dusk. In the predawn hours, less than twelve hours later, I experienced the divine call both as something heard and something seen—in the form of a vision and a voice. "This star is you; you are this star. The purification is of the people; all are one." This star was Venus, the morning star.

   The next morning at the Big Island's White Sand Beach, my native Hawaiian healer friend gave me a message from one of his ancestors who came to him during the burning. "My ancestor brought me a message…but it's for you. My ancestor said that you are a *kahuna po'o* (high priest)…you are a prophet bringing back 'first knowledge'—the lost knowledge and sacred teachings that have been misunderstood, forgotten, and corrupted. You have a message, path, and way to share with this world, but do not identify it as being from these islands or other lands. This only separates people and does not unite them. Name it whatever you like. Don't get discouraged with the resistance you will face; it's your destiny."

   The name I chose was Divine Humanity. Briefly, all things are divine with the spark—the starlight of God, the Great Mystery, the All—within them. In other words, the divine is within all things (seen and unseen), and all things are within the divine. This is radical nonduality or oneness, where spirit and matter, the absolute and relative, interpenetrate. One important aspect—there is no original sin, only original divinity.

   The oneness of interpenetrative radical nonduality sees a reality where there is no separation between mind and body, dark and light, or spirit and matter. The most profound and essential nature of things is not distinct from the things recognizable by our senses. In other words, our sacred selves and our profane selves are nondual and interpenetrate;

likewise, all other sentient beings' (things') sacred identities and profane identities are nondual and interpenetrate. This is true oneness.

Divine Humanity believes that each and every person has an immortal spark within him or her—an indestructible seed of divine light—the divine immanence. This indestructible seed of divine light may be likened to a mustard seed within our hearts.

3. http://www.primordialtraditions.net/.

4. G. Philippe Menos and Karen A. Jones Menos, *Revelation and Inspiration: Paranormal Phenomena in Light of the Kundalini Paradigm* (May 21–23, 1989): 3.

5. Marcus J. Borg, *Jesus: A New Vision*, 35.
6. *Henry R. Percival*, "Documents from the First Council of Nicea [the First Ecumenical Council], AD 325," http://www.fordham.edu/halsall/basis/nicea1.txt.

7. Paraphrased, Terry Brooks, *Sword of Shannara*, 494.

8. When I use the term church, I am referring to the total denominations of Christianity, not just the Catholics but all followers, including the Mormons.

9. "Our wealth has become so skewed that the top 1 percent possesses a greater collective worth than the entire bottom 90 percent, according to the Economic Policy Institute in Washington...Scholars from Harvard Business School and Duke University asked Americans which country they would rather live in—one with America's wealth distribution or one with Sweden's. But they weren't labeled Sweden and America. It turned out that more than 90 percent of Americans preferred to live in a country with the Swedish distribution...Not only do we aspire to live in Sweden, but we think we already do" (Nicholas D. Kristof, *Seattle Times*, October 6, 2012, A11).

10. John Hogue, *The Millennium Book of Prophecy*, 254–255.

11. http://www.wordreference.com/definition/revolution.

12. Richard Andrews and Paul Schellenberger, *The Tomb of God*, 398.

13. Ibid., 398–399.

14. Elizabeth Van Buren, *Refuge of the Apocalypse: Doorway into Other Dimensions*, 206.

15. My wife and I; sometimes the magical occurrences have happened in the presence of our two children.

16. Uranus (divine rebel with a pioneer spirit and consciousness and the qualities of freedom, independence, and rebellion) is the planet of my message and tied to my destiny.

17. Owls are spirit messengers representing prophecy, magic, and silence. The snowy owl has some extra, unique gifts, as it inhabits the realm of day. It has a special connection with the north direction (the same direction of the visitation). Finally, the "snowy owl carries messages from the elders, and people with this bird as a totem will channel this wisdom in some way for the benefit of the world, usually in the form of the written word" (Lesly Morrison, *The Healing Wisdom of Birds*, 108).

18. Ignatius Singer, *The Rival Philosophies of Jesus and of Paul*, 312–313.

19. Richard Andrews and Paul Schellenberger, *The Tomb of God*, 398.

20. John Hogue, *The Millennium Book of Prophecy*, 254–255.

21. John Davidson, *The Gospel of Jesus*, 124.

22. Adam McLean, *At the Table of the Grail*, 50–51.

23. Ibid, 51

24. Ibid.

25. William E. Phipps, *Muhammad and Jesus*, 135

26. Douglas Lockhart, *Jesus the Heretic*, 169.

27. Please use common sense. There are eight billion galaxies or more. Within each, there are an unknown number, probably billions, of stars. This is known creation. The earth sits in the corner of one of these galaxies—the Milky Way. It is the height of folly and arrogance to suppose that any human being or religious institution would have intimate knowledge and be able to identify the creator of our known universe within its concrete of dogma.

In fact, the dogmatic issue of "my god versus your god" has caused an unknown amount of suffering and bloodshed over the millennia. For just one example, "In 782 Charlemagne massacred 4,500 prisoners while others were enslaved or deported. Charlemagne destroyed pagan places of worship and decreed the death penalty for those who refused to be baptized or kept the pagan faith" (http://bio.sunyorange.edu/updated2/creationism/bad%20religion/3_forced_conversion.htm).

I acknowledge that the Creator, the Unknown and the Uncreated, cannot be identified or imagined in human terms, just in absolute terms, as it is the greatest mystery of all mysteries. I use the term God when referring to the Absolute, the All.

However, I am not referring to the concept of the Christian God—the Father, the Son, and the Holy Ghost—but to the Creator, the greatest Mystery of Mysteries, the Divine, the All, the Absolute, the Concealed and the Revealed, which is both immanent and transcendent and beyond human comprehension.

Thus, God, the One and Oneness of all, the Mystery of Mysteries, which is within us and outside of us, transcends our abilities even as divine human beings to comprehend the essence of what is the greatest mystery of all. God surpasses our dualistic view of reality and is neither male nor female but is the mystery of all that there is. God is love, not fear, both immanent and transcendent.

28. Douglas Lockhart, *Jesus the Heretic*, 9.

29. *Alaha* is Aramaic for God. Even though I would prefer to use the Aramaic name *Alaha* for numerous reasons, one being that it implies sacred unity or oneness, it may cause confusion, as it is similar to the Arabic Allah. Thus, throughout this book, I use the term God with the understanding that I am referring to *Alaha*—the Great Mystery, the Divine, the All, the Uncreated and the Created, the Concealed and the Revealed—please see the appendix.

30. Douglas Lockhart, *Jesus the Heretic*, 12.

31. This is God's natural, altruistic law: "I will put my law within them, and I will write it on their hearts" (*The HarperCollins Study Bible*, Jeremiah 31:33, 1174).

32. Fundamental awakening is "a way of collapsing the distance between mind and enlightened mind, and thus, abolishing the dualism that is itself the stuff of delusion." (Bernard Faure, *Visions of Power*, 16.)

33. I utilize the term pagan to emphasize Jesus's teachings connected with nature and conducted out in nature in rural Galilee and not within a temple, as well as his opposition to the Orthodox Judaism of his time. It is important to understand the meaning of paganism. "The term 'paganism' was revived during the Renaissance when writers were trying to differentiate the old traditions from their contemporary Christian faith. The term itself stems from the Latin paganus translated loosely along the lines of 'country dweller' or 'rustic'; thus it was initially a word describing a person of locality rather than a religion" (Ryan Stone, "The True Meaning of Paganism," November 9, 2014, http://www.ancient-origins.net/myths-legends/true-meaning-paganism-002306).

34. Marcus J. Borg, *Jesus: A New Vision*, 40.

35. H. P. Blavatsky, *Isis Unveiled*, 132.

36. Lynn Picknett and Clive Prince, *The Templar Revelation*, 295.

37. Ibid., 363.

38. Ibid., 287.

39. H. P. Blavatsky, *Isis Unveiled*, 150.

40. In 2009, the Catholic Church in Brazil came under fire for punishing an underaged girl who was raped and subsequently had an abortion. The Church couldn't excommunicate the girl herself because minors cannot be excommunicated, but the Church did excommunicate her mother. The Church also excommunicated the doctors who performed the emergency abortion. However, they did not excommunicate the girl's rapist.

In fact, the Catholic Church opposes abortion so vehemently that not only is it worthy of excommunication; the Church believes it's worthy of death in some cases. The Catholic Church has previously established that it would rather have a woman die than get a life-saving abortion. (Nathan Wold, "10 Secrets The Catholic Church Hopes You've Forgotten," March 10, 2015, http://listverse.com/2015/03/10/10-secrets-the-catholic-church-hopes-youve-forgotten/)

41. Matthew 23:27–28 (New International Version).

42. The original meaning of the Greek word was stage actors. In other words, a hypocrite is an actor on the stage of life. They are the ones that wear masks and are not authentic, which means what you see and hear is not necessarily what you will get. Some believe that in his incarnation, Jesus will be seen to possess a divine body. This is not true. Jesus will be in your presence, and you will not know it except that you will know that there is something different, unique, and enigmatic about

this person. Additionally, Mary the Magdalene will incarnate and be his partner (wife) once again. You will not know that you are in her presence except that there will be something different, unique, and enigmatic about her. Both will be connected with otherworldly signs and events that reveal their past incarnations.

43. A glaring view of church hypocrisy was publically aired when one of the princes of the church, Cardinal Keith O'Brien, the most senior Roman Catholic cleric in Britain and a condemner of homosexuality, admitted "that he had engaged in inappropriate sexual conduct after three priests and a former priest accused him of making improper advances decades ago" (Daniel J. Wakin, *New York Times* and *Seattle Times,* March 5, 2013, A4).

44. John Zarocostas, *Seattle Times*, February 6, 2014, A5.

45. Morton Smith, *Jesus the Magician*, 175.

46. Being a foundation does not negate the hoarding of wealth.

47. Ignatius Singer, *The Rival Philosophies of Jesus and of Paul*, 283.

48. The man responsible for the Vatican's finances says he has found millions of euros "tucked away" off balance sheets (December 4, 2014, http://www.bbc.com/news/world-europe-30339699).

49. Andreas Wassermann and Peter Wensierski, "Transparency vs. Money Laundering: Catholic Church Fears Growing Vatican Bank Scandal," http://www.spiegel.de/international/europe/a-growing-vatican-bank-scandal-threatens-catholic-church-image-a-842140-2.html.

50. Beware and be aware of the illusionary Pope Francis. The elite of the church knew they needed to take the focus off of the various scandals, so Pope Benedict stepped down, supposedly due to a message from God. Of course, the church elite consider themselves God. The dogma and doctrine are the same, just the message that the church cares about the poor,

and others, is illusionary. The dogma and doctrine will not change. And he is a Jesuit—just research their history.

51. The care she gave to the sick and poor in her hospices was observed to be wholly unsanitary, medical care was wholly insufficient, and crucial pain management for the dying was cruelly inadequate. Her hospices were found to not even distinguish between terminally ill patients and those who could be cured. Consequently, patients with curable illness died from the poor, unsanitary treatment they received from Mother Teresa's facilities.

Her motivation for setting these hospices may have been less compassion and more fundamentalism. Mother Teresa callously encouraged those who worked in her hospices to baptize dying patients, regardless of the patient's religious beliefs or consent. Mother Teresa's fundamentalism stretched beyond the subject of baptism. She claimed that abortion was "the greatest enemy of peace in the world," and opposed contraception even in the cases of rape and incest.

Mother Teresa also defended a pedophilic priest named Donald McGuire, trying to get him leniency after he was convicted of raping children. She wanted him to be reinstated as a priest despite his heinous crimes.
(Nathan Wold, "10 Secrets The Catholic Church Hopes You've Forgotten," March 10, 2015, http://listverse.com/2015/03/10/10-secrets-the-catholic-church-hopes-youve-forgotten/)

52. *Seattle Times* and *Newsline*, May 24, 2014, A2.

53. Maya Rhodan, June 2, 2014, http://time.com/2814527/pope-francis-dogs-cats-pets/.

54. http://en.wikipedia.org/wiki/Pope_Francis.

55. Junipero Serra sainthood: Native Americans protest at Carmel Mission cemetery on Easter Sunday – As Catholics celebrated Easter Sunday Mass in the packed Carmel Mission, nearly 200 Native Americans crowded into

the nearby cemetery to honor their ancestors buried there and to protest the impending sainthood of Junipero Serra, the friar who forced them into servitude.

The thick adobe walls of the mission separated the two cultures Sunday afternoon — as did the security guards stationed at the cemetery gate hired by the church to keep the peace. But their music strangely mingled: the church organ with the tribal drums, the "Alleluia" hymns with the native chants.

It was the first major protest of Native Americans since January. That's when Pope Francis announced that Serra, who founded California's string of missions in the 1700s and 1800s and is buried under the Carmel Mission altar, would be canonized in September in Washington, D.C. The pope praised him as the "evangelizer of the West," who converted thousands of natives to Catholicism and considered the landmark Carmel Mission his headquarters.

Many Native Americans consider Serra a "monster" who condoned the brutalization of their people, stripping them of their religion and languages, dragging them from their villages to work at the missions and punishing those who tried to flee.

"The truth needs to be told," said Laughing Coyote, a member of the Mono tribe in Fresno County who traveled to the mission for the rally. "For the pope to accord sainthood is such an obscene gesture on the part of the Catholic Church." (Julia Prodis Sulek, Junipero Serra sainthood: Native Americans protest at Carmel Mission cemetery on Easter Sunday, 04/05/15, http://www.santacruzsentinel.com/general-news/20150405/junipero-serra-sainthood-native-americans-protest-at-carmel-mission-cemetery-on-easter-sunday/2)

56. A lawsuit that is scheduled for trial later this year (2014) claims eleven Catholic nuns sexually abused ninety-five children at day schools and residential schools run by the Ursuline Sisters of the Western Province. The suit was filed in 2011 in Lewis and Clark County in Montana. Not

only does the lawsuit list 95 plaintiffs; it also includes placeholders for as many as 105 potential victims.

The trial is expected to begin on December 1, which is when the plaintiffs' attorneys will start trying to prove the eleven accused, who served at St Ignatius Mission School from the 1940s through the 1970s, abused students belonging to the Flathead Indian Reservation, emotionally, physically, and even sexually.

"It affected a whole generation of Native American kids," said Vito de la Cruz an attorney for the plaintiffs (Debapriya Chatterjee, "Lawsuit Against 11 Nuns Who Sexually Abused At Least 95 Children," October 23, 2014, http://www.atheistrepublic.com/news/lawsuit-against-11-nuns-who-sexually-abused-least-95-children).

57. Ignatius Singer, *The Rival Philosophies of Jesus and of Paul*, 288–289.

58. Dualism: In theology, the concept that the world is controlled by two opposing forces (i.e., good and bad, God and Satan). In philosophy, the idea that the world consists of two main components: thought and matter (http://www.spiritrestoration.org/Theological_Terms/Calvinism_to_Dualism.htm).

Philosophical belief that reality is essentially divided into two distinct kinds of stuff. Typically mind and body or the related pair, spirit and matter. One concept in each pair is often deemed superior to the other (http://www.thegreenfuse.org/glossary.htm).

A form of binary thinking that divides the world into good versus evil with no middle ground tolerated (http://www.publiceye.org/glossary/glossary_big.html).

Simplistic concept that all issues can be divided into either-or states such as good and bad, right and wrong, determinable and indeterminable (http://www.businessdictionary.com/definition/dualism.html).

The three major Western religions, Judaism, Christianity, and Islam, are based on the separation philosophy of dualism, with Christianity emphasizing the dualism represented by God and Satan, good versus evil.

59. John 10:30 (International Standard Version).

60. Kingdom does not imply or mean patriarchal. King is synonymous with queen. The usual analogy for the Divine is recognizable as operating on a vertical plane (an energetic norm descending or ascending) and male, even though the Divine, the All, the Absolute is neither male nor female. Thus, for convenience's sake and a terminology that most people will recognize, I use the term kingdom with the understanding that it is not patriarchal or one of male imagery. Its imagery may be considered stellar, as it is not one, solar (patriarchal), or the other, lunar (matriarchal), but both blended together as the seen and unseen universal cosmos.

61. This poem is dedicated to the wounded raven that hobbled by my window one wintry afternoon (Rev. Dr. J. C. Husfelt, 2002).

62. William G. Dever, *Did God Have a Wife? Archaeology and Folk Religion in Ancient Israel*, 159.

63. Even though the culture might have been steeped in orally transmitted knowledge where memorization of the spoken word was better in preliterate (oral) cultures rather than in written cultures, there is still room for error, and the reality that it is filtered through the beliefs, assumptions, expectations, and ego of the person transmitting the knowledge.

64. Harold Bloom, *Jesus and Yahweh*, 26–27.

65. Ibid 29.

66. http://changingminds.org/techniques/language/metaphor/metaphor_ definition.htm.

67. Shelley M. White, "Heart Based Consciousness: Using The Heart As An Organ Of Perception," April 10, 2015 (http://www. collective-evolution.com/2015/04/10/heart-based-consciousness-using-the-heart-as-an-organ-of-perception/)

68. More recently, it was discovered that the heart also secretes oxytocin, commonly referred to as the 'love' or bonding hormone. (http://www. healthwithconfidence.com/heart-hormones.html)

69. "There are many factors that go into a translation which are invisible and unknown to the reader of a translation. Most Bible readers assume that the English translation of the Bible is an equivalent representation of the original text. Because of the vast difference between the ancient Hebrews' language and our own, as well as the differences in the two cultures, an exact translation is impossible. The difficult job of the translator is to bridge the gap between the languages and cultures. Since the Hebrew text can be translated many different ways, the translator's personal beliefs will often dictate how the text will be translated.

"A translation of the Biblical text is a translator's interpretation of the original text based on his own theology and doctrine. The reader is then forced to use the translators understanding of the text as his foundation for the text. For this reason, readers will often compare translations, but are usually limited to Christian translations. I always recommend including a 'Jewish' translation when comparing texts, as this will give a translation from a different perspective. Yes, it will be biased toward the Jewish faith, but Christian translations are biased toward the Christian faith as well. A comparison of the two translations can help to discover the bias of each.

"To demonstrate how a Translator's interpretation of a text can influence the readers understanding of the text, let us examine two passages from the New International Version. 'Let the land produce living creatures' Genesis 1:24 'and the man became a living being' Genesis 2:7. From these passages the reader could conclude that animals are classified as 'creatures' and humans as 'beings' (The KJV uses the word 'soul' here). When the Hebrew text is uncovered, we find that the above 'interpretation' would never have occurred as we find that the phrase 'living creature' in the first verse and the phrase 'living being' in the second verse are two different translations of the same Hebrew phrase 'nephesh chayah'. Because of the translator's opinion that there is a difference between men and animals, the translation of these verses reflects the translator's opinions. The reader, not knowing the Hebrew background to the passages, is forced to base his interpretation on the translator's personal opinion" (excerpted from Jeff A. Benner's *His Name Is One: An Ancient Hebrew Perspective of the Names of…God*).

70. The decline in biblical literacy alarms clergy and the most devoted lay people. After all, how can people receive—and spread—the "good news" if they don't know it well themselves? "This is a very serious issue," said the Rev. Michael Bryant, dean of the Charleston Southern University's School of Christian Studies. "We have entered a new age that truly is post-Christian or anti-Christian" (Jennifer Berry Hawes, "Studies Show Many Americans Not Reading the Bible, Lack Basic Knowledge," November 1, 2014, http://www.postandcourier.com/article/20141101/PC1204/141109965/1177/studies-show-many-americans-not-reading-the-bible-lack-basic-knowledge).

71. Kurt Eichenwald, "The Bible: So Misunderstood It's a Sin," December 23, 2014, http://www.newsweek.com/2015/01/02/thats-not-what-bible-says-294018.html.

72. Ibid.

73. Ibid.

74. Ibid.

75. Ibid.

76. Ibid.

77. Marcus J. Borg, *Jesus: A New Vision*, 98.

78. Edmond Bordeaux Szekely, *The Essene Gospel of Peace*, 13.

79. Harold Bloom, *Jesus and Yahweh*, 50.

80. *The HarperCollins Study Bible*, Genesis 1:1–5, 6.

81. Jeff A. Benner, "Mechanical Translation of Genesis," http://www.ancient-hebrew.org/index.html.

82. Douglas Lockhart, *Jesus the Heretic*, 35–36.

83. Charisma may be either of two types. Where this term is fully served, charisma is a gift that inheres in an object or person simply by natural endowment. Such primary charisma cannot be acquired by any means. But charisma of the other type may be produced artificially in an object or person through some extraordinary means. Even then, it is assumed that charismatic capability can be developed only in which the germ already existed but would have remained dormant unless "awakened" by some ascetic or other means (http://www.e-reading.link/bookreader.php/145149/The_Sociology_of_Religion.pdf, 2).

84. http://www.e-reading.link/bookreader.php/145149/The_Sociology_of_Religion.pdf, 37.

85. Ibid., 37.

86. Marcus J. Borg, *Jesus: A New Vision*, 35.

87. Philo means loving; Sophia means wisdom. Philosopher is a lover of wisdom. Sophia is known as the goddess of wisdom and fate, black goddess, divine feminine, and the grail goddess.

88. The most well-known sacrifice of self to self was the Norse-Germanic all-father Ódhinn, who hung on the world tree, Yggdrasill, for nine days and nine nights.

89. Three submersions was the standard during Jesus' time; instead of three I was taught to do four.

90. Gershon Winkler, *Magic of the Ordinary*, 22.

91. Harold Bloom, *Jesus and Yahweh*, back cover.

92. "Our new account of the origins of Christianity only seemed improbable because it contradicted the received view. As we pushed further with our research, the traditional picture began to completely unravel all around us. We found ourselves embroiled in a world of schism and power straggles, of forged documents and false identities, of letters that had been edited and added to, and of the wholesale destruction of historical evidence. We focused forensically on the few facts we could be confident of, as if we were detectives on the verge of cracking a sensational 'whodunit', or perhaps more accurately as if we were uncovering an ancient and unacknowledged miscarriage of justice. For, time and again, when we critically examined what genuine evidence remained, we found that the history of Christianity bequeathed to us by the Roman Church was a gross distortion of the truth.

"One of the major players in this cover-up operation was a character called Eusebius, who, at the beginning of the fourth century, compiled from legends, fabrications and his own imagination the only early history of Christianity that still exists today. All subsequent histories have been forced to base themselves on Eusebins' dubious claims, because there has been little other information to draw on. All those with a different perspective on Christianity were branded as heretics and eradicated. In this way falsehoods compiled in the fourth century have come down to us as established facts.

"Eusebius was employed by the Roman Emperor Constantine, who made Christianity the state religion of the Empire and gave Literalist Christianity the power it needed to begin the final eradication of Paganism and Gnosticism. Constantine wanted 'one God, one religion' to consolidate his claim of 'one Empire, one Emperor.' He oversaw the creation of the Nicene creed—the article of faith repeated in churches to this day—and Christians who refused to assent to this creed were banished from the Empire or otherwise silenced.

"This 'Christian' Emperor then returned home from Nicaea and had his wife suffocated and his son murdered. He deliberately remained unbaptized until his deathbed so that he could continue his atrocities and still receive forgiveness of sins and a guaranteed place in heaven by being baptized at the last moment. Although he had his 'spin doctor' Eusebius compose a suitably obsequious biography for him, he was actually a monster—just like many Roman Emperors before him. Is it really at all surprising that a 'history' of the origins of Christianity created by an employee in the service of a Roman tyrant should turn out to be a pack of lies?" (Timothy Freke and Peter Gandy, http://www.pufoin.com/pufoin_perspective/jesus_mysteries.php).

93. HRH Prince Michael of Albany and Walid Amine Salhab, *The Knights Templar of the Middle East*, 4.

94. Michael Baigent, *The Jesus Papers*, 269–270.

95. Ignatius Singer, *The Rival Philosophies of Jesus and of Paul*, 14.

96. http://www.aspenchapel.org/sermon8-3-03.html.

97. http://www.allaboutarchaeology.org/.

98. From the *Kerygmata Petrou*, which originates from the Ebionites. In this account, the father of Christianity is described as "an apostate of the Law," the "spouter of lies," and "the distorter of the true teachings of Jesus." The events that occurred on the road to Damascus that resulted in Paul's "miraculous" conversion are given very short shrift, and are simply described as "dreams and illusions inspired by devils" (Marilyn Hopkins, Graham Simmans, and Tim Wallace-Murphy, *Rex Deus*, 71).

99. Ignatius Singer, *The Rival Philosophies of Jesus and of Paul*, 71–72.

100. Christopher Knight and Robert Lomas, *The Hiram Key*, 253.

101. All things in creation have consciousness. For example, trees have consciousness. This consciousness is of a oneness of existence; there is no separation. Thus, there is no need for awakening. However, human beings have a consciousness that views things dualistically, with an

egocentric self that only sees separatism. The divine spark represents the consciousness of unity or oneness. Thus, there is the need in humans to awaken it. This then awakens us out of our sleepwalking state of separateness into an awakened state of oneness. And as in all other things of creation, the awakening in humans is a gradual process that may eventually result in enlightenment, even though one will still have human frailties.

102. Douglas Lockhart, *Jesus the Heretic*, 44.

103. Dwight Goddard, *Was Jesus influenced by Buddhism?*, 198.

104. Colin Wilson and Rand Flem-Ath, *The Atlantis Blueprint*, 266–267.

105. Ibid., 267.

106. Ibid., 267.

107. Michael Baigent, *The Jesus Papers*, 38.

108. Michael Baigent, Richard Leigh, and Henry Lincoln, *Holy Blood Holy Grail*, 327.

109. "And Moses took the anointing oil, and anointed the tabernacle and all that [was] therein, and sanctified them" (Leviticus 8:10). Sanctification: "the procedure for making a person, place, or thing sacred" (Jonathan Z. Smith, *The HarperCollins Dictionary of Religion*, 957). Anointing equals sanctification equals sacred equals divine.

110. Margaret Starbird, *The Woman with the Alabaster Jar*, 36.

111. Laurence Gardner, *Bloodline of the Holy Grail*, 118.

112. Universal Mother Goddess.

113. David Fideler, *Jesus Christ Sun of God*, 171.

114. Ibid.

115. Elizabeth Van Buren, *Refuge of the Apocalypse*, 206.

116. This is a very rare occurrence where a spirit descends into a human, and he or she experiences the interpenetration of spirit and matter, the absolute and relative of creation—true oneness.

117. Jonathan Z. Smith, *The HarperCollins Dictionary of Religion*, 954.

118. Michael Baigent, *The Jesus Papers*, 84.

119. Ibid., 239.

120. Ibid., 239–240.

121. Jonathan Z. Smith, *The HarperCollins Dictionary of Religion*, 957.

122. Marilyn Hopkins, Graham Simmans, and Tim Wallace-Murphy, *Rex Deus*, 212.

123. "Nothing is older than water as an element of life and there is nothing more initial than its influence on the mind of man as an agent of destruction, of death, of an ending, the water of death being the natural antithesis to the breath of life.

"Water and Breath, in which baptismal regeneration finds its origin, are a symbolical representation of 'from out of the water into a new life,' or rebirth" (E. Valentia Straiton, *The Celestial Ship of the North*, 153).

124. Michael Baigent, *The Jesus Papers*, 214.

125. Since the nineteenth century, "important concepts of life were brought to the field of physiology such as homeostasis by Walter Cannon…Dr. Canon realized the importance of balance between acid and alkaline in the body

fluids, especially in the blood...An acidic condition inhibits nerve action and an alkaline condition stimulates nerve action. One who has an alkaline blood condition can think and act (decide) well. On the other hand, one who has an acidic blood condition cannot think well or act quickly, clearly, or decisively...For a long time I searched for a quick way to change an acidic to an alkaline condition. Finally, I found one through religious rituals. Japanese Shinto religion strongly recommends performing the *misogi* ritual, in which one takes a cold water bath or shower in a river, waterfall, or the ocean" (Herman Aihara, *Acid and Alkaline*, 1 and 109).

126. Jonathan Z. Smith, *The HarperCollins Dictionary of Religion*, 941.

127. H. P. Blavatsky, *Isis Unveiled*, 134.

128. Ibid., 135–136.

129. Marcus J. Borg, *Jesus: A New Vision*, 113.

130. James D. Tabor, *The Jesus Dynasty*, 149.

131. "The term *mikveh* in Hebrew literally means any gathering of waters, but is specifically used in Jewish law for the waters or bath for the ritual immersion. Ancient sages teach that the word mikveh has the same letters as Ko(v)Meh, the Hebrew word for 'rising' or 'standing tall,' therefore we see the idea of being baptized 'straightway.'

"The Essenes were anciently known as regular practicioners [*sic*] of daily immersion. In the Talmud these daily Mikveh practicioners [*sic*] are called tovelei shaharit or 'dawn bathers.' Not only Nasaraens, but several other Jewish groups observed ritual immersion every day to assure readiness for the coming of the Messiah. Epiphanius mentioned one of these groups called Hemerobaptists which means 'daily bathers' in Greek. The Clementine Homilees, or Recognitions of Clement, tell us that Peter always washed, often in the sea, before dawn which was no doubt a custom of all Nazarenes of his time...

"Ancient dawn bathing Nasaraens used at least three forms of Baptism, or mikveh purifications. We know this because the surviving remnants of these Nasaraens, the Nasorai sect (Mandeans), still preserve these forms of this ancient Nasarene purification rite once practiced and promoted by Yeshu (Jesus) and His messianic Spouse Maria…

"The Jewish baptism candidates were often immersed three times. The idea of total immersion comes from the Scripture in Leviticus 15:16 when it says, 'he shall wash all his flesh in the water.' One reason it was customary to immerse three times was because the word mikveh occurs three times in the Torah. We know this to have been an early Nazarene practice under Yeshu-Maria" (http://essenes.net/Mikveh.htm).

132. Bruce Chilton, *Rabbi Jesus*, 45.

133. Ibid.

134. Ibid.

135. Ibid., 48.

136. Mark 1:10.

137. My first physical experience of interpenetrative nonduality, the oneness of spirit and matter, occurred on a sacred mountain in Japan, Koyasan, at midnight in 1987 in front of the mausoleum of Kobo Daishi, the founder of Shingon Esoteric Buddhism. The story is told in my unpublished manuscript *Tequila and Chocolate*.

138. "The morning star went into Kobo Daishi's mouth" (Caption in Koyasan Museum).

139. Mark 1:12–13 (King James Version).

140. Jesus the Nazarene was the leader of a community of the "Way," and this was much like the "Way of the Wilderness" followed by the disparate Essene

groups as listed by Eisenman in his 1983 study of Maccabees, Zadokites, Christians, and Qumran (Douglas Lockhart, *Jesus the Heretic*, 62).

141. Gary P. Caton, "Astrology as if the Sky Matters: Venus Retrograde," May 14, 2012, http://mountainastrologer.com/tma/astrology-as-if-the-sky-matters-venus-retrograde.

142. http://www.bluecloud.org.

143. Christopher Knight and Robert Lomas, *The Book of Hiram*, 84.

144. Each letter in the Hebrew alphabet (or aleph-bet) has a numerical value. The first ten letters (consonants actually) have the values one to ten. The next nine letters are valued twenty, thirty...one hundred. The remainder are valued two hundred, three hundred, and four hundred. There is no representation for zero (http://www.i18nguy.com/unicode/hebrew-numbers.html).

145. According to Jeff A. Benner, http://www.hebrew-translation.org/hebrew-translation-locations/a-history-of-hebrew-part-12-the-alphabet-and-language-connection.

146. Rene Guenon, *Fundamental Symbols*, 110.

147. Ibid., 110–111.

148. The tarot is a system of symbolic cards possibly dating from the time of ancient Egypt. The cards are divided into Major and Minor Arcana. The word *arcana* has the meaning of hidden, secret, or mysterious.

149. Most people know this card as Temperance.

150. Sallie Nichols, *Angels and Mortals*, 198.

151. James D. Tabor, *The Jesus Dynasty*, 149.

152. The only time that Christians seem to do any ceremony or ritual before dawn is once a year at Easter. Even Peter, the supposed "rock" that Christianity is built on, supposedly practiced predawn ocean bathings.

153. Mark 1:10.

154. "Neanderthals were using red paint up to 250,000 years ago—far earlier than previously thought. Traces of the paint, made from ochre, were dug up in the Netherlands and dated to a quarter of a million years ago" (Ted Thornhill, http://www.dailymail.co.uk/sciencetech/article-2090718/Neanderthals-using-paint-250-000-years-ago—thousands-years-earlier-previously-thought.html).

155. http://www.thenazareneway.com/nazarene_or_nazareth.htm.

156. John Davidson, *The Gospel of Jesus*, 135.

157. http://wisdomintorah.com/bbpress/topic/ongoing-study-of-nazir-nazarite.

158. Kelly Washburn, http://tzvialane.blogspot.com/2010/02/kadoshsacred-nessserial.html.

159. Lynn Picknett and Clive Prince, *The Templar Revelation*, 276.

160. Ibid., 242.

161. Esoteric means "the 'inner' (eso-), in the sense of the inner consciousness; the contemplative, mystical or meditative transpersonal perspective. This is something different from the ordinary everyday understanding of things, and can only be understood by intuition or higher mental or spiritual faculties...

"Central to the distinction between Esoteric and Exoteric is that of states of consciousness. An Exoteric philosophy or religion as one which is based on the normal waking state of consciousness, or a modified state of consciousness which is still pretty close to the normal waking state. Any aspiration beyond the ordinary state of existence is discouraged. For example, according to the religious person, 'God created/loves you just as you are', so who are you to question what God has ordained for you by striving for some higher state of consciousness? While according to the skeptical Materialist, there is no higher state beyond the rational mind anyway (all non-rational states of consciousness being delusionary)" (http://www.kheper.net/topics/esoteric_and_exoteric.htm).

162. "For among Judeans there are three forms of philosophy. Now Pharisees are one sect, Sadducees another, but in fact the third, called Essenes, seems to be the most reverential discipline.—Josephus, Jewish War 2.119" (http://virtualreligion.net/iho/pharisee.html#sects).

163. Cult comes from culture and basically refers to a group of people with similar beliefs. With this definition, within the legal system, the bar association would be considered a cult.

164. Gnosis—knowledge; Gnostics—seekers of knowledge.

165. H. P. Blavatsky, *Isis Unveiled*, 127.

166. Ibid., 132.

167. Practitioners of magic.

168. H. P. Blavatsky, *Isis Unveiled*, 128.

169. A rule of Essene theology was "vegetarianism."

170. Philip Gardiner, *The Serpent Grail*, 96.

171. H. P. Blavatsky, *Isis Unveiled*, 132.

172. "Codex Nazaraeus or the Book of Adam (i.e., of man or humanity); the chief sacred scripture of the Nazarites and of the Mandaeans or Nasoraeans;

written in a Chaldeo-Syrian dialect mixed with the mystery language of the Gnostics" (http://www.babylon.com/definition/Codex_Nazaraeus/English).

173. Hermes (Mercury). Virgo is ruled by Mercury.

174. H. P. Blavatsky, *Isis Unveiled*, 132.

175. Ibid., 133.

176. Ibid., 561.

177. Gerald Massey, *Egyptian Book of the Dead and the Mysteries of Amenta*, 89.

178. Joseph Campbell, *The Hero with a Thousand Faces*, 319.

179. Ibid., 319–320.

180. Edouard Schure, *From Sphinx to Christ*, 272–273.

181. Despite the widespread, uncritical adulation of Paul by those who listen to others instead of thinking for themselves, independent-minded analysts of Jesus's teachings have often found great cause to find fault with Paul. One of the most famous criticisms comes from Thomas Jefferson, who wrote in a letter to James Smith, that "Paul was...the first corrupter of the doctrines of Jesus" (Works, 1829 edition, vol. 4, 327). George Bernard Shaw, the English playwright, is widely quoted as having said that "it would have been a better world if Paul had never been born" (http://www.wordwiz72.com/paul.html).

182. Security is one of the prime foundations of a person's ego. A faith-based person has an unhealthy ego where life is only seen through the prism of one's own personal safety and security and the arrogance that comes from being in the exclusive "club of Christianity," where wealth and external power are worshipped.

183. Douglas Lockhart, *Jesus the Heretic*, 261.

184. Ibid., 260.

185. William E. Phipps, *Muhammad and Jesus*, 224.

186. Bruce Chilton, *Rabbi Jesus*, 164.

187. Merkavah practice is, in the most precise sense, truly mystical (Arthur Green, *Keter: The Crown of God in Early Jewish Mysticism*, 40).

188. The immediate response that may pass through a person's mind to the religious philosophical principle of original divinity, that we are born with a divine, indestructible seed of light instead of original sin, takes the form of a question: "Why then do humans make war, kill, rape, and fly planes into buildings?"

    The short answer is that the divine spark or seed has not been awakened. Therefore, natural law has not been awakened within the person. Natural law is based on a belief in the inherent, natural, altruistic law of God that is found within each person. This natural law flows from the divinity within each individual but lies dormant until awakened by each person.

189. Jacques Duquesne, *Jesus, An Unconventional Biography*, 86.

190. Ignatius Singer, *The Rival Philosophies of Jesus and of Paul*, 313–314.

191. Judaism does not believe in the existence of original sin. "Saint Augustine (354–430) was the first theologian to teach that man is born into this world in a state of sin...Jews believe that man enters the world free of sin, with a soul that is pure and innocent and untainted" (http://www.jewishvirtuallibrary.org/jsource/Judaism/Original_Sin.html).

    "The basic tenets of Christian soteriology may be summarized as follows: humanity deserves damnation by God for the original sin, which it inherits by descent from Adam; each human also deserves damnation for his own actual sin. But because sin is regarded as also putting humans in the power of the Devil, Christ's work of salvation has been interpreted along two different lines. Thus, his crucifixion may be evaluated as a vicarious sacrifice offered to God as propitiation or atonement for human sin. Alternatively, it may be seen as the price paid to redeem humanity from the Devil. These two ways of interpreting the death of Christ have provided the major themes of soteriological theory and speculation in Christian theology. Despite this fluidity of interpretation, belief in the saving power of Christ is fundamental to Christianity and finds expression in every aspect of its faith and practice" (http://www.whatjewsbelieve.org/explanation5.html).

192. Gerald Massey, *Ancient Egypt*, 162.

193. Liz Greene, *The Astrological Neptune and the Quest for Redemption*, 41.

194. Ibid., 66.

195. Jim Walker, "Hitler's Religious Beliefs and Fanaticism," http://www.no-beliefs.com/hitler.htm.

196. You might be surprised that I am using knowledge from a Christian minster. Two points—first, as often happens in today's world, the person in the trenches, such as the voice on the phone that you are complaining to about some injustice connected with his or her company, or ministers, priests, imams, rabbis, and so forth, are only representatives of the institutions— many times they are not at fault. Let's not make them the devil. The devil and the fault are to be found in the greed-filled, materialistic paradigms and through the hierarchal leaders of institutionalized religion and capitalism.

197. http://www.aspenchapel.org/sermon8-3-03.html.

198. B. P. Grenfell and A. S. Hunt, *New Sayings of Jesus and Fragment of a Lost Gospel from Oxyrhynchus* (London, 1904); Oxy, 654, 9–21; and cf. NHC, 2:32:1933:5.

199. George Papadogeorgos, *Prominent Greeks of Antiquity*, 46.

200. http://www.salon.com/2014/11/01/the_sad_twisted_truth_about_conservative_christianitys_effect_on_the_mind_partner/.

201. Ibid.

202. Jonathan Z. Smith, *The HarperCollins Dictionary of Religion*, 392.

203. Carol Christian, "Houston Man Was Scheduled to Be on Missing Malaysia Flight," March 10, 2014, http://www.chron.com/news/houston-texas/houston/article/Houston-man-was-scheduled-to-be-on-missing-5303816.php.

204. Luke 12:15 (New International Version).

205. Marcus Borg and Ray Riegert, "East Meets West," *Bible* Review, November 30, 1999, 22.

206. John A. Sanford, *The Kingdom Within*, 96.

207. Ibid., 103.

208. Jerry Large, *Seattle Times*, March 17, 2014, B2.

209. Ibid.

210. Excerpted from the *Mountain Astrologer* (February/March 2008).

211. Here Jesus is referring to fulfilling the natural law of God (Matthew 5:17 [New International Version]).

212. "Priests' ecclesiastical missteps treated more sternly than abuse.

"Files detail cases in which L.A. Archdiocese officials displayed outrage over a priest's violation of canon law while doing little for victims of his sexual abuse.

"The archdiocese of Los Angeles learned in the late 1970s that one of its priests had sexually assaulted a 16-year-old boy so violently that he was left bleeding and 'in a state of shock.' The priest said he was too drunk to remember what happened and officials took no further action.

"But two decades later, word reached Cardinal Roger M. Mahony that the same priest was molesting again and improperly performing the sacrament of confession on his victim. The archdiocese sprang to action: It dispatched investigators, interviewed a raft of witnesses and discussed the harshest of all church penalties—not for the abuse but for the violation of church law.

"'Given the seriousness of this abuse of the sacrament of penance...it is your responsibility to formally declare the existence of the excommunication and then refer the matter to Rome,' one cleric told Mahony in a memo.

"The case of Father Jose Ugarte is one of several instances detailed in newly released records in which archdiocese officials displayed outrage over a priest's ecclesiastical missteps while doing little for the victims of his sexual abuse" (Victoria Kim, Ashley Powers, and Harriet Ryan, *Los Angeles Times* and the *Seattle Times*, February 3, 2013, A10).

213. "Retired Cardinal Roger Mahony and other top Roman Catholic Arch diocese of Los Angeles officials maneuvered behind the scenes to shield molester priests, provide damage control for the church and keep parishioners in the dark, according to church personnel files.

"The confidential records filed in a lawsuit against the archdiocese disclose how the church handled abuse allegations for decades and also reveal dissent from a top Mahony aide who criticized his superiors for covering up allegations of abuse rather than protecting children" (Gillian Flaccus, "LA Church Leaders Shielded Molester Priests, Records Show," Associated Press, http://usnews.nbcnews.com/_news/2013/01/22/16641582-la-church-leaders-shielded-molester-priests-records-show?lite).

214. Chris Tomlinson, *Seattle Times*, October 19, 2012, A17.

215. Bil Linzie, Uncovering the Effects of Cultural Background on the Reconstruction of Ancient Worldviews, 10 (http://heathengods.com/library/bil_linzie/cultural_background.pdf).

216. Ibid

217. "Judaism does not believe in the devil, but we do believe in Satan (who more properly should be called 'the Satan'). As this demonstrates, the Jewish view of Satan is very different than the Christian one. Here's a summary of the Jewish view; you can also find information at Alyza (Gretchen) Shapiro's website at http://www.geocities.com/alyzab/Jewish/satan.html.

"The word satan means 'challenger', 'difficulty', or 'distraction' (note that it is not a proper name). With the leading ha- to make haSatan, it refers to /the/ challenger. This describes Satan as the angel who is the embodiment of man's challenges. HaSatan works for G-d. His job is to make choosing good over evil enough of a challenge so that it can be a meaningful choice. In other words, haSatan is an angel whose mission it is to add difficulty, challenges, and growth experiences to life. Contrast this to Christianity, which sees Satan as God's opponent. In Jewish thought, the idea that there exists anything capable of setting itself up as God's opponent would be considered overly polytheistic—you are setting up the devil to be a god or demigod" (http://www.shamash.org/lists/scj-faq/HTML/faq/12-35.html).

218. *Seattle Times*, November 21, 2010, A19.

219. In 1978 in northwestern Guyana, a religious cult from California, the Peoples Temple, became internationally infamous when over nine hundred people died in a mass murder-suicide by drinking poison-laced Kool-Aid. This was all orchestrated by their leader, Jim Jones.

220. "Notwithstanding the arguments that time will never come when the Church will be able to dispense with hell, it is idle and hypocritical to argue as we have heard so many persons do, upon this point. 'I am a Christian,' says one.—'Then you believe in Hell and the Devil?'—'Oh, no, indeed; for this doctrine is ridiculous and long since exploded.'—'Then you are not a Christian, and your Christianity is but a false pretence'—is our answer.—'But, indeed, I am one, for I believe in Christ.'—'In a Christ god or a Christ man?' 'If you believe in him in this latter capacity, then you are no more a Christian than a Jew or a Mohammedan; for both believe in their own way that such a man lived from the year 1 to the year 33; the one holding him as an impostor, and the other condescending to see in Jesus a prophet though far lower than Mohammed. Yet for all that neither of these call themselves Christians—nay, they loathe the very name! And if, agreeing with your Church, you see in the crucified 'Man of Sorrow' your saviour, the very God himself, then are you compelled by this very fact to believe in Hell.'...'But why?'—we will be asked. We answer by quoting the words of the Chevalier des Mousseaux, in his Moeurs et pratiques des démons, a book which has received the approbation of the late Pope and several cardinals. 'THE DEVIL IS THE CHIEF PILLAR OF FAITH, he says. He is one of the grand personages whose life is closely allied to that of the Church; and without his speech which issued so triumphantly from the mouth of the Serpent, his medium, the fall of man could not have taken place. Thus, if it were not for him [the Devil], the Saviour, the Crucified, the Redeemer, would be but the most ridiculous of supernumeraries, and the Cross an insult to good sense! For—from whom, would this Redeemer have redeemed and saved you, if not from the Devil, the "Bottomless pit"—Hell' (p. x). 'To demonstrate the existence of Satan, is to re-establish one of the fundamental dogmas of the Church, which serve as a basis for Christianity, and, without which, Satan would be but a name'—says Father Ventura di Raulica of Rome, the Examiner of Bishops, etc." (H. P. Blavatsky, *The Theosophist* 2, no. 7 [April 1881]: 152–153).

221. Dualistic religions also feed off of the emotional, dualistic thinking of people, such as right and wrong and good guy versus bad guy. It is easy for people who have fear and revenge, with a touch of arrogance thrown in, within their hearts to believe that a person such as Osama bin Laden would end

up in hell for an eternity. (According to one survey, 69 percent of Americans believe bin Laden is in hell.) But the ones that used 9-11 as justification to begin a war that ultimately caused much more death, destruction, and sufferings of thousands would not end up in hell but in heaven.

222. According to the *Merriam-Webster* online dictionary, bogeyman is defined as, "a monstrous imaginary figure used in threatening children; a terrifying or dreaded person or thing." You may not be aware of it, but the bogeyman is very much alive and doing extremely well in today's world.

This bogeyman takes many guises and wears many faces. In fact, with a little stretch of the imagination, the bogeyman may be seen as the predominate paradigm of our culture and of the twenty-first century—even though he has been hanging around for millennia causing fear and dread. And how do I know that this bogeyman is male? Read on, and you will discover the answer.

This bogeyman is unique in its true identity: dualism. Bogeyman dualism is nothing more than the separate, dualistic beliefs and paradigms of humanity, such as God versus Satan; good versus evil; light versus dark; and finally, the big one, heaven versus hell. Even though the dualism is illusionary, the bogeyman makes you think that it's real.

Bogeyman dualism feeds itself purely on the illusion of separation and the fear that the dualistic imagery provokes. It has been, and still is, very destructive to humanity's efforts toward world peace.

Fear is very effective in controlling others. And where there is separation, such as good versus evil, there is fear. You may have already guessed that each and every institution and paradigm that bows down to bogeyman dualism is dominated by patriarchal leadership—thus the reason the bogeyman is the "man."

Pure and simple, bogeyman dualism is utilized by various institutions, such as Christianity, to elicit fear for power and control and to justify their dogma, doctrine, laws, practices, and policies.

223. Dwight Goddard, *Was Jesus Influenced by Buddhism?*, 198.

224. This example is in reference to the work of the physicist David Bohm (1917–1992), a colleague of Albert Einstein. He theorized a different view of the universe than the one that is commonly accepted by science. Briefly, he theorized a model of wholeness that constituted reality, which consisted of two orders: the explicate order and the implicate order. The explicate order is the manifest realm of the physical universe in space and time. The other order, implicate, is the unmanifested, unseen (hidden) universe that has an unknown number of layers. The primary universe is not the explicate order but the implicate order. Additionally, he conceived of a "deeper," hidden, unmanifested layer of the implicate order, which he named the superimplicate order—the eternal order. Bohm also utilized an approximately comparable term for the implicate order—the holomovement. This indicated that the implicate order was always in dynamic flux.

From his research and from his own intuitive side, Bohm concluded that the universe, seen and unseen, is an inseparable whole that is full of energy and contains an unknowable number of universes enfolded, intertwined, and interpenetrated into each other.

225. "The expression 'Divine spark' can be misleading, as can any metaphysical term taken too literally. The word 'spark' gives an image of a fiery particle thrown away from a central fire. Some have taken this literally, seeing humanity as 'sparks' that originated in the Light, but which have flown out and away from the Source. This view is contrary to the witness of the Sages and the teaching of the Mysteries. The term 'Divine spark' refers to the Immanence of God within each heart. But the Infinite One is not a pie that can be cut into slices. Where the Indivisible One is, at any single point (or spark) there the All-Holy abides in the fullness (pleroma) of Wisdom and Love and in the plenitude of Divine Power" (David Goddard, *The Tower of Alchemy*, 147).

226. "The kingdom of heaven is like to a grain of mustard seed, which a man took and sowed in his field. Which is the least indeed of all seeds; but when it is grown up, it is greater than all herbs, and becometh a tree, so that the birds of the air come, and dwell in the branches thereof" (René

Guénon, *Fundamental Symbols*, 298). Additionally, the tenth letter of the Hebrew alphabet is yod, symbolically represented as a flame or seed. "The yod is the smallest of all the letters of the Hebrew alphabet, but from it, nevertheless, are derived the forms of all the other letters...It is the seed which is contained in all things" (René Guénon, *Fundamental Symbols*, 300). Furthermore, there is the symbolism of the yod inside the heart. "The yod, while having the meaning of 'principle', also has that of 'seed'. The yod in the heart is in a way, therefore, the seed enclosed in the fruit" (René Guénon, *Fundamental Symbols*, 297).

227. "No one after lighting a lamp puts it under the bushel basket, but on the lampstand, and it gives light to all in the house. In the same way, let your light shine before others so that they may see your good works" (Matthew 5:15–16).

228. Koyasan University, *Mikkyo, Kobo Daishi Kukai and Shingon Buddhism*, 34.

229. John A. V. Strickland, "Jesus's Religion: The Greatness of God in All Humankind," *Unity* (August 1993): 52.

230. Ibid., 53.

231. Joseph Campbell, *The Power of Myth*, 57.

232. http://theawakenedstate.tumblr.com/post/32317620623/the-torus-the-code-to-the-universe.

233. Ibid.

234. Athon Veggi and Alison Davidson, *The Book of Doors*, 13.

235. Ibid., 11.

236. David Fideler, *Jesus Christ Sun Of God*, 22.

237. Bruce Chilton, *Rabbi Jesus*, 164

238. The full story is contained in one of my books, *The Greatest Lie Ever Told.*

239. The majority of my research consisted of analyzing my astrological birth chart. According to physicist David Bohm (1917–1992), a colleague of Albert Einstein, "Astrology is seen as a valid and sacred science." His groundbreaking work bankrupted the basic philosophy of reductionism in orthodox science.

    "In analogy to holography but on a much grander scale, Bohm believes that each part of physical reality contains information about the whole...Evidence for this kind of holographic structure in nature has emerged recently in the burgeoning field of chaos theory and its close cousin, fractal geometry...

    "Bohm proposes that the holomovement consists of two fundamental aspects: the explicate order and the implicate order...what we call matter is merely an apparent manifestation of the explicate order of the holomovement...In other words, the explicate order is the manifest realm; it is the physical space-time universe in which we live. This explicate order is the surface appearance of a much greater enfolded or implicate order, most of which is hidden. Thus, the implicate order is the unseen, or the un-manifest realm.

    "Another point that Bohm emphasized was that empty space is part of the wholeness—this unbroken flowing movement. Empty space is not just some giant vacuum through which matter moves, but rather, space and matter are intimately interconnected.

    "Contemporary physics and, indeed, most of science deals with explicate orders and structures only, which is why physics has encountered such great difficulty in explaining a variety of phenomena that Bohm would say arise from the implicate order...

    "In reference to the alchemical axiom of 'as above, so below,' the microcosm has all the elements, essentially of the macrocosm. It is important to emphasize that each part does contain the whole, not at a manifest level but at a process level.

"This all leads to a kind of metaphorical understanding of how astrology might work, and it works in a way that is not mechanistic. This is very important to understand. It's not that Pluto (planet) sends rays down to your brain, which acts as a radio receiver, picks them up, and goes and does Plutonic things. And it's not that Pluto is in you, in the sense that the physical Pluto is much too big to be contained in your physical body. It's that the process that's going on in Pluto is also going on in you. Literally so, Pluto is literally contained in you, and in me, but at the process level, not at the manifest level" (the preceding is excerpted from two sources: http://www.vision.net.au/~apaterson/science/david_bohm.htm and the *Mountain Astrologer* [October/November 2009]).

240. One of the primary spiritual teachings is to listen, look, and learn.

241. Marcus J. Borg, *Jesus: A New Vision*, 111.

242. Donald Tyson, *Tetragrammaton*, 14–15.

243. Ibid., 16.

244. Hezekiah was the fourteenth king of Judah. His reign was between 715 and 686 BC. According to the Hebrew Testament, Hezekiah introduced religious reform and reinstated religious traditions. He resolved to abolish idolatry from his kingdom, and among other things that he did to this end, he destroyed the high places (or bamot) and "bronze serpent" (or "Nehushtan"), recorded as being made by Moses according to the command of Yahweh (Numbers 21:8), which became an object of idolatrous worship (2 Kings 18:4). In place of this, he centralized the worship of Yahweh at the Jerusalem Temple (http://en.wikipedia.org/wiki/Hezekiah).

245. Micha F. Lindemans, http://www.pantheon.org/articles/s/seraphim.html.

246. This is paraphrased from Revelation 22:13 and 22:16.

247. Ancient term for initiates.

248. H. P. Blavatsky, *Isis Unveiled*, 254.

249. Matthew 15:11 (*Aramaic Bible in Plain English* [2007]).

250. Elisabeth Haich, *Wisdom of the Tarot*, 167.

251. The Hawaiians of days past taught that there was a "cave of the beast" within us that was "localized from the stomach down through the sex and evacuation organs" (David Kaonohiokaala Bray, *The Kahuna Religion of Hawaii*, 43).

252. Abuse, physical or sexual, is a behavior of the destructive side of the beast, which in some cases may have been triggered as a result of the person's own experience of being abused as a child.

253. "And God saw that the light was good; and God separated the light from the darkness" (Genesis 1:4).

254. "Jung appeared to be undecided in his own mind about the question of the ontological status of the archetypes (see e.g., 1968d [1936], 58; see also Dourley, 1993); and this state of affairs has led to considerable controversy. But I believe that the ambiguity was necessitated by Jung's inability to scientifically reconcile his conviction that the archetypes are at once embodied structures and bear the imprint of the divine; that is, the archetypes are both structures within the human body, and represent the domain of spirit. Jung's intention was clearly a unitary one, and yet his ontology seemed often to be dualistic, as well as persistently ambiguous, and was necessarily so because the science of his day could not envision a nondualistic conception of spirit and matter.

"Jung's dualism is apparent in his distinction between the archetypes and the instincts which required for him a polarization of the psyche into those products derived from matter and those derived from spirit. He imagined the psyche as the intersection at the apex of two cones, one of spirit and the other of matter (1969a [1946], 215)" (Charles D. Laughlin, http://www.scientificexploration.org/journal/jse_10_3_laughlin.pdf).

255. Diana L. Paxson, *Taking Up the Runes*, 185.

256. This is connected with the concept that our conscious minds consistently seek power. The definition of power is individualistic. In our society, most people equate power with external, materialistic things, such as status, position, title, money, possessions, and even physical attractiveness; consider the amount of cosmetic surgery and the money spent on cosmetics.

257. "Evangelical Pastor convinced followers his penis contained HOLY MILK, arrested! Now this one has got to be an all-time worst Everything Is Going Down, But The Word Of God reports…This is worse than the woman that took the stand in court and said it was her Godly duty to allow Bishop Earl Pulk to have sex with her while she was married to one of the elders at the church. However the following report coming out of Brazil takes the cake! Read it below:

"BRAZIL—January 28, 2013—Religion is a virus. The world is quickly finding out the damage and crimes that the Vatican and its little harlots—all other religions—have caused worldwide.

"Just when you think you had heard it all, another malicious and alarming crime committed by a criminal priest, nun, minister or pastor, surfaces. This one has to be one of the most shocking yet…an Evangelical Pastor managed to abuse victims after convincing them that his penis contains HOLY MILK. The criminal: Valdeci Sobreni Picano of Brazil.

"Valdeci Sobreni Picano is a Brazilian Evangelical Pastor. He has been arrested after deceiving the faithful using the name of the 'Holy Spirit', by using these foolish lies. This criminal pastor claimed that the Holy Spirit would secrete from his penis in the form of 'sacred milk'. This pastor said that his penis was blessed and that 'the Lord had consecrated him with divine milk of the Holy Spirit' and, of course, he had to release it in order to 'evangelize'. 'He has convinced us that only God could come into our lives through our mouth and that's why he would do what he did'. Often, after worship, pastor Valdeci would take us to the where the funds were kept at the back of the Church and asked us to have Oral sex with him until the Holy Spirit would come through ejaculation'. This is the testimony

of one of his victims" (https://obnoxioustv.wordpress.com/2013/01/31/
pastor-in-brazil-convinced-his-members-his-sperm-was-holy-milk-has-
been-arrested/).

258. *Seattle Times*, November 21, 2010, A19.

259. If we were to ask the average New Age practitioner the meaning of chakra,
the response would probably be: energy vortexes. That would be correct
if we are talking about the exoteric meaning. But what many do not know
is the original esoteric meaning. The original name meant 'discus,' as in
the lethal throwing weapon, with the meaning of destroying the passions
that hinder a person's journey towards enlightenment. Passions mean
anything that disrupts the tranquility of the mind.

The common most number of chakras is seven. However, some systems of
thought may have five or eight. It is believed that chakras are deposito-
ries of memory. Our emotional wounding's and the past issues connected
with those wounding's may be locked away within the various chakras.
These blockages will definitely affect and inhibit the energy flow throughout our body. Over time this disharmony will affect the body's various
health systems such as the organs and glands and will ultimately result in
a state of unhappiness and disease.

The 1st chakra is the named the Root Chakra. It is located at the base of the
spine and deals with issues of security, basic needs, basic human survival,
profane sex and inappropriate sexual activity (un-awakened beast) and
one's sense of 'roots' and family and connection to the earth (an unawakened first chakra views earth/nature as hostile). This is the chakra
of dualism. Endocrine System: Reproductive Glands/Adrenals. The color
symbolism is red.

260. Sallie Nichols, *Jung and Tarot*, 203.

261. A term used by psychologists referring to empathy leading to helping
activity.

262. Natural law may be likened to the concept of a "moral compass." A form of natural law is alluded to in the Declaration of Independence and is sometimes referred to as "natural rights." These concepts were championed by Thomas Jefferson, who used natural-rights ideas to justify declaring independence from England and justified the Revolutionary War by appealing to "the law of nature and Nature's God." According to the National Center for Constitutional Studies, "The Declaration of Independence of 1776 established the premise that in America a people might assume the station 'to which the laws of Nature and Nature's God entitle them...' The Founders saw these as moral duties between individuals."

263. Marcus J. Borg, *Jesus: A New Vision*, 97.

264. Ibid., 110.

265. Michael R. Burch, http://www.thehypertexts.com.

266. William E. Phipps, *Muhammad and Jesus*, 231–232.

267. Ibid., 231.

268. Lynn Picknett and Clive Prince, *The Templar Revelation*, 295.

269. Ibid., 363.

270. Ibid., 352.

271. Ignatius Singer, *The Rival Philosophies of Jesus and of Paul*, 297.

272. David Fideler, *Jesus Christ Sun of God*, 134–135.

273. Marcus J. Borg, *Jesus: A New Vision*, 142.

274. Duncan Holcomb, *The Gospel According to Us*, 92.

275. Joseph Campbell, *The Power of Myth*, 110.

276. Swine is a person concerned only with materialism and wealth; today the swine would include the capitalist elite.

277. Jesus recognized the divine purity in children and their beauty and limitless potential, whereas "in the biblical view, a child is not a being that is born with amazing capabilities that will emerge with the right conditions like a beautiful flower in a well-attended garden. Rather, a child is born in sin, weak, ignorant, and rebellious, needing discipline to learn obedience. Independent thinking is dangerous pride" (Marlene Winell and Valerie Tarico, AlterNet, http://www.salon.com/2014/11/01/the_sad_twisted_truth_about_conservative_christianitys_effect_on_the_mind_partner/).

278. Peter Kirby, http://www.earlychristianwritings.com/thomas/.

279. This is from a foreword by Gabriel Cousens from Rabbi Gershon Winkler, *Magic of the Ordinary*, xv.

280. "Almonds and walnuts contain the necessary healthy fats and nutrients that are required in the production of sex hormones. Without these critical nutrients one can experience depression and can negatively affect mood, desire, and focus.

"Almonds have been described as a sexual stimulant but have also been found to reduce infertility and miscarriages. These nutrient-dense nuts also provide critical minerals such as selenium, zinc and provide a great source of vitamin E" (Cory Couillard, http://www.care2.com/greenliving/5-foods-that-improve-your-sex-life.html#ixzz2CDZ8K8KO).

281. Fred Hageneder, *The Meaning of Trees*, 36.

282. Ibid., 37.

283. http://www.bible-history.com/tabernacle/TAB4The_Golden_Lampstand.htm.

284. Symbol of ascent.

285. David Goddard, *The Tower of Alchemy*, 93.

286. René Guénon, *Fundamental Symbols*, 153.

287. A form of rabbinic literature.

288. Rabbi David A. Cooper, *God Is a Verb*, 295.

289. However, in one sense it is the "end of time"—that is, linear time. Awakening to the reality of radical nondualism is also awakening to the knowing of the states of timeless and timelessness.

290. Rocco J. Gennaro, "Consciousness," *Internet Encyclopedia of Philosophy*, http://www.iep.utm.edu/consciou/.

291. Charles D. Laughlin, http://www.scientificexploration.org/journal/jse_10_3_laughlin.pdf, 381.

292. By all accounts Moses would have been awestruck with this "proof" of the oneness of creation—the divine and intrinsic nature of all things and their interpenetration. Of course, I can't prove that this was his thinking or revelation from this divine visionary experience. Neither can it be disproved, as we are discussing orally transmitted stories, teachings, and legends that were written down hundreds of years after the actual events had taken place.

But our reason and common sense, without the influence of the dogma and the doctrine of organized religion, would have to acknowledge that Moses would have been greatly impressed with this proof of divine oneness and intrinsic identity. Moses was spiritually evolved, intelligent, and wise. In addition, he had been schooled in the Egyptian mystery religion of his time and married to a daughter of a priest (shaman) of Midian. Would not this indicate that he understood this vision as one of divine oneness—the interpenetration of spirit and matter?

293. Moses's concept of oneness did filter down to the Jewish belief in the divine spark. According to internationally renowned professor, theologian, and spiritual leader Rabbi Jack Bemporad, "Judaism teaches us that all human beings are created in the divine image and therefore are linked to God by the Divine Spark within them" (http://theollendorffcenter.org/principles.html).

294. According to Michael Baigent, the belief in one god "has been seen by some scholars as deriving from ancient Mesopotamia: the name of the god of the Assyrians, Ashur (*Assur*), means the 'One,' the 'Only,' the 'Universal God'" (Michael Baigent, *The Jesus Papers*, 217).

295. Refer back to chapter 1 and the section "Genesis Translated from the Ancient Hebrew"—"In the summit 'Elohiym [Powers]' fattened the sky and the land…"

296. This concept is the same as Shingon Esoteric Buddhism, where the relative realm is the "body" of the supreme deity Dainichi Nyorai—Great Sun, Great Universal Light. Additionally, according to Rabbi Geoffrey W. Dennis, "The design of the **Tabernacle** and the **Temple** are microcosms of **Creation** (Ex. R. 35:6; Num. R. 12:13). The human body also embodies the entire universe in microcosmic form" (*The Encyclopedia of Jewish Myth, Magic, and Mysticism*, 57).

297. Erik Hornung, *Akhenaten and the Religion of Light*, 92–93.

298. I resolved this paradox by my belief that we are not made in the image of God or the Absolute, but we are, as are all other things of creation, a reflection of the original divine unity. Instead of a substance, such as semen, it was the reflection of itself that then produced creation. Thus, "first divine pair, and thus plurality, resulted from the original emanation. (1 + 1[Reflection] = 2, 1[reflection] + 2 = 3) This concept of reflection is indicated in the first letter of the Jewish Alphabet—Aleph."

299. Erik Hornung, *Akhenaten and the Religion of Light*, 91–92.

300. There is further consideration to the fact that the Israelites were recognizing and honoring the goddess Asherah (Venus) until King Hezekiah "removed the high places, smashed the sacred stones and cut down the Asherah poles. He broke into pieces the bronze snake Moses had made, for up to that time the Israelites had been burning incense to it" (2 Kings 18:4 [New International Version]).

This indicates that the Israelites were following in the footsteps of Moses by recognizing the one and the many by their worship of the goddess Asherah. Additionally, they recognized the sanctity of nature (many), as indicated by their practice of worshipping in sacred groves and high places, but not in temples. Why would they not do this, since one of their prophets received his vision while out in nature sleeping on the ground and using a stone for his pillow?

301. Earth, nature, and the feminine are subordinate, second-rate, and second-class citizens to these patriarchal monotheistic religions, which first and foremost highlight and stress the preeminence of heaven and the masculine. We are witness to the legacy of thousands of years of the rule of these patriarchal monotheistic religions through ever-present war, destruction of indigenous peoples, the ever-widening destruction of the biosphere, and the ongoing suppression and repression of women.

Of the three patriarchal monotheistic religions, Judaism, by far, is less patriarchal and is friendlier to the earth and nature, with more equality between men and women than the other two Western religions.

302. *Mountain Astrologer*, October/November 2008.

303. Rabbi Joel C. Dobin, "To Rule Both Day And Night: Astrology in the Bible, Midrash, & Talmud," http://jhaines6.wordpress.com/2012/04/20/history-of-astrology-in-judaism-christianity-a-fantastic-article-that-helps-to-correct-some-of-our-false-history-j/.

304. Ibid.

305. Ernest L. Martin, "Astronomy and the Birth of Jesus: Scripturally Connected by Mt. 24:30 and Rev. 12:1-2," http://deeperwalk.lefora.com/2010/07/03/the-astronomical-sign-of-the-son-of-man/.

"And there appeared a great wonder in heaven; a woman clothed with the sun, and the moon under her feet, and upon her head a crown of twelve stars..." (Revelations 12:1 [King James Version]).

"The essential factor in interpreting the symbol of Revelation 12:1–5 is the identification of the woman...the woman in the first three verses is featured as being in heaven and both the Sun and the Moon are in association with her...the important factor is the birth of the man-child and the Woman's relationship with the heavenly signs while she is symbolically in heaven. (The first three verses of Revelation 12 shows the Sun clothing her, the Moon under her feet and the Twelve Stars on her head)

"The 'birth' of the Messiah is associated with this heavenly spectacle...

"Since the Sun and Moon are amidst or in line with the body of this woman, she could be, in a symbolic way, a constellation located within the normal paths of the Sun and Moon. The only sign of a woman which exists along the ecliptic (the track of the Sun in its journey through the stars) is that of Virgo the Virgin. She occupies, in body form, a space of about 50 degrees along the ecliptic. The head of the woman actually bridges some 10 degrees into the previous sign of Leo and her feet overlap about 10 degrees into the following sign of Libra, the Scales. In the period of Jesus's birth, the Sun entered in its annual course through the heavens into the head position of the woman about August 13, and exited from her feet about October 2. But the apostle John saw the scene when the Sun was 'clothing' or 'adorning' the woman. This surely indicates that the position of the Sun in the vision was located somewhere mid-bodied to the woman, between the neck and the knees...

"The only time in the year that the Sun could be in a position to 'clothe' the celestial woman called Virgo (that is, to be mid-bodied to her, in the region where a pregnant woman carries a child) is when the Sun is located between about 150 and 170 degrees along the ecliptic. This 'clothing' of the woman by the Sun occurs for a 20-day period each year. This 20 degree spread could indicate the general time when Jesus was born. In 3 B.C.E., the Sun would have entered this celestial region about August 27 and exited from it about September 15…

"This heavenly woman called Virgo is normally depicted as a virgin holding in her right hand a green branch and in her left hand a sprig of grain. In the Hebrew Zodiac, she at first (in the time of David) denoted Ruth who was gleaning in the fields of Boaz. She then later became the Virgin when the prophecy of Isaiah 7:14 was given in the time of King Hezekiah and the prophet Isaiah. This Virgin held in her left hand a sprig of grain. This was precisely where the bright star called Spica is found. Indeed, the chief star of the constellation Virgo is Spica.

"Bullinger, in his book The Witness of the Stars (29–34), said that the word 'Spica' has, through the Arabic, the meaning 'the branch' and that it symbolically refers to Jesus who was prophetically called 'the Branch' in Zechariah 3:8 and 6:12. And Bullinger (and Seiss in his book The Gospel in the Stars) maintains that this sign of Virgo designates the heavenly witness for the birth of the Messiah (Jesus).

"Jesus was born in early evening, and Revelation 12 shows it was a New Moon day.

"What New Moon could this have been? The answer is most amazing. It is almost too amazing! September 11, 3 B.C.E. was Tishri One on the Jewish calendar. To Jewish people this would have been a very profound occasion indeed. Tishri One is none other than the Jewish New Year's Day (Rosh ha-Shanah, or as the Bible calls it, The Day of Trumpets⊠Leviticus 23:23–26). It was an important annual holy day of the Jews (but not one of the three annual festivals that required all Palestinian Jews to be in Jerusalem).

"What a significant day for the appearance of the Messiah to arrive on earth from the Jewish point of view! And remarkably, no other day of the year could astronomically fit Revelation 12:1–3. The apostle John is certainly showing forth an astronomical sign which answers precisely with the Jewish New Year Day. John would have realized the significance of this astronomical scene that he was describing" (Ernest L. Martin, "Astronomy and the Birth of Jesus: Scripturally Connected by Mt. 24:30 and Rev. 12:1–2," http://deeper-walk.lefora.com/2010/07/03/the-astronomical-sign-of-the-son-of-man/).

306. Excerpted from *Tequila and Chocolate: A Guide to a New Consciousness— the Awakening of Our Divinity and Humanity*, an unpublished manuscript by Rev. Dr. J. C. Husfelt.

307. Marcus J. Borg, *Jesus: A New Vision*, 98–99.

308. Paul Broadhurst, *Tintagel and the Arthurian Myths*, 24.

309. Amanda Froelich, "Science Proves Hugging Trees Is Good for Health," June 23, 2014, http://www.trueactivist.com/science-proves-hugging-trees-is-good-for-health/.

310. Philip Gardiner, *The Serpent Grail*, 136.

311. John Dart and Ray Reigert, *Unearthing the Lost Words of Jesus*, 55.

312. *Sacred Writings, Judaism: The Tanakh*, 1289; Proverbs 3:13–15

313. Rabbi Geoffrey W. Dennis, *The Encyclopedia of Jewish Myth, Magic and Mysticism*, 239.

314. E. Valentia Straiton, *Celestial Ship of the North—[1] The Mother Mystery*, 6.

315. *Sacred Writings, Judaism: The Tanakh*, 105; Exodus 13:21.

316. "We see in…early accounts of Jesus's healing in the Gospel according to Mark an emphasis on touch. He grasps the fevered women's hand; in another episode he spits on his fingers, sticks them into a deaf mute's ears and mouth, then grabs his tongue and says in Aramaic, 'Ephatha (Be opened up)'

(Mark 7:31–37); and in yet another story, he spits right into a blind man's eyes and lays hands on them in a healing that takes two treatments to be effective (Mark 8:22–26). This tactile focus of Jesus's Chasidic power, the shamanic side of his practice, is greatly diminished in the Gospels, which were written later. There, Jesus is logocentric: he just speaks and healing happens spontaneously (see, for example, Matthew 8:16). As Christianity took on an increasingly Hellenistic character, its portraits of Jesus became more cerebral, almost philosophical. He no longer spat or grabbed hands and tongues; the carousing drunkard became a divine oracle. The earthiness of his rabbinic persona was lost" (Bruce Chilton, *Rabbi Jesus*, 109 and 130–131).

317. Excerpted, William Temple, *Nature, Man and God*, 46.

318. A shaman is a person with the ability to connect the profane or earthly existence to the sacred, the heavens, and thus provide a link between heaven and earth. He or she is a visionary and what I call a "pathfinder to the soul." Shamans are dreamers, philosophers, and non-dogmatic religious guides and teachers. But they are probably best known as healers, specifically wounded healers, which means that the shamans have been doing their own healing of their past wounding's. A shaman is also a "person of power" who dream-voyages to the otherworld for knowledge and freedom. The original shaman not only was a healer but also fulfilled the role of priest, wizard, and spiritual leader.

319. The following is an account of an exorcism of a spirit in the form of a serpent I performed on one of our apprentices in 1997 after the visitation—in her own words:

"From the start it was a strange injury. I do several sports; karate, where I was a purple belt, and tennis, which I play competitively at the club level. And so I always have plenty of opportunities to get injured. But I didn't get injured while I did a sport. I didn't even get injured within several days of doing one of my sports. I just woke up one morning and my heel hurt. Within two days my leg started to hurt, and within hours I couldn't put any weight onto my leg at all. I had ruptured my calf muscle. Recovery involved about six weeks in an air cast and physical therapy that included everything from swimming to special stretches.

"After about three months, I began returning slowly to my sports. After about nine months, I was back fully to my sports. There was, however, a nagging tightness and sometimes aching in my leg that never seemed to fully leave me. After a strenuous workout, it would even develop spasms, and at times I had full range of motion and didn't seem to be hindered sports-wise other than the discomfort, so I knew that something else was going on. I spoke to J. C. and asked if he would do a healing on my leg.

"Early one August morning, after a very powerful baptism ceremony, J. C. performed the healing. I don't know what energy he was tapping into; I did feel tingling up and down my spine. It was excruciatingly painful when he put his hands on my leg and pulled off whatever it was he was pulling off. That night when everyone had gone to bed at my house, I went into my meditation room to do some chanting and ceremony. My chanting kept getting interrupted because I felt like snakes were crawling over my body. I knew from the rational world that there were no snakes in my room in my house. But they felt so real that I couldn't concentrate. Finally, after several fruitless attempts, I decided to call it a night. As I was closing up my altar, I suddenly heard a very distinctive hissing sound coming from the corner of the room. I couldn't see anything, but the noise had a distinctly otherworldly feel to it. It made the hair on the back of my head stand on end, and my blood instantly ran cold in my veins. It had the effect that a good horror film will have on someone—paralyzing. I ran out of the room, closed the door, and called J. C. even though it was near midnight. Normally J. C. and his wife have an answering machine on so they do not have to answer the phone at night. But on this night J. C. had fallen asleep downstairs by the phone and had gotten up and was standing by the phone when it rang at midnight. I remember sobbing to him that something was hissing at me and I was terrified. J. C. said that he had taken a serpent off of my leg that morning and had cast it away, but sometimes this serpent energy will follow the person and 'stalk' him or her. He taught me a secret mudra (a hand position), a mantra (a vocalization or prayer), and a movement to chase it away.

"When I touched the doorknob of the room, I immediately felt the same cold horror. My hair stood up, and my blood felt chilled again. I walked carefully into the room with my arms crossed in front of me and my hands tightly holding onto the mudra. In the corner where the energy was most intense, I performed the combined movement and mantra twice.

"Immediately, my blood warmed up and the fear dissipated. Since this time, my leg has been wonderful. Other than occasional bouts of stiffness, I am able to move much more energetically, and I can feel the energy flow has returned to its normal levels. I am very grateful."

320. H. P. Blavatsky, *Isis Unveiled*, 48.

321. "Consequently the most important magical parallel to the gospels is that to Jesus's life and legend as a whole. This we saw in the comparison of Jesus and Apollonius, but even when Jesus's career does not parallel that of Apollonius, it is consistently paralleled by other magical material, and the parallels *are not haphazard*; they fit together. Taking the gospel material supported by such parallels, we get the following coherent, consistent and credible picture of a magician's career.

"After undergoing a baptism...Jesus experienced the descent of a spirit upon him—the experience that made a man a magician" (Morton Smith, *Jesus the Magician*, 180–181).

322. "Jesus had already been acknowledged in Galilee as a rabbi: a master of *halakhah* whose actions were equal to his words. His teaching had made him seem like other Galilean rabbis, who were known as *chasidim*...These rabbis cured sickness and relieved drought through prayer...*Chasidim* were ancient Judaism's shamans, faith healers, witch doctors, and sorcerer...

"We see in...early accounts of Jesus's healing in the Gospel according to Mark an emphasis on touch. He grasps the fevered women's hand; in another episode he spits on his fingers, sticks them into a deaf mute's ears and mouth, then grabs his tongue and says in Aramaic, '*Ephatha* (Be opened up)' (Mark 7:31–37); and in yet another story he spits right into a blind man's eyes and lays hands on them in a healing that takes two treatments to be effective (Mark 8:22–26). This tactile focus of Jesus's chasidic power, the shamanic side of his practice, is greatly diminished in the Gospels, which were written later. There, Jesus is logocentric: he just speaks and healing happens spontaneously (see, for example, Matthew 8:16). As Christianity took on an increasingly Hellenistic character, its portraits of Jesus became more cerebral, almost philosophical. He no longer spat or grabbed hands and tongues; the carousing drunkard became a divine oracle. The earthiness of his rabbinic persona was lost" (Bruce Chilton, *Rabbi Jesus*, 109 and 130–131).

323. David Stern, "Masters of Ecstasy," http://ngm.nationalgeographic. com/2012/12/shamans/stern-text?source=podrelated.

324. Namrata Anand, "First Reference to Christ?," http://www.msnbc.msn. com/id/49075679/ns/technology_and_science-the_new_york_times/.

325. Marcus J. Borg, *Jesus: A New Vision*, 101 and 118.

326. Rabbi Gershon Winkler, *Magic of the Ordinary*, 22.

327. This is Jacob's awakening.

328. Torah, Genesis 28:16–22, 31:13, 35:14.

329. Theodor Reik, *Pagan Rites in Judaism*, 6.

330. Lynn Picknett and Clive Prince, *The Templar Revelation*, 287.

331. Rosemary Clark, *The Sacred Magic of Ancient Egypt*, 2.

332. Ibid., 2–3.

333. True philosophy and divine truth are convertible terms. A religion which dreads the light cannot be a religion based on either truth or philosophy—hence, it must be false. The ancient Mysteries were mysteries to the profane only, whom the hierophant never sought nor would

accept as proselytes; to the initiates the Mysteries became explained as soon as the final veil was withdrawn. No mind like that of Pythagoras or Plato would have contented itself with an unfathomable and incomprehensible mystery, like that of the Christian dogma (H. P. Blavatsky, *Isis Unveiled*, 121).

334. Lynn Picknett and Clive Prince, *The Templar Revelation*, 296.

335. Ibid., 296.

336. Timothy Freke and Peter Gandy, *The Complete Guide to World Mysticism*, 67.

337. Jean Doresse, *Gospel of Thomas Saying 77*. She further writes, "Cf. the Gnostic Gospel of Truth (Codex XIII of Chenoboskion, 17): 'The All has been in search of Him from whom he came forth; and the All was within him, unseizing, unthinkable!' One might also mention the Acts of Peter, Chapter XXXIX: 'Thou art the All, and the All is in thee, and thou art! And there is nothing else that exists, except thou alone!' The same allusion is found in Col. III, 11: 'Christ is all and in all'" (*The Secret Books of the Egyptian Gnostics*, 376, excerpted from http://www.earlychristianwritings.com/thomas/gospelthomas77.html).

338. Malcolm Godwin, *The Holy Grail*, 211.

339. Brian Leigh Molyneaux, *The Sacred Earth*, 10.

340. Riane Eisler, *The Chalice & the Blade*, 75.

341. Ibid., 75.

342. Ibid., 89.

343. My common-sense theory is that Moses, in seeking the homeland of his people, did not leave Egypt and do a "right turn" (southeast), traveling through the wilderness of the Sinai Peninsula, but instead followed Abraham's route, paralleling the Mediterranean Sea to Canaan, where

he discovered his future father-in-law, Jethro, near the Sea of Galilee. Of course, if Moses had a lousy sense of direction, he could have wandered all over the Sinai Peninsula through the wilderness of Shur, the wilderness of Sin, and the wilderness of Paran and then traveled around the Gulf of Aqaba into Arabia, where he stumbled on Jethro and his family. These are all lands where Abraham and his ancestors had never set foot. It doesn't make sense, and I don't think Moses was brain-dead!

344. Venus.

345. Riane Eisler, *The Chalice & the Blade*, 87–88.

346. Malcolm Godwin, *The Holy Grail*, 212.

347. "According to a new report by Rainforest Action Network the banking sector is a major source of climate disruption, perpetuating the reliance on dirty energy sources and enabling polluters. The report states that despite the fact that the insurance industry has identified climate change as a significant risk of loss, banks like Bank of America and JPMorgan Chase continue to invest in polluting energy industries like coal at the expense of renewables like wind and solar.

"The big banks will do whatever the big banks need to do to turn a profit. And that usually comes at the greatest cost to middle class lives and livelihoods. In that respect Hurricane Sandy is a little like the foreclosure crisis: both were created by Wall Street and in both Wall Street has somehow managed to escape accountability" (Jessica Pieklo, "How the Big Banks Helped Cause Hurricane Sandy," November 1, 2012, http://www.care2.com/causes/how-the-big-banks-helped-cause-hurricane-sandy.html).

348. "Australia's most prominent Islamic cleric vowed Thursday to stand strong against widespread outrage over his description of women who don't wear head scarves as 'uncovered meat' who invite rape" (Rohan Sullivan, "Rape Comment by Islamic Cleric Stirs Up a Storm," *Seattle Times*, October 27, 2006, A15).

349. Marcus J. Borg, *Jesus: A New Vision*, 133 and 134.

350. Michel Onfray, *Atheist Manifesto: The Case Against Christianity, Judaism and Islam*, 101–102.

351. William E. Phipps, *Muhammad and Jesus*, 136.

352. Douglas Lockhart, *Jesus the Heretic*, 235 and 237.

353. Michael Baigent, *The Jesus Papers*, 112.

354. Malcolm Godwin, *The Holy Grail*, 210–211.

355. Lynn Picknett and Clive Prince, *The Templar Revelation*, 249.

356. Ibid.

357. Laurie Goodstein, "Historian Says Piece of Papyrus Refers to Jesus's Wife," *New York Times*, September 18, 2012.

358. Vilhelm Gronbech, *The Culture of the Teutons*, 148.

359. Marcus J. Borg, *Jesus: A New Vision*, 134.

360. Michel Onfray, *Atheist Manifesto: The Case Against Christianity, Judaism and Islam*, 102–103.

361. Larisa Epatko, "Banned documentary examines brutal Delhi gang rape," Mar 11, 2015, http://www.pbs.org/newshour/rundown/documentary-india-gang-rape/.

362. Elizabeth Dias, "Vatican Strengthens Ties with Evangelicals and Mormons against Gay Marriage," November 20, 2014, https://time.com/3597245/vatican-evangelicals-mormons-gay-marriage/.

363. Ibid.

364. Ibid.

365. Ibid.

366. Jonathan Dudley, "How the Bible Began Saying Life Begins at Conception," November 19,2012, http://www.huffingtonpost.com/jonathan-dudley/how-the-bible-began-saying-life-begins-at-conception_b_2132951.html.

367. Julie Pace and Steve Peoples, *Seattle Times*, October 26, 2012, A4.

368. http://www.jewfaq.org/divorce.htm.

369. Genesis 2:7 (King James Version).

370. John Ashton and Tom Whyte, *The Quest for Paradise*, 58.

371. http://wiki.grassrootinstitute.org/mediawiki/index.php?title=NHSC_Native_Hawaiian_Religion.

372. "The Bible Tells Us When a Fetus Becomes a Living Being," October 31, 2012, http://www.thechristianleftblog.org/tcl-blog/the-bible-tells-us-when-a-fetus-becomes-a-living-being.

373. "The symbolism of dew, closely connected with that of rain by its very nature, is likewise related more especially to the giving of life; and this symbolism is common to numerous traditional forms—Hermetism, the Hebrew Kabbala, and to the Far Eastern tradition" (Rene Guenon, *Fundamental Symbols*, 246).

374. "The information of your DNA is carried in your voice, and you can get a sound [with family] that you never get with someone who's not blood related to you" (Randy Lewis, "Obituaries," *Los Angeles Times*, January 3, 2014, http://www.latimes.com/obituaries/la-me-phil-everly-20140104,0,2345470.story#ixzz2ppSbk5gG).

375. Duncan Holcomb, *The Gospel According to Us*, 82.

376. Bruce Chilton, *Rabbi Jesus*, 79.

377. Rhyd Wildermuth, "Book Review: This Should Change Us," November 30, 2014, http://wildhunt.org/2014/11/guest-book-review-this-should-change-us.html.

378. Neil McMahon, "Ásatrú: The old Norse religion practised by Iceland´s early Viking settlers," Jan 26 2015, http://icelandmag.com/article/asatru-old-norse-religion-practised-icelands-early-viking-settlers.

379. Elohim (one of the names of God) אלהים, has a numerical value of 86. The Hebrew term for "the natural world" is Ha'teva הטבע. This is also 86. In other words, "the natural world" is also a name of God—God and the Natural World or Creation are one!

380. Bruce Chilton, *Rabbi Jesus*, 19.

381. Edmond Bordeaux Szekely, *The Essene Gospel of Peace Book Two*, 31

382. Liz Greene, *The Astrological Neptune and the Quest for Redemption*, 222.

383. Primordial tradition portrays universal themes, principles, and truths.

384. Marcus J. Borg, *Jesus: A New Vision*, 27.

385. Ibid., 27–28.

386. This is the "well" of knowledge from the most ancient of civilizations, which spread throughout the world and is known to us through the patinas of many different cultures and their writings.

387. http://www.primordialtraditions.net/.

388. G. Philippe Menos and Karen A. Jones Menos, *Revelation and Inspiration: Paranormal Phenomena in Light of the Kundalini Paradigm* (May 21–23, 1989): 3.

389. Malcolm Godwin, *Angels: An Endangered Species*, 237.

390. I use the feathered serpent as an animal or earth archetype for a divine human. For many ancient and current spiritual traditions, the serpent or dragon has symbolized wisdom, enlightenment, and immortality.

391. Ibid., 25.

392. Harold Bloom, *Omens of Millennium*, 67.

393. Ibid., 68.

394. Sallie Nichols, *Angels and Mortals*, 190.

395. When reincarnation is not one of the beliefs of a religion then the metaphoric "gates of hell" are flung wide-open. The present day most vivid result of this is exemplified by Islamic jihad and is equated to a one way ticket to paradise even though you may have blown up innocents while achieving jihad.

396. Nancy B. Detweiler, History of Astrology in Judaism & Christianity, http://jhaines6.wordpress.com/2012/04/20/history-of-astrology-in-judaism-christianity-a-fantastic-article-that-helps-to-correct-some-of-our-false-history-j/

397. Early followers of Jesus's message and teachings not connected with Saul and predating the First Council of Nicaea.

398. John Davidson, *The Gospel of Jesus*, 415.

399. Paul Broadhurst, *Tintagel and the Arthurian Myths*, 99–100.

400. Elisabeth Haich, *Wisdom of the Tarot*, 88.

401. Ibid., 89.

402. Characteristics or emanations.

403. "Malkuth means Kingdom. It is associated with the realm of matter/earth and relates to the physical world, the planets and the solar system. It is important not to think of this sephirah as merely 'unspiritual,' for even though it is the emanation furthest from the divine source, it is still on the Tree of Life. As the receiving sphere of all the other sephirot above it, Malkuth gives tangible form to the other emanations. It is like the negative node of an electrical circuit. The divine energy comes down and finds its expression in this plane, and our purpose as human beings is to bring that energy back around the circuit again and up the Tree...

    "In comparing with Eastern systems, Malkuth is a very similar archetypal idea to that of the Muladhara chakra. In this manner, Malkuth is again associated with the anus, although technically the Muladhara is located in the sacram bone. In Shakta tantra, which is also associated with the Earth, the plane in which karma is expressed.

    "Although Malkuth is seen as the lowest Sefirah on the tree of life, it also contains within it the potential to reach the highest. This is exemplified in the Hermetic maxim 'as above, so below'" (http://en.wikipedia.org/wiki/Malkuth).

404. Elisabeth Haich, *Wisdom of the Tarot*, 89.

405. There is a Hopi prophecy connected with the Blue Star. This is the return of Pahana or "True White Brother."

406. "Daniel W. E. Green of the Harvard-Smithsonian Center for Astrophysics stated that the latest orbital calculations indicate that the Hale-Bopp comet last passed through the inner solar system about 4210 years ago.

An Arutz-7 correspondent noted that according to the ancient Jewish text Seder Olam Rabah, the comet's previous appearance was approximately the same year that Noah began building the ark" (http://www.spiritoftruth.org/j31.html).

407. I use the male identity for literary reasons and intrinsic identity, even though angels and archangels are neuter and neither male or female.

408. Hamish Miller and Paul Broadhurst, *The Sun and the Serpent*, 32.

409. Paul Broadhurst, *Tintagel and the Arthurian Myths*, 52–53.

410. Ibid., 53.

411. Ibid., 180.

412. The spiral is one of the oldest spiritual symbols and reflects the inward and outward consciousness of the kingdom of God and the universal pattern of growth and evolution. Spirals are common in nature and the product of phi (ϕ), which is also called the "golden section" or the "golden mean."

413. This is a state of being or consciousness where the mind does not attach externally or internally to the sensory input, even though it is still a part of our consciousness, and we do not attach to the senses or the passions that arise from them. Passions are things that disturb the tranquility of our mind, such as fear.

Furthermore, this is the Japanese concept composed of two interpenetrating concepts: immovable mind and no mind. Mastery is encoded within these two concepts, each with an ocean of meaning and understanding. The highest level of body-mind skill is only attainable through a mind that is ever present with total sensory input (without mind chatter—no mind) but detached—a mind and heart that is ever flowing but does not attach and thus remains immovable.

Our eyes every day attach and judge with various emotions arising from this attachment and judgment—our minds constantly chatter. Contrary to this, the highest level of martial or spiritual ability is to "see but not see" the other person or persons—no attachments, no judgments (i.e., win or lose, live or die).

414. Lono is lord of the east and the god of learning. "Lono in Hawaii is associated with cloud signs and the phenomena of storms. In prayers to Lono the signs of the god are named as thunder, lightning, earthquake, the dark cloud, the rainbow, rain and wind" (http://www.luckyulivehawaii.com/myths3.htm).

"In Hawaiian mythology, Lono is a fertility and music god who descended to Earth on a rainbow to marry Laka. In agricultural and planting traditions, Lono was identified with rain and food plants. He was one of the four gods (with Ku, Kane, and his twin brother Kanaloa) who existed before the world was created. Lono was also the god of peace. In his honor, the great annual festival of the Makahiki was held. During this period (from October through February), all unnecessary work and war was kapu (taboo).

"Some Hawaiians believed that Captain James Cook was Lono returned and indeed this fact may have ultimately contributed to Capt. Cook's death. There was a tradition that such a human manifestation of the god [Lono] had actually appeared, established games and then departed to 'Kahiki,' promising to return" (http://www.mythichawaii.com/tiki-gods.htm).

415. An individual's unique song of power; it is composed of vocalizations, not words, and only attained through rigorous spiritual and mental training. This leads to mastering the power of the "mind-song." The most powerful songs are the ones of long-dead shamans—this is the song that I carry.

416. Proof of being in the presence of the heavenly or divine power of the three pillars of light is reflected in the increase in size of the stones. Indigenous cultures believe in the spiritual power of stones. The Japanese believe that sacred power is often manifested within a sealed vessel that may grow. The vessels that contain this sacred power are known as ut-subo. The stone is an utsubo vessel. It contains a sacred force that may grow under the right circumstances. Even the Japanese National Anthem contains these words addressed to the emperor: "May your reign last for thousands of years until pebbles have become moss-covered rocks."

417. "And they will say to the dwellers of this land, as they have heard, that you Yahweh are within this people who saw you Yahweh, eye to eye, and your cloud stood over them and you walked before them in the pillar of cloud by day and in a pillar of fire by night" (Numbers 14:14).

418. H. P. Blavatsky, *Isis Unveiled*, 488.

419. Rabbi Geoffrey W. Dennis, *The Encyclopedia of Jewish Myth, Magic and Mysticism*, 171.

420. Malcolm Godwin, *Angels: An Endangered Species*, 25.

421. James R. Lewis and Evelyn Dorothy Oliver, *Angels A to Z*, 279.

422. Cover photo taken by Jim Kalnins

423. The various accounts are taken from the American Bible Society, *Angels and Miracles*, 17.

424. Beatrix Murrell, http://www.bizcharts.com/stoa_del_sol/plenum/plenum_3.html.

425. Ibid.

426. Ibid.

427. Bohm's theory of the implicate order stresses that the cosmos is in a state of process. Bohm's cosmos is a "feedback" universe that continuously recycles forward into a greater mode of being and consciousness.

428. One of our apprentices took a picture of me during the day while we finished building the stone death spiral. No one saw what the camera picked up. The picture is not of pillars of light. It is an intense and immense light off to my left in the woods with two globes of light suspended above. The light has a shape almost like a sword in its center with golden rays coming

off of it. It's been verified that it is not a reflection of the lens of the instant camera that took the picture.

429. Alvin Boyd Kuhn, *Esoteric Structure of the Alphabet*, 20.

430. Ignatius Singer, *The Rival Philosophies of Jesus and of Paul*, 297.

431. Dwight Goddard, *Was Jesus Influenced by Buddhism?*, 198 (paraphrased).

432. Bruce Chilton, *Rabbi Jesus*, 19.

433. Today, one of the most dreaded diseases is cancer. "The body is made up of trillions of living cells. Normal body cells grow, divide to make new cells, and die in an orderly way. Cancer cell growth is different from normal cell growth. Instead of dying, cancer cells continue to grow and form new, abnormal cells" (http://www.cancer.org/cancer/cancerbasics/what-is-cancer).

Philosophically, as well as materialistically, every part of the body dreams—including cells. If there has been major wounding from the past, this memory is encoded somewhere within the body—within the cells. And woundings of the same nature could possibly be in the same set of cells. Conducting the following spiritual, mental, and physical tool of release may possibly reprogram the cells and let them die naturally, reflecting the "mental or spiritual death" of the wounding and its cellular memory.

"Dropping the stone" is a process that is both manifest and visceral for healing our internal wounds. We have to identify the various woundings or "stones" within us. A few of these stones may indeed be boulders. To begin any healing, we need to choose a more recent "wounding," one that is not too large. We want to begin with a small stone, not a large boulder from our distant past. The boulders take time to release. This is the reasoning behind the need for patience and persistence. The following is the process of "dropping the stone":

❖ Focus your intent on the forgiveness and the wounding (issue or emotion) you want to release.

❖ Find a stone in nature and ask permission with your mind to use it. Then take the stone and sit with it alone (preferably in nature) and talk your feelings and emotions—cry, shout, yell, whatever it takes—into this stone. You may only spend a few minutes doing this, and then put the stone away in a special place, or you may even carry it with you.

❖ When you are ready to say more words of healing to the stone, re-peat as often as necessary. This process may take hours, days, weeks, or months (depending on the "size of the stone"). But when you feel ready to release, visit a stream, lake, or ocean. It can be at any time of the day, but dawn is the best symbolically.

❖ Sit by the water's edge and relax. More words may need to be said and more tears shed. When you are ready, let go, forgive, and re-lease—drop (or toss) the stone into the stream, lake, or ocean. As you let go of the stone, you are letting go of the *stone*, the wounding within, in your bowl of light. If you are unable to open your fingers and release the stone, it just means that you have more work to do on this wounding. Keep this stone, and take it back home again. Repeat talking to your stone. When you feel you are ready again, re-visit the stream, lake, or ocean and release. When you have forgiven and let go of this past wounding, sit by the water's edge and feel the lightness within you. Bless the experience and the place, give thanks, and leave an offering before you depart. Bless, thank, and love your-self for having the courage, wisdom, and love to forgive and let go.

This process may be used with any woundings, not solely the ones connected with "turn the other cheek."

434. Luke 9:62 (New Living Translation).

435. The Norse hero Sigurd accidentally tasted dragon's blood, which gave him the ability to understand the language of birds. In the Jerusalem Talmud, Solomon's proverbial wisdom was due to his being granted

understanding of the language of birds by God. The language of birds is the mystical pure divine speak—a song of light.

436. Arthur Cotterell, *The Encyclopedia of Mythology*, 132.

437. Anne Wright, http://www.constellationsofwords.com/Constellations/Crater.html.

438. "Neanderthals were using red paint up to 250,000 years ago—far earlier than previously thought. Traces of the paint, made from ochre, were dug up in the Netherlands and dated to a quarter of a million years ago" (Ted Thornhill, http://www.dailymail.co.uk/sciencetech/article-2090718/Neanderthals-using-paint-250-000-years-ago—thousands-years-earlier-previously-thought.html).

439. http://www.webexhibits.org/pigments/intro/reds2.html.

440. Hank Harrison, *The Cauldron and the Grail*, 24–25.

441. Ibid., 80 and 84.

442. Andrew Sinclair, *The Discovery of the Grail*, 181–182.

443. The Inquisition is known today as the Congregation for the Doctrine of the Faith of which Pope Benedict was the head before becoming pope.

"In 2010, as allegations of pedophilic priests continued to swirl, Christopher Hitchens decried individual and institutional corruption within the church's sacred walls. The following is excerpted from the original:

"'Very much more serious is the role of Joseph Ratzinger, before the church decided to make him supreme leader, in obstructing justice on a global scale. After his promotion to cardinal, he was put in charge of the so-called "Congregation for the Doctrine of the Faith" (formerly known as the Inquisition). In 2001, Pope John Paul II placed this department in charge of the investigation of child rape and torture by Catholic priests. In May of that year, Ratzinger issued a confidential letter to every bishop. In it, he reminded them of the extreme gravity of a certain crime. But that crime was the reporting of the rape and torture. The accusations, intoned Ratzinger, were only treatable within the church's own exclusive jurisdiction. Any sharing of the evidence with legal authorities or the press was utterly forbidden. Charges were to be investigated "in the most secretive way… restrained by a perpetual silence…and everyone…is to observe the strictest secret which is commonly regarded as a secret of the Holy Office…under the penalty of excommunication." (My italics) Nobody has yet been excommunicated for the rape and torture of children, but exposing the offense could get you into serious trouble. And this is the church that warns us against moral relativism!

"'Not content with shielding its own priests from the law, Ratzinger's office even wrote its own private statute of limitations. The church's jurisdiction, claimed Ratzinger, "begins to run from the day when the minor has completed the 18th year of age" and then lasts for 10 more years. Daniel Shea, the attorney for two victims who sued Ratzinger and a church in Texas, correctly describes that latter stipulation as an obstruction of justice. "You can't investigate a case if you never find out about it. If you can manage to keep it secret for 18 years plus 10, the priest will get away with it"'" (Christopher Hitchens, *Slate*, http://www.slate.com/articles/news_and_politics/fighting_words/2010/03/the_great_catholic_coverup.htm)

444. Andrew Sinclair, *The Discovery of the Grail*, 14.

445. This quote is paraphrased: Arthur Edward Waite, *The Secret Doctrine in Israel: A Study of the Zohar and Its Connections*, 139.

446. "Introduction of The Book of Zohar," http://www.kabbalah.info/eng/content/view/frame/110106?/eng/content/view/full/110106&main.

447. Jeremiah 31:33.

448. Natural law is based on God's natural, altruistic law written on our hearts and souls. It is not about the external aspects of life, such as Islam's sharia law that requires women to be covered fully or to wear a head covering, which in some countries is enforced by religious police.

449. John 10:34 (Aramaic Bible in Plain English).

450. John 10:37–38 (English Standard Version).

451. No firsthand knowledge or experience of the otherworld is necessary to be the archbishop of Canterbury, just the ability to wear a mask of spirit as a hypocrite that others, the faithful, believe.

452. Henry Chu, *Seattle Times*, November 9, 2012, A6.

453. Luke 11:39 (New International Version).

454. Torah, Exodus 3:2.

455. Ibid., Exodus 3:14.

456. According to Jeff A. Benner's *A Mechanical Translation of the Book of Genesis*, Eh'yeh is translated as Exist (I will Exist) (http://www.ancient-hebrew.org/index.html).

457. Anything may be inserted, such as I am that star I am; I am that bird I am; I am that person I am; I am that blade of grass I am; I am that cat I am, and so on.

458. The ancient motto of Husfelt (Scottish-Norse earthly lineage) is "In Time," with the image of an hourglass.

459. Jeff A. Benner, *His Name Is One*, 63–64.

460. Ibid., 64–65.

461. http://biblesuite.com/greek/5590.htm.

462. Thing refers not only to human beings but all things of the universe. "I exist in that star I exist; I exist in that person I exist; I exist in that cat I exist."

463. Joseph Campbell, *The Power of Myth*, 57.

464. Tachibana Takashi, *Kūkai and the Astronaut, Mikkyō*, 45.

"Atman refers to the essence of each individual living thing—its soul or primary living energy. Each living thing—people, animals, plants—have an atman that forms each thing's eternal essence. The atman is not the body; the body is not eternal. The body houses the atman until the body dies. Atman is immortal and eternal.

"Brahman is 'world soul' or 'cosmic soul.' It is the eternal essence of the universe and the ultimate divine reality. It is the life source of all that has been, is and will be throughout the entire cosmos. It is not an individual being—it is more like the primal ground or reality of all being and existence.

"So, the phrase 'atman is Brahman' is saying, quite simply, that the individual soul is the world soul.
    "In other words, each individual soul—say, yours or mine—comes from and is made of the same reality as the world soul. There is no distinction between us, on the one hand, and the ultimate divine reality, on the other.

"It basically means that in our deepest selves, we are divine. All living things are divine in their deepest selves. Now, that divine self may be hidden or covered over by hatred, envy, fear or other negative things. But, it is there nonetheless and it is our 'true' and 'eternal' selves" (Dr. Jill Carroll, *Atman & Brahman*, http://www.world-religions-professor.com/atman-brahman.html).

465. http://gnosis.org/naghamm/thunder.html.

466. "Pluto transited through Capricorn from December 24, 1515 until the end of 1532...these years saw the dawn of the Protestant Reformation (1517) in Western Europe...Although the Reformation was essentially a religious movement, it had a massive impact on the human psyche and, consequently, on human activities...John Calvin praised work and effort as part of his religious doctrine...It wasn't too long before a lot of effort was invested in one's occupation and in the results of this effort—that is, success or failure in business. Success became a sign of God's grace, and failure a sign of damnation...In the old order, there was no particular urge to work more than was necessary to maintain the traditional standard of living...Work did not have the abstract character of producing some commodity that might be profitably sold on the market. What was new in modern society was that people came to be driven not so much by external pressure but by an internal compulsion that made them work as only a very strict master could have forced them to in other societies. Moreover, earnings were not to be enjoyed but had to be reinvested ad infinitum...

"Therefore, it can be said that this shift enabled a flourishing of capitalism that simply could not have developed had not the greatest part of people's energy been channeled in the direction of work. This new attitude toward work as an aim in itself may be assumed to be the most important psychological change since the end of the Middle Ages... The last Capricorn ingress of Pluto took place in early January 1762; Pluto stayed in this sign until the spring of 1777...In 1765, James Watt invented the steam engine that powered the Industrial Revolution... The American war for independence kicked off in the spring of 1775 after much bickering about unfair taxation from Great Britain. The arbitrariness of such a situation was inherent in the lunacy of relatively rich people who saw their wealth as a sign of God's love and therefore also saw themselves as naturally privileged. This, in turn, was challenged by a nascent nation that functioned according to the same lunacy and whose wealth was largely obtained by the exploitation of African slaves. Consequently, with so many humans being victims of genocide and slavery for the sake of wealth, the notion of human freedom became a burning issue, for the human psyche can only cope with so much abuse.

'Those who can make you believe absurdities can make you commit atrocities,' aptly wrote Voltaire at the time...To sum up, most of humankind responded to the passage of Pluto in Capricorn by expanding and increasing their consumption of natural resources according to their cultural patterns. A new relationship with the divine emerged from 1517 for a growing portion of humanity that equated wealth with divine salvation. The Reformation movement considerably increased and manipulated fundamental existential fears and anxieties and channeled most of the resulting energy in the direction of work—the so-called Protestant work ethic. This initiated an unparalleled period of frantic activity that enabled the birth of capitalism as a doctrine of exploitation of people and natural resources...A massive increase in military operations ensued, carving huge colonialist empires that yielded an unprecedented accumulation of wealth and power concentrated in a few nations and families...The coupling of this ruthless exploitation with military power gave rise to the military-industrial complex that currently dominates the world, promoting fierce economic competition, arms races, and wars among nations. Native populations were either eliminated or brutally enslaved...To this day, entire continents still have not recovered from this. Pluto's transit through Capricorn approximately every 230 years always 'heralds a long period of deep transformation of the collective'" (excerpted from the *Mountain Astrologer* [February/March 2008]). Please note that currently, Pluto is transiting Capricorn once again from January 2008 to 2023.

467. I use various symbolic words to describe the fragment of God or the Absolute within us, as purely written or spoken words alone are inadequate to express the Absolute. "There is no question about the affability of our word of reality, for we communicate with each other about the various phenomena which occur in this world by means of language. But when it comes to the absolute realm, the world of enlightenment, language is no longer a suitable mode of expression...on the other hand, the realm of the absolute is also expressible, although not of course by means of the written or spoken word, but through symbols" (Mikkyo Kobo Daishi, *Kukai and Shingon Buddhism*, 34).

468. "No one after lighting a lamp puts it under the bushel basket, but on the lampstand, and it gives light to all in the house. In the same way, let your light shine before others so that they may see your good works" (Matthew 5:15–16).

469. "Like the Bhagavad-Gita's composite symbol of man—Krishna (god Self), Arjuna (human self), and the Chariot (body)—each component of this integral partnership is seen as necessary for man to exist as a functional whole and to fulfill his individual and collective reason for being.

"Nevertheless, the story of how the One becomes the many, and how each of us rediscovers both the many and the One in ourselves—and in others—is the story of evolution, providing insights and clues as to how we may creatively participate in this grandest story ever told" (http://www.theosophy-nw.org/theosnw/human/hu-wtst2.htm).

470. Hawaiian shaman-priests.

471. David Kaonohiokaala Bray, *The Kahuna Religion of Hawaii*, 24.

472. "Pantheism is the belief that the universe (or nature as the totality of everything) is identical with divinity, or that everything composes an all-encompassing, immanent God.

"Panentheism (from Greek πᾶν (pân) 'all'; ἐν (en) 'in'; and θεός (theós) 'God'; 'all-in-God') was formally coined in Germany in the 19th century in an attempt to offer a philosophical synthesis between traditional theism and pantheism, stating that God is substantially omnipresent in the physical universe but also exists 'apart from' or 'beyond' it as its Creator and Sustainer.

"Pandeism is another word derived from pantheism and is characterized as a combination of reconcilable elements of pantheism and deism. It assumes a Creator-deity which is at some point distinct from the universe and then merges with it, resulting in a universe similar to the pantheistic one in present essence, but differing in origin.

"Panpsychism is the philosophical view held by many pantheists that consciousness, mind, or soul is a universal feature of all things. Some pantheists also subscribe to the distinct philosophical views hylozoism (or panvitalism), the view that everything is alive, and its close neighbor animism, the view that everything has a soul or spirit" (http://en.wikipedia.org/wiki/Pantheism).

473. W. Winwood Reade, *The Veil of Isis*, 64.

474. F. H. Colson and G. H. Whitaker (trans), *Philo De Opificio Mundi*, vol. 1, 13.

475. Dennis Overbye, "Three Physicists Win Nobel Prize for Developing New Light Source," *Seattle Times*, October 8, 2014, A2.

476. The colors themselves contain hidden meanings and teachings, which is not the province of this book. However, it is revealed in my book *Tequila and Chocolate*.

477. Dennis Overbye, "American and 2 Japanese Physicists Share Nobel for Work on LED Lights," October 7, 2014, http://www.nytimes.com/2014/10/08/science/isamu-akasaki-hiroshi-amano-and-shuji-nakamura-awarded-the-nobel-prize-in-physics.html?_r=0.

478. These are patterned after Shingon Esoteric Buddhism's levels of consciousness.

479. Just as humanity in Divine Humanity represents not only the human race but all things of creation, brother or sister means all things of creation.

480. Malcolm Godwin, *The Holy Grail*, 38.

481. Ibid., 247.

482. Anna Murdoch, *The Sovereign Adventure: The Grail of Mankind*, 52–53.

483. "The most ancient peoples believed that God gave Revelation, and was the One Supreme, the Eternal, the Infinite, pervading all places and exalted in a super-celestial place of Divine Light, that He was spiritual in essence, self-existent, uncreated, yet was made manifest to all as the most tender love and truth, which they received in their lives on earth with happiness and joy. Born of this Supreme One was She of celestial loveliness and purity, Divine in nature, whom they called the Spirit of God, the Dove, the Virgin Spirit, the Logos which is the Word of God, the earliest first Mother, whose name came to represent the essence of all that was beautiful and pure, and of most divine love. She was, in the Talmud, 'The Spirit of God that hovered over the water like a dove, which spreads her wings over her young.' She was the Shekinah, a mystic word often variously typified as a Lotus, a Rose, an Egg, and by symbols that were oval, as a Cup, a Boat or a Moon" (E. Valentia Straiton, *Celestial Ship of the North*—[1] *The Mother Mystery*, 6).

484. "The solution to this paradox regarding the beginning of creation was that the original divine unity secreted something of his substance, whether as spittle, sweat, tears, semen, or even as the word that went forth from his mouth. The first divine pair, and thus plurality, resulted from this original emanation. As early as the Coffin Texts, this process was described with a 'trinitarian' formula: 'when he was one, when he became three.' Multiplicity and the plurality of divine forms were thus derived from an original unity" (Erik Hornung, *Akhenaten and the Religion of Light*, 91–92).

485. "We are part of this universe; we are in this universe, but perhaps more important than both of those facts, is that the universe is in us" (Neil deGrasse Tyson, http://www.huffingtonpost.com/2012/03/12/most-astounding-fact-universe-neil-degrasse-tyson_n_1339031.html).

486. The planet "Neptune can symbolize the highest and most exalted manifestations of love... and creative vision of which human beings are capable in those moments when the earthbound illusion of separateness is replaced by a recognition of ultimate unity" (Liz Green, *The Astrological Neptune*, xvii).

487. Liz Green, *The Astrological Neptune*, 306.

488. Martin Luther King's 1967 speech against the war in Vietnam

489. Steve Lohr, *Seattle Times*, June 24, 2013, A10.

490. Beware of "wolf in sheep's" clothing – The Breakthrough Institute: "We believe that technology and modernization are at the foundation of human progress." Theirs is a human centric vision of the future -the full corporatization of all earth's resources and the end of wild places. (http://thebreakthrough.org/about/mission)

About the Author

Rev. Dr. JC Husfelt, author of *I Am a Sun of God and So Are You*, *The Return of the Feathered Serpent*, and *Return of a Green Philosophy*, is a philosopher, shaman, and mystic as well as a poet, martial artist, visionary, and exemplary prophet.

Since 1964 Husfelt has undertaken a literal and metaphorical journey through the mystical and practical aspects of the martial arts, mystery, myth, and spiritual lore of indigenous cultures throughout the world. He and his wife have traveled across the Americas to the icy plateaus and volcanoes of Iceland, through the windswept barrens of the British Isles and the Orkneys, and across Norway, Europe, the Mediterranean, Asia, and the Polynesian Islands.

Husfelt's teachings grew from his firsthand experience with multiple cultures and their spirituality. For more information, please e-mail him at spirit@divine-humanity.com or visit any of his websites:

www.divinehumanity.com
www.revolutioninreligion.com
www.spartanwarriorphilosophers.com

www.ingramcontent.com/pod-product-compliance
Lightning Source LLC
LaVergne TN
LVHW051223080426
835513LV00016B/1376